OAKWOOD LIBRARY OF RAILWAY HISTORY

The Kendal & Windermere Railway

Gateway to the Lakes

by
Robert Western

THE OAKWOOD PRESS

British Library Cataloguing in Publication Data
A Record for this book is available from the British Library
ISBN 978 0 85361 721 1

Typeset by Oakwood Graphics.
Repro by PKmediaworks, Cranborne, Dorset.
Printed by Information Press Ltd, Eynsham, Oxford.

In memory of
Cornelius Nicholson

'... one of the chief pioneers of railway work in England'.

The Illustrated London News, 17th August, 1889

By the same author

The Ingleton Branch (1990) first published as *The Lowgill Branch* (1971)
The Eden Valley Railway (1997)
The Cockermouth Keswick & Penrith Railway (2001, revised edition 2007)
The Coniston Railway (2007)

Front cover: Stanier class '5MT' 4-6-0s were a frequent sight on the branch in the latter days of steam. Here No. 44727 is passing through Burneside in March 1960. *Margaret Duff Collection*

Title page: Kendal & Windermere Railway Company Seal. *National Railway Museum*

Rear cover, above: This postcard shows one of the many different scenes on the cards issued in the early 1900s by the London & North Western Railway to meet the needs of the tourist industry. *Author's Collection*

Rear cover, below: Railway Clearing House map from the Grouping era showing the Windermere branch and surrounding railways. *Oakwood Collection*

Published by The Oakwood Press (Usk), P.O. Box 13, Usk, Mon., NP15 1YS.
E-mail: sales@oakwoodpress.co.uk
Website: www.oakwoodpress.co.uk

Contents

A view of the junction of the Windermere branch and the West Coast main line at Oxenholme on 4th August, 1960. Stanier 'Duchess' class 4-6-2 No. 46225 *Duchess of Gloucester* is seen with a northbound main line freight. *Derek Cross*

Prologue

The English Lake District is a place of outstanding natural beauty. Over the years, especially in the 18th and 19th centuries, this beauty has provided the inspiration for poets, writers and painters, who have recognized it as a place where there is calm and tranquillity, moving the emotions of those who are sensitive to its grandeur. But could it really be a place where the less sensitive would actually benefit from the inspirational experience which it has to offer? Would such people simply disturb this haven of peace and spoil it for those who could properly appreciate it? Perhaps, on the other hand, by being able to visit the Lake District and experience its beauty, those reckoned as less sensitive might actually develop an awareness and sense of appreciation which would enhance their lives and make them better people.

When the line of railway from London to Scotland was being planned and when it was eventually mooted that a railway from the main line should be built into the Lake District, this debate became one of the key issues. Railways were still beyond the experience of most and whilst there was the anticipated advantage of a line being able to bring in and take out commodities with an ease not experienced before, so improving, in a number of ways, the standard of living for those who lived locally, could this really more than balance the disadvantage (as seen by some) of the better ease of communication which would bring more visitors flocking into the Lake District; visitors who could well spoil this idyll?

The proposal to build the first railway into the Lake District initially envisaged a line which would reach the shores of Lake Windermere and the outcome was a saga which, during the planning stage, was destined to become a very contentious one. It had aspects which might seem remarkable in this 21st century. For example, this may well have been the only railway over which a war of words involved the Poet Laureate and about which poetry was used significantly as a means of protestation!

The early history of Britain's railways is alive and richly coloured with flamboyant characters; men of vision whose dreams and enthusiasm brought about a transition in the area where they lived and sometimes beyond; a transition which was so far reaching that, frankly, it is difficult, if not impossible, to grasp it fully. Fortunately, such men were to be found in the northwest of England and among them is numbered Cornelius Nicholson.

The name Cornelius Nicholson would be destined to be linked for ever with the Kendal & Windermere Railway. He was a man who was highly motivated and had seemingly boundless energy; a man with the gift of convincing rhetoric and one who was not easily distracted from his objectives in the face of opposition or adversity.

So; the line of railway from Euston was moving northwards. Soon it would be nudging the borders of the Lake District. It was heralding in a new era - but not an era welcomed by all ...

The ornate drinking fountain in front of Windermere station and depicted in the postcard showing the station in LNWR days (*see page 172*) was saved for posterity. It can now be seen in the grounds of the Brewery Arts Centre in Kendal. *Author*

Chapter One

The Move North Begins, 1837 to 1844

The London & Birmingham opens

On 20th July, 1837, the first 25 mile section of the railway from Euston to Birmingham was opened. It went as far as Boxmoor. So began an important era as far as travel to and from the capital to the North of England and beyond to Scotland, was concerned. Some idea of how important this new mode of travel would be is reflected in the fact that in a contemporary account it was reported (by Wyld) that on the first day passenger receipts amounted to £1,423; a significant sum of money for that period. On Monday 16th October, the line was opened as far as Tring and on 17th September, 1838, once the sections from Euston to Denbigh Hall had been linked to the section between Rugby and Birmingham, the railway facility was opened throughout. Yet discussions about linking London with Scotland had started even before the line from Euston to Birmingham had been opened; indeed it can be argued that there had been deliberations about doing this before the plan to build this railway had been finally conceived.

The discussions and events which took place during this period form a backcloth for what was to follow as far as Kendal was concerned because it involved a very active group of people from that town. Prior to the plans which would lead to the final route for the West Coast main line being decided, there had been considerable debate in Kendal about the role of the town in the scheme of things. In later years, Kendal was to be styled as the 'Gateway to the Lakes' but even in this period, it would seem that this was an embryonic idea in the minds of some, when considering provision for a rail link for the town. It becomes clear from the exchanges taking place that there was much anxiety in some quarters about Kendal missing out on a rail link, given certain schemes which had been proposed. There were those in Kendal, as in so many other places where the prospect of the coming of a railway was beginning to have an impact, who could see that prosperity would almost certainly be linked to the arrival of such a facility. It stood to reason, they argued, that incoming commodities would be more plentiful and cheaper and the ability to move goods, made in Kendal and district, to a wider market, would very much enhance the town's economy.

Once ideas started to be formulated in practical terms, the proposal to link London with Scotland involved considering which the most favourable route north of Lancaster might be. The terrain of much of Westmorland and Cumberland meant that there appeared to be no obvious and straightforward solution. When the mountainous regions were considered, it seemed that, in principle, there were three possible ways to move forward. Taking Lancaster as a starting point, the first would be to avoid the high terrain by sweeping through an arc eastwards, a second would be to do the same but by going westwards. The third would be to find a more direct route somewhere between these two, though this possibly presented more of a challenge. All these were considered, together with modifications, over a period of time. The easterly option would be to go round the mountainous region by taking the line to the east via Kirkby Lonsdale, Sedbergh and the Lune Valley. The coastal route, to the west, would have to take account of Morecambe Bay, at the very least. There was certainly an aversion, by some, to the use of tunnels and on the coastal route tunnels did not pose a problem. However, for what became referred to as 'the inland routes', tunnelling would become something of an issue.

1835 and 1836 – Joseph Locke and George Stephenson

In 1835 the Directors of the Grand Junction Railway requested Joseph Locke, their Chief Engineer, to put forward ideas about a possible line of railway between Preston and Carlisle. There had, in fact, already been some discussion, initiated by the editor of the *Carlisle Journal*, about this, as part of a link to Scotland. Locke, a man of experience who had trained under Stephenson, acted quickly and by November had carried out a preliminary assessment. He subsequently tendered a report in January 1836. In this report he has occasion to mention the town of Kendal, suggesting that it was reasonable to assume that, given its status, it would be a contender to be on the line. There is, however, he notes, a problem. Whilst it would not be difficult to bring a railway into Kendal, the terrain was such that it would not be so easy to determine a route out of the town. A better understanding of this problem can be gained by climbing to the top of the Helm which is a hill just south of Kendal. For anyone in reasonable health, the climb is not a demanding one. From the top, looking in a southerly direction it is possible to see the comparatively easy terrain through which the railway has been built. Turning gradually northwards and looking towards and beyond Kendal gives an idea of how the terrain beyond would be challenging for anyone wanting to take a railway northwards out of the town of Kendal.

Locke does consider the possibility of using a stationary engine or making a long tunnel but these solutions would not seem to be ideal. A route that might be a solution would be to take the line through Longsleddale and then to Haweswater. However, this would also involve tunnelling. Locke certainly dismisses any thought of taking a line through the Lake District; he saw this as being impractical. Events would show that there was no satisfactory way in which a route north could actually pass right through Kendal. The issue would become which scheme would bring it as near as possible to make the railway have a real impact on the town. There is, however, as Locke sees it, another way. This would be to make an eastern sweep and take a line through the area of Kirkby Lonsdale, Sedbergh, Orton on to Shap Fell and thence to Penrith. A drive along the A683 from Lancaster towards Kirkby Lonsdale alongside the River Lune and then on towards Sedbergh, may well suggest the terrain would have made it an eminently suitable route.

One proposal in this last scheme was to start the line just south of Lancaster, with the town being provided with a branch onto the main line. The worthies of Lancaster were not happy about this! Another aspect of this easterly route was that it would not include Kendal. There would be opposition on both these counts and, in addition, there would be threats of opposition by the landowners of the fertile Lune Valley, unwilling to have their 'territory' invaded.

In the meantime there were those on the west coast of what is now Cumbria, who had other ideas. A line of railway round the coast would best serve their interests. In September 1836, George Stephenson was asked to put forward ideas (in effect, at this stage, no more than that) about the suitability of such a scheme and he produced a report the following year. The proposal, for many, made a lot of sense because at the time the west coast (at Whitehaven and Millom, for examples) was becoming a thriving industrial area. Stephenson was also asked to comment on the proposal of an eastern route. As far as the latter was concerned, he made much of the problems which he perceived would be caused by the effects of severe winters on some sections of the higher ground, whereas the coastal route, being flat, would not be faced with such circumstances. He felt the coastal route would be cheaper and the works required to place a railway over Morecambe Bay would not be insurmountable. In view of these factors (and perhaps not surprisingly, given the group he was advising) he recommended the coastal route.

A route to accommodate Kendal

As the months went by, a great deal of effort went into the matter of trying to resolve which of these routes would be preferable, with the various parties vying for the scheme which would best suit them. One of the outcomes was that, during the period from 1835 to 1843, considerable modifications were made by a number of individuals, especially to the routes originally put forward by Locke.

The longer the debate went on, the more concerned those who had interests for Kendal became. Some of the schemes would effectively isolate the town. Locke had implied that Kendal had a good case to be on the railway (or close to it) so why not? It was, after all, a place of some standing, as Locke himself had stated, and there were those whose philosophy of railway development seemed to involve linking together such places.

1837

Towards the end of 1837, there was also growing concern in Penrith about the way in which events might develop. In order to discuss the various issues, five magistrates, John de Whelpdale, E.W. Hasell, Sir George Musgrave, Henry Howard and Thomas Scott, were petitioned to call a meeting. The strength of feeling can be judged by the fact that 86 people signed this petition. The response was to call a meeting at 2.00 pm on Tuesday 7th November at the Crown Inn, in Penrith. The meeting again reflected the considerable support for a scheme which would include Penrith, when about 300 people packed into the assembly rooms of the Crown. In the chair was the Lord Lieutenant of the Counties of Cumberland and Westmorland. The first of a number of proposals really summed up the main purpose of the meeting. This was put forward by Sir George Musgrave and stated:

> That the interests of the public at large, and especially of all classes in this district, would be materially benefitted by a line of railway from Lancaster to Carlisle and Glasgow, passing near the town of Penrith.

The only real threat, as far as Penrith was concerned, was the coastal route; Penrith was included in all the others. Even so, after much deliberation, a committee was set up to discuss with the Directors of the Grand Junction Railway, the best way forward. The committee was a large one, consisting of 21 members.

What is perhaps significant is the comment in the press report which expresses the hope that Kendal will follow the example set by the inhabitants of Penrith. A further incentive was given for Kendal to act by a meeting held in Appleby on 11th November, which supported the easterly route; one which would to some extent favour that town. Once again the report in the press expresses an expectation that the worthies of Kendal would soon hold a meeting as well.

What was needed now was a champion for the cause for Kendal. Enter: Cornelius Nicholson.

Cornelius Nicholson and his pamphlet

Cornelius Nicholson was to fall into that auspicious group of men from what is now Cumbria, who would campaign to realize railway facilities for the area; men like E.W. Hasell of Dalemain and Admiral Russell Elliot, of Appleby; promoters extraordinaire. Nicholson was a man of considerable energy. Born in Ambleside, his father had died when he was still a boy. This had resulted in the young Cornelius getting only a basic education but he had grit and determination and by the time the railway project was being mooted, he was already well-known in Kendal for what, today, would be seen as having an entrepreneurial attitude. He was a visionary and, in his view, a railway for Kendal was essential if the town was going to develop and be successful. When an advertisement appeared in the press on 2nd December announcing that,

> THIS DAY IS PUBLISHED (Price Twopence)
> A PAMPHLET
> ENTITLED
> THE LONDON AND GLASGOW RAILWAY
> Through Westmorland and Cumberland
> THE INTERESTS OF KENDAL CONSIDERED
> BY CORNELIUS NICHOLSON

the press in Kendal positively whooped with joy, seeing it as potentially offering an important contribution to what was deemed to be 'a very exciting issue'.

The pamphlet was published by Hudson & Nicholson and would be for sale, it seemed, just about everywhere in the area. It is very lengthy. In it Nicholson displays a remarkably erudite style and shows a keen understanding of the economic argument, which he puts forward with considerable zeal, at times showing a certain impatience with what he perceives to be lethargy on the part of those whom he considers should be promoting the cause. He points out the importance, as he sees it, of making every effort to ensure that the line passes through Kendal and whilst he argues mainly from a commercial standpoint, at the same time he is at pains to put forward a case which looks carefully at the ramifications of the commercial success a railway should bring to the town in terms of the improvement in the standard of living which all might enjoy. He compares the lot of Kendal to that of places like Huddersfield and Halifax and his belief that Kendal could, with proper communications (which, for Nicholson, means a railway), compete in manufacturing terms with such places. He bases part of his argument on the benefits which followed the opening of the Lancaster & Kendal Canal (which he sees as 'bringing in a new era' and being 'a powerful stimulant') but reasons that benefits brought by a railway would greatly outweigh those that the canal brought:

> If the manufacturers of Kendal will not exert themselves to secure the advantages of a Railway other towns who better understand their interests will rob us of our trade.

He develops this at considerable length, with various examples. He then goes on to re-emphasize the need for a railway:

> What we want as essential to the continuance or extension of our prosperity - cheap and punctual conveyance of raw material of manufactures and of coals into the town with the transport of manufactured goods and agricultural produce out of the town; and moreover a steady and certain mode of *personal intercourse* [his italics] with the markets (distant as they are) on which we are entirely dependent.

He then argues that beneficial though the canal has been it cannot meet these requirements. He also has things to say about the high costs incurred. This section concludes with the assertion: 'Hence we argue the *necessity* for a railway on particular grounds as well as on general principles'.

Nicholson has by no means finished with this statement. He then goes on to argue the case that a further outcome will be the increase in the value of property and land in the district. This argument is followed by a discussion about how the poorer people of the district would fare. There may be those, he surmises, who will say that certain foods will be dearer (because the demand for them to be taken elsewhere will tend to push up local prices) and so the poor will be even worse off. Whether or not his counter argument to this is reckoned to be plausible, it certainly displays a sharply analytical mind:

> I anticipate, certainly, that meat would be dearer and that bacon, butter, fowls, eggs and all other agricultural produce would be dearer. Not only could the consumption of these commodities be greater at home but our distance by connection with the railway from the great hives of industry would be so trifling. But many of the farmers of Westmorland might send their produce to those markets in less time than they now bring them to Kendal and the Lancashire markets would consequently rule the prices here. But I rule this as the very opposite of an objection. Whenever prices of native produce are maintained at a high rate by great consumption the means of payment are sure to be proportionate to the demand; for that labour which consumes the food is the creative power of wealth. And again, should our market be in some measure thinned of meat and fowls we shall in lieu thereof have fish as an addition to our supplies. At present Kendal is ill supplied with sea fish. What we do get is generally tainted before it arrives here (by the tedious conveyance of horse and cart) and it is charged a great price even

> in that condition. But with Railway communication we should have fish of all kinds - for the poor as well as the rich - fresh and at a moderate price.

Clearly Nicholson was going to leave no stone unturned in his case for a railway.

He then goes back to matters relating to the canal and expresses the view that prices for carriage of goods would fall because there would be competition. He refers, in particular, to coal and makes the point that if the price of coal came down it would balance the possible increase in the cost of meat so the 'poor' would not be worse off. There is then the practicability of the scheme and whether it would be one which would benefit the shareholders. He suggests that the way forward would be to employ an engineer who should 'deliberately and accurately' survey lines up the vale of Kent, through Kentmere and up the vale of the Sprint, through Longsleddale to Penrith. If such a survey indicated that the scheme was impracticable he concedes it would be madness to proceed, but again he issues a caveat,

> But it appears to me that it would be a great reflection on the people of Kendal if they neglect the opportunity of putting this experiment to the test.

Nicholson then embarks on a sort of contrived dialogue about the scheme, debating what might be possible and what might be probable. In the process, he attempts to overcome the views of those who might raise objections about the perceived impracticalities by pointing them to the obstacles which had to be overcome when building the Manchester and Liverpool and also the Carlisle and Newcastle railways. There is another verbal swipe at the people of Kendal:

> The mistake with many persons in the neighbourhood of Kendal is that they cannot look farther than between Penrith and Lancaster and they can see *no means* within this compass of cutting through the hills and supporting a Railway.

He then dismisses suggestions that there would be trouble caused by snow, asserting that locomotives would easily plough through it. After yet more discussion about the impact that a railway might have on turnpike road and canal trade, he expresses a view about the possible construction of a railway to Scotland on the eastern side of the country and is clearly of the opinion that the Government would only sanction one route:

> Have you not seen the vigorous efforts that have been made and are at this moment being made on the Newcastle side of the country, to get the whip hand of us, and carry the English and Scotch connecting Railway through their district and suppose that by our inactivity they first get the ear of Parliament and succeed in their object, then, 'A long farewell to all our greatness'.
>
> This is the grand point for our consideration. I am in my own mind as certain as I ought to be of any event which has not actually transpired that before many years have elapsed, a railway will be constructed on one side of the country or the other, connecting the manufacturing districts of England and Glasgow with Edinburgh. But Parliament can never be expected to sanction *two lines* ...

In a final appeal he states, 'I recommend the people of Kendal to shake off their lethargy - to call a public meeting ...' And this is precisely what happened.

A meeting in Kendal ... momentum gathers

William Gelderd, the mayor of Kendal, received a petition to which 75 names were attached. It requested him to call a public meeting 'for the purpose of adopting such means as may then be deemed most advisable to second the efforts now making in our neighbourhood towns in favour of the LONDON and GLASGOW RAILWAY through Westmorland and Cumberland'. The last name on the list is Cornelius Nicholson. The mayor responded promptly and called a meeting for Tuesday 19th December. The venue would be the town hall; the time two o' clock.

The meeting was well attended, although reports indicate that some of the notaries on the petition were not present; possibly a source of surprise and disappointment. However, as expected, Cornelius Nicholson did attend. A considerable number of the 'working classes' turned up and it was thought more might have been present if a more convenient time for them had been chosen. The mayor was appointed the Chairman (his first such public event, it would seem) and the opening spokesman was Edward Wilson. Wilson had certainly done his homework thoroughly and gave a well informed and clearly stated analysis of the present state of affairs. The language was inclined to be rather florid, as was often the case in this era when trying to make a point forcibly. He suggested that if the railway passed 13 miles from Kendal 'I should think that the sun of our greatness had set forever and we might be compared to the pelican in the wilderness and our town would speedily become a deserted village'. This remark earned him considerable applause. He argued the case for the route which Locke had first proposed and whilst acknowledging that Locke had been concerned about the route out of Kendal, Wilson felt the problems could be overcome. A tunnel from Kentmere High Street to Haweswater, some two miles in length, would present no more difficulties and expense, in his view, than the tunnel which was one and a quarter miles long in Liverpool. In conclusion, Wilson dismissed both the coastal route and the route via Kirkby Lonsdale and Kirkby Stephen as likely to be more costly and, not least, because they would not pass through Kendal! He sat down to great applause. Joseph Banks seconded the motion proposed by Edward Wilson, namely,

> That this Meeting, viewing the almost general adoption of railway communications throughout the country and regarding, in connexion with this subject, the interests of the town of Kendal and neighbourhood, considers it expedient that surveys should be made of the country between Kendal and Penrith, to maintain if a practicable line of Railway can be found through this district.

The resolution was carried unanimously. It was then the turn of James Gandy to propose that the gentlemen named on the petition should form a committee, with the power to add to their number. He was followed by Cornelius Nicholson who would second this motion. However, Nicholson did not miss the opportunity to express his feelings about the matters in hand. Perhaps reflecting on what he had written in the pamphlet and feeling vindicated in urging his fellow Kendalians to stir from their lethargy he commented on the number present at the meeting, saying that he felt 'it was an assurance that the people were duly alive to the welfare of the town'. He then proceeded to wave a copy of the reports which Stephenson had prepared for the coastal route and another prepared by a Whitehaven Committee. Whilst he did not call into question Stephenson's ability as an engineer, Nicholson, nevertheless, pointed to the fact that having been hired by the Whitehaven Committee, it was clear that Stephenson would recommend a scheme which was in their favour. Nicholson then indulged in what clearly proved to be a popular observation,

> If the Whitehaven people hired Mr Stephenson to say all that could be said most pleasing to them, then they had no reason to grumble if he charged them pretty high for his services. He had given them a whistle to pipe on for a length of time to come but he wished that, after all they would not pay 'too dear for their whistle'.

Following this, he read extracts from Stephenson's report. He dismissed Stephenson's objections raised about the route through the Lakes and asserted that in Stephenson's argument it seemed that it was a matter of any stick to beat a dog. Nicholson almost gets to the point of ridiculing Stephenson when considering the comments and says:

> Here [Stephenson says] it [the terrain] is too barren and there it is too fertile - here it is too thinly inhabited and there it is too thickly crowded with houses and seats and gentlemen's mansions - here it is too barren and there it is beautiful over much.

By this point the room was cheering and feelings were starting to run high. It is quite clear that Nicholson intended to use this to the full. Whether this speech had been planned (surely some thought had gone into it) or whether, in the main, it was an impromptu oration, Nicholson now launched into a lengthy discourse. It was almost as though this was some sort of performance and he was determined to be the star turn. The speech is extremely protracted and deals further with the objections of Stephenson and others; of what Nicholson believes to be the idle gossip aimed at defeating the proposition. At the end he came up with what would be a most effective piece of rhetoric:

> Never cease to think upon it: never cease to talk about it. It is said that a person may be talked into love for another, and even into a marriage, though there was never any appearance of a spontaneous flame and so we may talk the Glasgow and Lancashire people into a 'happy union' with us. Let your converse, therefore, be always on the railway till you are made happy with it. There are no difficulties, as I believe, but such as a spirited, a united, a persevering people may not – will not easily overcome. But if, unhappily, obstacles should present themselves which we do not foresee, if by the mighty cataclysms which have occurred in the womb of the earth, mountains have been up heaved and thrown in our way, such as we can neither subdue nor avert, then, given in that case, we have at least this consolation that, 'Tis not in mortals to command success. But we've done more, Horatio, we've deserved it'.

During this oration there were laughter and cheers and as Nicholson sat down there was further loud cheering. He had clearly made his mark as a very forceful proponent of the cause.

When the meeting had settled again, John Wakefield proposed that George Gibson be appointed treasurer and Cornelius Nicholson the Secretary. Robert Benson seconded this and took the opportunity to point out to the assembled company that if a survey was to be carried out, it would have to be paid for. He hoped those present would contribute to the cost and those who were wealthy would do so liberally. This lead nicely into the next proposition put forward by Isaac Braithwaite that a subscription should be entered into for the purpose of defraying the cost of the survey and for the payment of such expenses as may be incurred. Again the opportunity was taken to make observations on the proposed scheme when compared to Stephenson's. As far as the latter was concerned, Braithwaite expressed the view that those who traversed a long extent of sand soon became weary. He felt the Kendal and Kirkby Lonsdale routes more preferable and, understandably, supported the former. This proposal was seconded and a further proposal that various notaries should be solicited for support was also passed. Following a discussion about the effect that snow might have on the route under consideration by the committee, Nicholson had one last dig at Stephenson's rationale for the coastal route:

> The advocates of the Morecambe Bay line contend that the sea breezes will keep the rails free from snow while they forget that the same agency would keep them clear of trains.

The meeting over, the committee met to discuss further strategy and then, between them, £100 was raised towards the cost of a survey. As the year drew to a close there was much optimism and confidence in the direction things were moving. Similar committees were set up in Penrith and Carlisle.

The work of Job Bintley

There had been some progress on another front. Towards the end of the year, Job Bintley, a local man, was asked to carry out a preliminary survey for a route through Longsleddale (following Locke's observations) and he would continue this work in the following year. The route he would propose did not actually pass through the town of Kendal, again given the restraints imposed by the terrain, but it would pass nearer than the other schemes already being considered.

1838

In January, there appeared, at first sight, to be a further boost for those in Kendal; one which seemed to indicate that success was a little nearer. On 13th January, a letter appeared in the *Westmorland Gazette*. It was written by Cornelius Nicholson and had a very marked tone of triumph about it. It is headed, 'THE RAILWAY, DEATH WARRANT OF THE MORECAMBE BAY SCHEME'. It is not clear whether these words are Nicholson's or those of the newspaper's editor. The message, however, is very clear in the letter which follows:

> Sir,
> I have this morning been favoured, by a friend in Cumberland, with a copy of the reply of the Lords of the Treasury to the hopeful and much vaunted memorial [petition] of the West-liners. The following is a copy.
> I am, Sir,
> Yours respectfully,
> Cornelius Nicholson
>
> Cowen Head, Kendal Jan 11, 1838

25902 Treasury Chambers 27th December 1837

Gentlemen, - The Lords Commissioners of Her Majesty's Treasury had under their consideration your Memorial, praying that a Government Survey be made for a Railway from Carlisle to London. I have it in command to acquaint you that my Lords do not consider that they should be justified in interfering as requested by you.
I am,
Gentlemen,
Your obedient servant
T. Baring

There follows a quite remarkable statement in the newspaper and again it is not altogether clear who is the writer:

Addressed to a Gentleman in Maryport
This is the 'unkindest cut of all'. The last resort defeated! The best of hopes blighted! The weak and broken-spirited project abandoned by the public, and the public Treasury! Alack a day! But the 'mountaineers' are not so cruel-hearted as to exult over a prostrate and death-stricken rival. No! They are prepared to sing its requiem with charitable feelings. Peace, peace to its manes.*

This was quite a premature piece given that no real decisions about a route had yet been made and not least because the 'Morecambe Bay' route, in particular, had yet to be surveyed by Hague. It was really far from 'dead'. It seems to have appeared to some, for a moment, that it was now all down to a decision between the route round by Kirkby Lonsdale and the Eden Valley, on the one hand and, on the other, the one the Kendal Group was hoping would eventually be the chosen scheme (although this, also, had yet to be properly surveyed). More correspondence now appeared in the press, including an extremely protracted letter from someone who wanted to argue the case for a line through the Eden Valley. The whole matter was still very much in the air. In July, Locke produced a further report.

Locke begins this report:

Gentlemen
I have attended to the instructions which I received from you, namely to survey on behalf of the Committee at Penrith, the line by Kirkby Lonsdale, Tebay and Sunbiggin Tarn to Penrith: and for the Kendal Committee, the line by Kendal and Longsleddale. The former line was, according to your directions, explored and levelled by Mr Larmer, and the latter by Mr Bintley. Their sections were some time ago presented to me and after some modifications and improvements in the levels, were finally submitted for my examination. Having personally examined both lines of country, and become acquainted with the important features of the measure, I beg to lay before you the following report.

* The use of this comparatively obscure word, 'manes', may well give a clue to the writer. Clearly, whoever penned this was a person of considerable literary ability; that could well point to Cornelius Nicholson who seemed very fond of using this type of vocabulary and did so frequently. The word means the shade of a departed person as an object of reverence but here it certainly applies to the plan for the coastal route!

Locke points out, by way of a reminder, that he did, in fact, carry out a survey some two years previously and on that occasion he had come down on the side of a line which passed by Kirkby Lonsdale and then to Tebay, beyond which it went under Shap by means of a tunnel and so on to Penrith. The aim of the report now in hand was to consider the removal of the need for a tunnel under Shap and also to address the requirements of Kendal. He then goes on to outline the two routes now under consideration.

The first, which he now chooses to call the Appleby Route, will, when it reaches the area, go to the west of Kirkby Lonsdale, east of Killington and Sedbergh and on to Tebay. It will then turn eastwards to Sunbiggin Tarn (which will be the summit) and then descend by way of Great Asby, King's Meaburn, Morland, Cliburn, Eamont Bridge and to Penrith. This route would take it just over two miles from Appleby.

The second route, 'The Kendal Line', approaches by Stainton, passes east of Natland then to Oxen Holme [*sic*] and Larch Hill, leaves Kendal about a mile to the west and then takes the high ground to Meal Bank, crosses the River Mint, takes a western detour by Garnet Fold to Otter Bank, over the River Sprint at Cat Barrow, thence along to Longsleddale and Back Barrow, where there will be a tunnel. The line then passes on the west side of Hawes Water and on to Thornthwaite and Bampton and by way of the valley of the Lowther, eventually to Penrith.

The line via Kendal is 10 miles shorter (between Lancaster and Penrith) and the gradients present a more favourable case. However, according to Locke, there are other considerations which swing the balance. Crossing the Mint and Sprint and, especially, the tunnel, are seen by Locke as the 'most formidable' elements of this route. The tunnel could present major engineering demands but he also thinks that the length of it (2¼ miles) will 'be considered objectionable by passengers'. (Although he concedes that they will no doubt become reconciled to it.) Locke recognises that the Appleby Route is not without its problems and in summing up leaves the matter rather open-ended:

> Were it a matter of certainty that no better line could be obtained, then I should then give it as my opinion, considering the importance of the thriving town of Kendal, and the shortness of the line, that the route by Kendal is preferable: but even in this case, considering the nature of the works, I should recommend that the line be modified, with a view to avoid expense, even though the gradients require to be somewhat steeper.

He then states what has probably been in the back of his mind throughout the exercise:

> On the whole, I do not see that the original line by Shap has been improved; and on a careful reconsideration of that line it is susceptible of some improvement.

Locke goes on to justify this view and makes the point that he feels he must put the schemes into context. If what was being considered was a 'local' project it might be easier to resolve the issue but what is being considered here is, in his words, 'a great national work'. This factor must influence the decisions that are to be made. In the concluding section of the report he considers the route north of Penrith.

The view of the Kendal Committee on receiving Locke's report seems to be that in some way it implied the route would take into account the needs of Kendal, although on the face of it this was a rather misguided and over-optimistic assessment. There is a hint of a suggestion by the Committee that it was not really within Locke's brief from the two committees to introduce comparisons with his Shap route and so this is not up for consideration. If the two schemes are considered side by side, Locke would, it is argued, prefer the Kendal route against that which passes easterly towards Appleby. The review of the report, given in the *Westmorland Gazette* was optimistic, yet this optimism was tinged with caution. There was an admission, that whilst Locke continued to hold the view that the needs of Kendal should be a consideration in the debate, there was still a strong case for the line to go over Shap. However, the *Westmorland Gazette* was not going to miss an opportunity in lauding the efforts of the Kendal group.

> ... the active men of Kendal who have bestirred themselves on this subject have 'done the town some service'. If no steps had been taken to survey a line through or near to the wealthiest and most thriving town in the county, a burning and lasting stigma would have rested on its spirit.

Ever keen to promote the route passing near Kendal, the *Westmorland Gazette* launches into considerable detail about other reasons why the Kendal route is preferable and the Appleby route is not. Wealthy landowners in areas such as Rigmaden will vigorously oppose the plan. The writer questions the accuracy of Locke's geological assessment as far as the Shap line is concerned and then goes on to point out that the Kendal route has only been hurriedly surveyed once by Mr Bintley (whom, it concedes, is considered to very proficient). It is reasoned that there is a case for a more detailed survey, which even Locke has suggested, and this may result in a stronger case for the Kendal route. The proposals concerning the Morecambe Bay route (of which more would be heard later) leads the writer of this piece to resort to the sort of florid language needed when 'factual' aspects were seemingly exhausted:

> But considering the tunnel - the man that can undertake to throw an embankment over Morecambe Bay, would take as mere child's play a tunnel of two and a quarter miles to be made through clay slate; the frightful scarecrow tunnel! Is this an unheard of conception? Are we arrived at the middle of the nineteenth century - the glory of science and human enterprise - and are the talents and energies of the commercial Great Britain petrified at the sight of Gate Scarth? Out upon such a libel on the age.

The piece concludes with a mild criticism of Locke, followed by a resounding claim that Kendal will get its railway and 'will exult in its consequences'. The Committee decided that the Longsleddale route offered the best option as far as Kendal was concerned and that it needed more detailed consideration. Job Bintley, as seen earlier, had been invited to survey the route and this he had agreed to do.

At this point there is something of a lull in the proceedings. The worthies of towns and cities up and down the country, including Kendal, were turning their attention to an appropriate way to celebrate the coronation of Queen Victoria, who had ascended to the throne the previous year. The Victorian Era was about to begin; an era which would see rapid progress in many aspects of Britain's industrial life. Yet, whilst the 'Railway Era' has often been seen as virtually synonymous with the 'Victorian Era' a great deal had already been planned and achieved by railway pioneers during the reign of King William.

In September, George Stephenson no doubt raised a few eyebrows amongst all parties over in the west not least those who were still of the opinion that Parliament would probably sanction only one scheme to Scotland. He told the people of York that he hadn't the slightest doubt that a railway to the North would pass through the city 'as no other line can be found so eligible'. So much for his previous thoughts on the coastal route.

In the meantime, Hague had been at work carrying out a survey in connection with the coastal route. At the beginning of the year, in February, he had done some preliminary work but later, in June, having been given a more detailed brief, he carried out further work and prepared a report of his findings. There was a great deal of speculation in the press, by way of correspondence, and elsewhere, about the possible outcome of Hague's survey. At the beginning of August, someone using the *nom de plume* 'Agricola' wrote to the *Westmorland Gazette* expressing optimism that the survey, once completed, would demonstrate that a route across the bays would be both feasible and preferable. In the same letter, 'Agricola' chastises the *Westmorland Gazette* for being too partisan but concedes that this is understandable. The writer also suggests that if the coastal route is realized, a branch to Kendal would not only be across level ground but would make the town, in effect, a sea-port. Towards the end of the year, Hague issued his report. It is addressed to: 'Sir H. Le Fleming Senhouse, and the Gentlemen forming the Provisional Committee of the "Caledonian,* West Cumberland and Furness Railway".'

Hague points out that he has enlisted the help of Mr Padley 'of London who has a great deal of experience', and goes on to give a careful account of the work he has undertaken. Very early in the report he feels able to point out that:

> Upon a careful examination and consideration of all the circumstances and localities, I am of the opinion that the object the Committee have in view is perfectly feasible, and that there is not any difficulty, in an engineering point of view, in carrying a railway across these two bays.

The two bays being referred to are Morecambe Bay and the estuary of the Duddon. The plan was to create embankments. The one across Morecambe Bay would be just over 10 miles long; the one across the Duddon Estuary nearly two miles. The former was a particularly ambitious scheme and would involve driving four rows of piles the width of the railway, 21 ft apart from centre to centre, across the bay, with longitudinal timbers on the top to be strengthened by diagonal struts or braces from the piles to the underside of the timbers. The piles would be secured by cross braces at the upper ends. The piles would be driven through the sand to the clay and to a depth that would make them safe. The work would be done using a machine designed for the purpose. It was envisaged this would be on a platform some 60 ft long and mounted on wheels and would move

* The reference to 'Caledonian', here, has nothing to do with the railway which was later to bear this name. It was simply a reference to the fact there was to be a Scottish connection in the scheme.

forward as the work progressed. The device would have a stationary condensing engine of some 40 hp and this would be used to create a vacuum which would drive in four piles simultaneously. After the rails had been laid, the engine would advance 12 ft and repeat the process. When the halfway stage had been reached, the procedure would be repeated from the other side and the two sections joined in the middle. There would be a carpenter's shop on the platform which would be weatherproof, so enabling the work to be carried out in all conditions. The rails would be laid on the longitudinal timbers. On the sea side of the piles it was planned to fix sheet piling. This would be as high as the line of sand and sunk two feet into the clay. The reason Hague intended to do this was to stop water making its way through the loose sand and undermining the foundations. Simultaneously with this work there would be the construction of bridges, tide gates and 'coffer dams' (caissons). Once this stage was completed, the embankments would be made. This would be done by running wagons along the railway and depositing stones between the piles, so filling up the hollows. Hague was convinced that as the embankments rose, nature would take its course and in so doing would enhance the building up of them. He gave a detailed account of the mechanism he believed would do this. He also outlined the manner in which the tide gates and sluices would be used as the tides ebbed and flowed. This is not all. Land would be reclaimed (in the region of 52,000 acres) in this scheme and also the port of 'Ulverstone' would be enhanced by the manner in which the rivers Leven and Crake would be diverted. Hague seemed reluctant to make comparisons with the other schemes which were being put forward but he appeared to be of the opinion his would be favourably received by the Government not least because it involved the reclamation of so much land.

In spite of what, on the face of it, was an impressive report, the *Westmorland Gazette*, commented:

> ... we confess that independently of the physical obstacles which present themselves, in attempting to deprive old Neptune of a portion of his demesnes [land rightfully belonging to him] in Morecambe Bay, it appears to us that in Mr Hague's plan of embanking, there is something which is not very feasible.

The writer went on to explain why this would appear to be so and concludes with the plea: 'Keep the railway on *terra firma* and let the steam ships contend with the ocean'. It is clear, yet hardly surprising, that the paper is very much in support of a line through Kendal.

When surveying other sections of the route, Hague and his team had encountered a measure of hostility, especially in the Poulton area where, it is said, they experienced some 'bullying'. Even by this time those who carried out surveying work for the railway companies were not always welcome.

1839 ... a significant step is taken

There is a certain amount of 'marking time' during 1839 as the various schemes in the offing were adjusted in an attempt to give them more credence. As the year progressed the line from Preston to Lancaster moved nearer to completion and it was anticipated the railway would open the following year. Coach companies took the opportunity, in the interim, to fill the gap between Kendal and the nearest points on a railway.

Two new services were introduced during the year and given titles with a railway flavour. The first was called 'The Engineer' and commenced in June. It linked Kendal with Preston where passengers could join the train and travel on to London, the journey time being put at 16 hours. It left Kendal at 11.00 am and called at Milnthorpe, Lancaster and Garstang. There was also a coach for the north leaving at 12.30 pm which went to Edinburgh and called at a number of places including Penrith and Carlisle. A coach for Kendal also connected with the train at Preston and left there at 8.00 am (or 'immediately after the arrival of the train from London'). The second service, which commenced in late September, was named 'The Locomotive' and plied between Kendal and Carlisle with connections for the trains to Newcastle. Whilst 'The Engineer' was a daily service, 'The Locomotive' was limited to running north only on Tuesdays, Thursdays and Saturdays, leaving at 10.00 am. Return runs were on Mondays, Wednesdays and Fridays, leaving Carlisle at 4.30 pm.

On 21st August, 1839 a significant event took place which would move the whole project forward. At the close of the proceedings of the House of Commons, Mr Hind, the MP for Newcastle, moved for and obtained leave for, an address to Her Majesty,

> ... praying that she will be pleased to give directions that an engineer or engineers may be appointed to enquire and report upon the relative merits and the preference which ought to be given to the respective and already surveyed and projected railways between London and Edinburgh following namely, *via* Newcastle upon Tyne and Berwick, *via* Newcastle upon Tyne and Hexham, *via* Lancaster, Whitehaven, and Carlisle, *via* Lancaster, Penrith, and Carlisle.

Matters were beginning to take on a broader perspective. The group selected to carry out the enquiry was headed by Lieutenant-Colonel Sir Frederic Smith, of the Royal Engineers, and Professor Barlow. In the months ahead they would carefully examine the various plans and drawings prepared for each of the routes and talk with those responsible for producing them. They would also talk with some of the men who were promoting the different projects. In the meantime there was a good deal of honing of the schemes.

George Larmer's Report

George Larmer, who had been working for the Penrith Committee, published a report in November in which he put forward his views on the possible route north of Lancaster. He compared his own proposals for a route which left Lancaster and after passing near Kirkby Lonsdale went through the Lune Valley, passing near Orton and on to Shap, with the 'coastal route'. He concluded, not surprisingly, that the 'inland' route would be preferable. It would not only be shorter but avoid the use of major undertakings such as the embankment over Morecambe Bay. He also considers the needs of Kendal and comments:

> This Inland Line is also well adapted for forming branches to the east and west and while upon this part of the subject I shall take the opportunity of alluding to the thriving town of Kendal which, though the difficulties are great in taking a line in that direction I do not think they are impracticable or greater than the West Coast Line; but if the one by the Lune Valley should be thought the most feasible, a branch could be taken from it to that town of not more than 10 miles in length; when if more accurate surveys should be made these lines will be better compared, and though the Kendal Line would have a tunnel to contend with nearly 2½ miles in length, yet the gradients would be better than on the Lune Line; but as the same parties will support either it is immaterial at present which is the most feasible.

So, in Larmer's view, a route taking in Kendal is not completely ruled out at this stage.

1840

The prospect of the Commissioners' investigations produced a flurry of letters in the local press. Cornelius Nicholson, as may have been anticipated, was not slow in putting his thoughts onto paper and, on 16th March, wrote a long letter to the *Westmorland Gazette*. In view of the length of this missive, it appeared in two parts; the first being printed in the edition of 21st March. Nicholson tackles Larmer's proposals and finds it hard to believe that Larmer, having been so ready to say how he felt it important to consider the needs of Kendal in a scheme, now seems to be favouring one which would result in a line passing 10 miles distant from Kendal, even though Larmer seems to see a link line as an important part of the project. Nicholson is at pains to point out that if the problem for Larmer is one involving the tunnelling entailed in each of the routes under consideration (on the one hand the tunnel under Orton Scar on the Lune Valley route and the other under Gatescarth on the Kendal route) Larmer has 'got it wrong'! For example, Nicholson suggests that when it comes to the tunnel at GateScarth on the Kendal line, Larmer, in calculating the time needed for constructing it and possible cost, seems to assume that the tunnel (two miles and seventeen chains long) is at 1,200 ft below the surface for the whole of its length and in the letter there is a sketch showing that whilst the highest point is at 1,200 ft, the land tapers off on each side! In characteristic style, Nicholson points out,

> Now you will see that if the cap or apex had in height exceeded the 'skiey head of blue Olympus' - if it had been 120,000 instead of 1,200 feet, this would not have retarded the opening of the Tunnel one single day. The extreme altitude of the hill is of no importance at all.

Nicholson is even prepared to go as far as to say that Larmer 'commits himself either to a charge of wilful deception or an imputation of ignorance'. He asks why this is the case and comes up with the conclusion that Larmer,

> ... wants all the glory of finding out a line for himself and cannot brook to yield the merits of his contemporary Mr Bintley's line. Thus for the petty jealousies of a Surveyor

is the public mind to be divided and the public interests to be tampered with? Mr Larmer states that the Lune line is not a 'competitor' against that through Kendal. Oh! no, he is quite in love with the Kendal line in one sense. A specimen of love, I ween, such as is mentioned by Rochefaucaulde: love having the effects of dislike.

For one who was to a large extent self taught, Nicholson, who readily quotes the words of a French writer and philosopher, shows a remarkably wide breadth of reading and, in spite of being very cutting in his language, a capacity to be extremely eloquent. There would be many such fine words, both spoken and written, as the saga of a railway for Kendal unfolded.

Nicholson goes on to address the matter of costs. He challenges Larmer's calculations and dismisses some aspects as a 'delusion'. Larmer had put the cost of the Orton tunnel at £50 a linear yard and come to the conclusion the cost would be £121,000. Nicholson disputes this because he feels Larmer has not taken into account the sections of cutting at the ends of the tunnel which, in being excavated, would increase the cost significantly, even, he argues, as much as the tunnel itself. And as to Larmer's claim that the material taken out from the excavation of the tunnel would be useful for building elsewhere, Nicholson dismisses this suggestion as 'talking very unadvisedly' and takes the example of the Littleborough tunnel on the Manchester & Leeds Railway where similar material had come out in small fragments. He then discusses, at some considerable length, the manner in which the material which would be handled in opening the Gatescarth tunnel could be dealt with, quoting the methods used by quarrymen. The conclusion reached is that the tunnel would cost £40 for each lineal yard and the cost would come out at £150,000 a mere £29,000 more than the Orton tunnel. He asserts Locke has verified these figures.

Nicholson then gives the following resume:

Mr Larmer's main line is	51	miles	long
The tentacle thrown out for catching Kendal	10	"	"
	61	miles	
The direct line *through* Kendal is not quite	47	"	
Kendal line shorter by	14		

To this Nicholson comments,

So that Mr Larmer's notable scheme is to construct, and keep in constant repair, fourteen miles of extra length of Railway, that he may save £29,000 ! ! ! According to his own way of reckoning it, at £14,000 per mile, he would spend £196,000 in the *first cost,* and travel over fourteen miles extra length, which is a perpetual burden, for the laudable purpose of saving £29,000 at another point. And mark what an immense sum this ingenious scheme *sacrifices* in losing the transit of coal to Kendal. But I have said enough for the present, and, by your leave will enlarge on this point next week.

There follows the phrase 'to be continued'!

A further letter, signed quite simply 'Philo' describes the joy that would be experienced by viewing the scenery when travelling on the line proposed through Kendal. Philo mildly chastises the editor for apparently showing waning enthusiasm in supporting the Kendal scheme and exhorts him to show more.

In the third letter published in this edition of the *Westmorland Gazette* and signed 'H', there is a proposal for yet another route north. The writer puts forward a scheme which would pass near to Levens, go to Newby Bridge and thence on the west side of Lake Windermere. There would be a tunnel at Borrowdale. Kendal would be served by a spur five miles long from Levens. Such a line, it is argued, would better serve the copper, slate and other industries of the area.

On 28th March, Cornelius Nicholson's continuation to the letter of the previous week was published. In typical Nicholson style it starts with a flourish carrying the heading 'Linea Recta Brevissima' and deals with the subject of the provision of coal supplies by the two routes proposed. Larmer, Nicholson points out, has made much of the manner in which the Lune line will result in the supply of the 'black diamond' (Nicholson) becoming cheaper for the places it will serve. Nicholson challenges the reasoning in this. He asks which places Larmer has in mind and rules out Crosby Ravensworth, Orton, Sedbergh and Kirkby Lonsdale because these places are already well served by coal from places such as Garsdale, Ingleton and Bentham. Kendal, Nicholson concludes, is the only place which is in need of better and cheaper supplies and the Lune line will not facilitate these. Once again Nicholson becomes very critical of Larmer and writes:

> Altogether, the boast and promise of coal by the Lune line is most futile, and shews an utter ignorance of the country and its requirements which I did not expect Mr Larmer to display. The Railway would neither benefit nor be itself benefitted by the conveyance of coal to any extent beyond a point of ridicule.

Nicholson then moves his attention to what he describes as the direct line through Kendal and, not surprisingly, comes up with an argument outlining why this is the preferred route as far as the supply of coal is concerned. He examines in detail the costings that he envisages, with the resulting savings for those who use the commodity. Once again, Nicholson reminds his readers of the importance Larmer gave to Kendal when first considering a possible route. There is, however, another side to all this, namely the revenue to be gained by the railway and given the projection that the consumption of coal in Kendal could well (Nicholson assures his readers he has been reliably informed) 'soon' double. Although he determines to underestimate this suggestion, it would still be a great loss in revenue to a line which took the Lune route. At the end of the letter, by way of a 'P.S.', Nicholson states:

> I have, in these letters, treated Mr Larmer's project of a branch line from Kirkby Lonsdale to Kendal as if it were practicable and probable; but I have the authority of our Surveyor for stating that there are very great engineering difficulties between Kendal and Kirkby Lonsdale. That there would be a tunnel of considerable length is certain and that the line would be unusually expensive would be equally certain. But I am almost ashamed of treating such a project with any degree of seriousness. In two senses it is 'quite beside the question'.

Towards the end of March the Kendal Committee enlisted the help of Francis Whishaw who carried out an examination of the Longsleddale route. The Directors of the Lancaster & Preston Railway clearly approved of this course of action and they paid £50 towards the survey which was carried out. However, at a later date, Bintley took issue with Whishaw's findings.

In May 'H' came up with a more detailed scheme to support his earlier suggestions regarding an alternative route but this was not really a serious contender.

By now, the Commissioners were certainly given a lot to think about.

The Commissioners carry out a review

The Commissioners worked steadily through the early part of 1840. They examined the plans and proposals for the coastal route and were very complimentary about the way these had been prepared and presented. When it came to an examination of the two inland routes the Commissioners were less impressed by the material they were given and described them as 'insufficient for fairly testing the relative merits of the several projects'. In view of this they called for additional information. This was provided by 18th February and enabled them to make headway with their assessments. When looking at the coastal route they found many of Hague's proposals were open to question; however, it did have an advantage as far as gradients were concerned. On the calculations they made, it was estimated that the coastal route would serve a smaller population with a resulting lower passenger potential (over 13,000 per annum was envisaged). In comparing the merits and possible disadvantages of the two inland routes, the tunnels were an issue and to assist them in their deliberations they called in Lieutenant Huw Dalrymple Fanshawe (of the 12th Foot). The lieutenant carried out various detailed observations and with a consideration of the material of which each hill was comprised, the limestone of Orton was seen to be preferred, not least because there would be greater scope when deciding on the number of bore holes. This fact suggested that the Lune line was preferable to the Kendal line and things were not looking too good for the Kendal Committee. With their work completed, the Commissioners issued a report on the 16th May with their findings. It is addressed to Robert Gordon MP, Secretary to the Treasury and is lengthy. It looks in great detail at the proposals being put forward by the various bodies, for a route to Scotland, north of Lancaster. The report is very thorough and indicates that a considerable amount of work has gone into reaching the conclusions which are made. The various schemes have been carefully scrutinized and the advantages and disadvantages of each one are weighed carefully.

The first scheme to be rejected is the coast line, thus leaving one of the two 'inland' lines as being preferable. Based on the engineering difficulties anticipated with the Kendal line in the Longsleddale section, the line through the Lune Valley is the one which the Commissioners reckon to be the best option. There had been some discussion, at the time, about whether it might be possible to combine certain elements of Bintley's and Larmer's schemes. The suggestion was that Bintley's plans should be adopted from Lancaster to Kendal and Larmer's from Penrith down to Burrow Bridge with a link made from this point to Kendal. The result would also have removed the possible problems as far as Bintley's projected section from Kendal though Longsleddale were concerned. However, Larmer rejected the proposals on the grounds of cost. In the meantime, the Kendal

Committee had decided to approach Larmer (in spite of Nicholson's scathing comments on his earlier proposals!) with a view to looking at other possible alternatives. Larmer came up with a modification to his plan and proposed a route which would pass nearer to Kendal and go via Grayrigg before turning north. At the eleventh hour, the Kendal Committee approached the Commissioners with this latest idea but by this time the report was too far advanced in its preparation. Nevertheless the Commissioners did note:

> … we have no hesitation in saying that if a line has been found which would afford the advantage of direct railway communication with Kendal without either materially increasing the cost of construction or the length of the line between Lancaster and Carlisle and which would be free from other great defects it might be more beneficial to the public than the Lune line. This, however is a subject for future consideration …

So it was the Lune line which won the recommendation of the Commissioners but there still appeared to be room for manoeuvre. The report is signed by Frederic Smith, Peter Barlow and the Secretary, Henry Amsinck (Lieut RN). There is a telling comment at the end of the report:

> In conclusion, we have only to state that in our inspection of the coast line, we were accompanied throughout the whole distance by Mr Brisco, an assistant to Mr Rastrick, and in our examination of Morecambe Bay by Mr Hague, the engineer, and by Mr Yarker, the solicitor, besides other gentlemen interested in this project. Mr Larmer pointed out the Lune line and we were also accompanied by the secretary and several members of the Kendal Committee, all of whom evinced every desire to facilitate our enquiry; but it is to be regretted that more time and means had not been at the disposal of the surveyors of the inland lines to have enabled them to prepare their plans and other drawings in an equally perfect and satisfactory manner with those of the coast line.

Later the Commissioners would review their findings in the light of further petitioning.

Job Bintley's Objections

On 21st May Job Bintley sat down and wrote a lengthy report for the Kendal Committee about the decision of the Commissioners. Bintley was clearly disenchanted, even aggrieved, with some of the conclusions and findings in the Commissioners' report and he sought to take issue with them and put the record straight.

Bintley briefly outlines the history of the events; of Locke's involvement in 1836 and of his own in the latter part of 1837 and early 1838. He challenges the findings based on Larmer's work, stating that the report has been based on 'imperfect data' and that it is this matter which has prompted the writing of the report. He goes into considerable detail in attempting to show that much of Larmer's findings are unreliable and that his projections on costings are not sound. He starts by considering the Lancaster end of the scheme and deals with the proposals for the links with the Lancaster and Preston Railway. Bintley takes great exception to the Commissioners' comment that, 'The result is that this gentleman [Mr Larmer] has considerably modified and improved that part of Mr Bintley's line south of Kendal'.

Bintley sees this as very prejudicial against him. He goes on to justify his recommendations for the Longsleddale route and questions the unfavourable comparison made with the Orton route. He feels that Francis Whishaw indulged in 'vague calculations' and he seeks to justify his conclusions regarding the nature of the rock formations in both schemes, having sought expert advice. He also takes issue with the Commissioners because, in his view, they looked only at his earlier 1837 report and subsequent modifications seem to have been ignored or overlooked. He claims that in view of this he has been 'unfairly' treated. He even offers to enter a wager,

> If I do not prove to him [Larmer] the truth that he is in error I will pay him something handsome for the time he devotes, to set this matter at rest, viz. two guineas a day and expenses.
>
> He cannot but say that my proposals are liberal, and as such ought to accept them, keeping in mind that if he does not substantiate the correctness of his survey, he must pay me two guineas per day and expenses for the time devoted to the Grayrigg line.

When Bintley's views were made public, they carried a very telling postscript:

> Since writing the above, a gentleman belonging to the railway committee suggested to me how desirable it might be to let this matter rest and not bring it before the public. To that gentleman my best thanks are due, as every word uttered was, I have no doubt, given in true friendship and regard for my weal. From what transpired I could easily understand that he was jealous I had stated something reflecting on the character of the committee and which was calculated to create enmity. However, I trust there is not a word tending to rouse their animosity against me; they had a right to employ any professional man they pleased. This article is not against the committee, neither is it written to wound the feelings or injure the character of any one but to cut the matter short, *it is in self defence.*

This was not published in the *Westmorland Gazette* until 29th May, 1841 (i.e. one year later). The item is headed, 'MR BINTLEY'S REPORT ON THE RAILWAY FROM LANCASTER BY KENDAL TO PENRITH' and although matters had moved on by then, it did invoke a response.

Lord Lowther champions the cause

It was Lord Lowther who further embraced the cause for a line of railway which would better serve the needs of Kendal. He supported the proposition to take a line by Grayrigg which would join the Lune line at its northerly end. In this the Kendal Committee was also backed by those in Penrith and Carlisle. On Tuesday 23rd May, only days after the Commissioners report was out, his lordship was successful in carrying a motion in the House of Commons which enabled the Commissioners to examine this possibility.

The Lancaster & Preston Railway opens

Meanwhile, the railway link from London moved steadily northwards as the Lancaster & Preston Junction Railway brought railway communications to the doorstep of Westmorland. It was originally announced that this section of the link, which would eventually become part of the West Coast main line, would open on 8th June but in the event, it opened on Thursday 25th June, 1840. There were five trains a day in each direction between Lancaster and Preston. The company was destined to have a somewhat chequered career during the early years of its existence.

With interest in railways no doubt growing, the *Westmorland Gazette* reported on 20th June that 'three splendid first class carriages passed through the town'. They were destined for the Ayr & Glasgow Railway and had been built in Lancaster. A taste of things to come. By the beginning of July a new coach service had been introduced to connect Kendal with the trains at Lancaster. It was billed as 'the cheapest coach of all others' and left Kendal at 10.00 am on every day except Sunday and left Lancaster for a return trip at 6.00 pm or immediately following the arrival of the train. Fares from Kendal to Preston (road and rail included) were four shillings. A new 'light omnibus' was also introduced to link this service with Bowness and Ambleside. Not to be outdone, fares on the Swift Packet Boats between Kendal and Preston were reduced to four shillings and sixpence, 'first cabin' and three shillings, 'second cabin'. There would also be connections with the trains on these services. So communications to and from Kendal were being strengthened and competition was creeping in as this happened. Yet it must have been realized that these steps could only be transitory; a railway from Lancaster, northwards, must surely be inevitable. The competition between different operators of coaches soon became a matter for concern because it was alleged that the vehicles were being driven recklessly. A correspondent to the *Westmorland Gazette* who signed simply 'Viator' expressed dismay in a letter published on 8th August:

> Mr Editor, - The speed at which the opposition coaches between Lancaster and Kendal are running - or rather racing - is not only extremely dangerous to persons travelling thereby, but very perilous to passengers along the line of road they travel, more particularly in the towns of Kendal and Kirkland. In addition to this, the great cruelty to the animals by the furious driving of the conductors of the vehicles to which the dumb and abased beasts are harnessed, calls loudly for magisterial interference.

The idea of these coaches racing 'Ben Hur' style around Kendal puts a strain on the imagination but the practice was clearly an issue. Horses were known to drop dead after having been raced hard. The writer goes on to air other grievances about the various practices adopted and calls for action to be taken.

Whilst coachmen were careering between Kendal and Lancaster and coach firms vying with the packet boats for custom, the promoters of a railway which would serve Kendal were far from idle. The success of Lord Lowther's petition in Parliament, for further investigations into the route through Grayrigg, led, in August, to the Commissioners being instructed by Parliament to carry out a review. Frederic Smith arrived in Kendal on 23rd October to re-examine the schemes and only a week later the *Railway Times* was able to report that following a reappraisal of the routes it appeared likely that the Grayrigg route would be favoured. This would provide a better link for Kendal than the previous plans. When the Commissioners issued their findings on 14th November this indeed proved to be the case. Once again there is much play on the fact that Kendal is a place which merits railway facilities. They point out that on their previous visit and in their subsequent report, they were aware that there was another scheme in the offing but felt unable, at the late stage at which it was mooted, to consider it properly in their recommendations. Now it had been possible. Larmer had called his latest proposal 'Grayrigg Junction'; the Commissioners preferred the title 'Grayrigg Line'. This scheme was compared with Bintley's proposals and south of Kendal one element which was seen to be preferable was that Larmer's plans involved a head-on connection with the existing line at Lancaster whereas, as mentioned previously, Bintley's had a junction about two miles south of the terminus, creating the need for an extra length of line and also possible inconvenience to travellers. However, it was in the area of Kendal that Larmer's scheme made more sense if Kendal's needs were to be seriously taken into account. Although the line would not pass through the town, it would pass barely more than a mile east of it and in doing so would not significantly lose height. To the north of Kendal the line would go in a north-easterly direction, through Docker Garth and then east for a distance before turning in a northerly direction where it would follow one of Larmer's original schemes. The Commissioners felt this to be the route that, all circumstances being considered, would be preferable and therefore the one they recommended. Understandably there was much excitement in Kendal with this decision. The *Westmorland Gazette* hailed it as 'a great triumph for the interests of Kendal'. Even so, in spite of the Commissioner's recommendation of this route, the issue was by no means completely closed. Time would show that there were still some obstacles which would have to be overcome.

1841 – The Commissioners report again

On 15th March the Commissioners issued their fourth and final report. It dealt with railway communications between London, Dublin, Edinburgh and Glasgow. There was no threat, here, to the proposals relating to the route between Lancaster and Carlisle, indeed it is further endorsed. A line through eastern England was seen as a possible alternative should the former fail for any reason. However, the interests of those in Kendal were soon aroused by this report because in it there is a reference to a proposal for a railway from Lancaster to Edinburgh. In August, a committee was formed consisting of 39 men, many of them already familiar now with railway projects. The last named is Cornelius Nicholson. He would act as secretary.

It was at the end of May that the article written by Job Bintley appeared in the *Westmorland Gazette* and there were those who sympathized with him and felt he had been shabbily treated. One such person wrote under the pseudonym of 'Fair Play'. Whoever penned the letter felt that 'Mr Bintley has been ill-used' and 'his professional character implicated'. So convinced was the writer that the Longsleddale route was the preferable one that it was felt it should be given the title 'Bintley's Line'. The hope was expressed that because he was a young man with a family to support, the Kendal Committee would take up his cause and raise a subscription for him to make up for any loss of income which might be incurred. Job Bintley, latterly, had been advertising in the *Westmorland Gazette* as a 'Land Valuer and Surveyor' but within a short time the bold part of the advertisement styled him as a 'Woollen Draper' with 'Surveyor' in smaller print. Clearly, Job Bintley was a man of diverse talents.

In June, yet another coach service was introduced. With titles such as 'The Engineer' and 'The Locomotive' already in use, this one went the whole hog and was called 'The Railway'. It ran between Keswick and Lancaster every morning except Sunday and passed through Ambleside and Kendal arriving in Lancaster in time 'to proceed by the Railway Train at One p.m. to Manchester, Liverpool &c &c and returning from J.Dunn and Sons Coach Office, Lancaster, at Two o'clock p.m. Kendal at Five, p.m. Ambleside at Seven, p.m. and arrives at Keswick at Nine, p.m.' There is a note. 'One Coachman - No Guard'.

Now that the way seemed clear to formulate in more detail the plans for the building of the railway, a meeting of the Carlisle Committee was held in Carlisle Town Hall on 2nd October. The Kendal and Penrith Committees were also represented with John Wakefield and Cornelius Nicholson representing the former. Other groups were also present including those from the Grand Junction Railway. No less a person that Captain Huish, Secretary of the Grand Junction, represented that company. It was a protracted meeting with much rhetoric about the importance of the line and the intention to get ahead of schemes which might be forthcoming for the east of the country. There was discussion, too, about the plans north of Carlisle and also a need to get the London & Birmingham Railway involved. Nicholson spoke at some length. He sang the praises of Larmer (again, much in contrast to his earlier views) in coming up with a scheme which the Commissioners had been able to recommend but there was a hint that Huish was rooting for Locke. Any decision about who would be given the responsibility of carrying out a detailed survey in readiness for presenting a Bill to Parliament was left until a meeting could be held in Glasgow. The meeting in Glasgow was held on the 22nd December. In the end Locke was given the job, acting, as he later claimed, for the Grand Junction Railway.

1842 – Joseph Locke springs a surprise – Support and opposition

By the beginning of September, Locke was able to present a report on the surveys he had carried out. In a preamble, he points out that there had been certain problems which had arisen and which had delayed the completion of it. He remarked on the Commissioners' findings and the facts that those findings were based upon. He suggested that the Commissioners' objectives were limited by certain factors and also by the requirements of certain groups. He then states,

> ... in consequence of this circumstance, that I, on undertaking to make the present survey, felt it necessary, with due deference to the Commissioners, and to the very able Report which they furnished, to require that my investigations should not be restricted to the line recommended by them, but that I should be at liberty to make such further surveys as seemed likely to settle definitively the best route for the Railway in question.

Members of the Kendal Committee and those in the Kendal camp reading this report probably guessed what was coming! Sure enough, their fears would be justified on reading further. Locke does make a careful comparison between the possible routes in this area. He is sympathetic to the needs of Kendal and realises that there is much to be gained for the prosperity of that town by the coming of a railway and, also, the revenue that might be generated for a railway which would serve Kendal. Yet in the final analysis he has this to say:

> I am still of the opinion, that, in an Engineering point of view, the Lune line is the best, it is shorter, cheaper, and has better gradients than the Kendal ... [He does concede] but these advantages are not probably so important as are the considerations to which I have just alluded.

It could be argued that what Locke is saying, in effect, is that he was right the first time even though the first inspection he had carried out was, in his own word, 'cursory'. Certainly Locke was of the opinion that he was dealing with part of what was to become a major trunk route and that this must be the prime consideration when determining which way that route should be taken. So, it would seem that Locke had really got his own way in the end. Here was something of a twist in the tale. Whilst the Commissioners had been carrying out their investigations to establish which route between Lancaster and Carlisle they would recommend, they had consulted a number of people involved in putting forward the various proposals. The names mentioned include Hague, Rastrick, Bintley and Larmer as those chiefly responsible for setting out the various schemes. Thus, in spite of the work that he had done in the early part of the planning process, Locke is overlooked by the Commissioners. It is Larmer who seems to get the credit for the route which was initially recommended. Then it was also Larmer who, on the request of the Kendal Committee, came up with the plan involving the Grayrigg route, which was ultimately the one preferred by the Commissioners. By being appointed as the Engineer for the Lancaster and Carlisle line, Locke had made, as it were, a come back. Having done so, Locke chose to ignore the Commissioners' final recommendation and decided to recommend a line along the route which he had originally preferred, namely the one which included Kirkby Lonsdale and the Lune Valley; the scheme which did not include Kendal. In acting like this, was Locke implying that he knew better than the Commissioners and their advisers? Did he simply feel strongly that his route was the best one or was he attempting to make a point about Larmer?

Whatever the rationale, the Kendal Committee simply could not risk letting this decision stand. Once again there seemed to be a possibility that a railway link for Kendal might be in jeopardy.

The debate re-ignites

Despite the fact that the Commissioners had made it clear which route they felt should be adopted, the whole debate now erupted again with each side marshalling its arguments once more. It was almost as though the Commissioners had never reported, except that, where it was deemed to support a particular group, their work and conclusions were included in the argument.

There could have been a hint of what might happen when, in March, a notice appeared, headed 'The Caledonian Railway'. The notice states that there is an intention to make an application to Parliament in 'the next ensuing session for an Act or Acts for making and maintaining a Railway or Railways'. This railway or railways would start at the junction with the Lancaster & Preston but options are very much left open at this stage about the route. It lists Kirkby Lonsdale, Barbon, Casterton, Mansergh, Middleton, Firbank, Howgill, Marthwaite and Sedbergh but then it also includes Kendal. A route could not take in the former group and also include Kendal. Kendal was therefore possibly a contender for a branch from the main line.

Locke was no doubt aware, when conducting his surveys, that there had already been a lot of opposition to the Lune Valley Line. There had been a public meeting at The Royal Hotel in Kirkby Lonsdale as early as the 3rd February, at which a group of landowners made it clear that the project would be vigorously opposed. The meeting had resolved:

> That whereas the projected Railway through this district would intersect and materially injure many private grounds, cut up and destroy the most fertile portions of the Valley and mar the generally admired beauties of the Lune, and is not called for by the wants of the District and whereas another Line has been surveyed by way of Kendal, more likely to subserve the interests of Commerce, for which railways are avowedly designed, and calculated a much larger population, it is therefore the opinion of this Meeting that a decided opposition should be offered to the Line proposed by the Lune valley.

A committee was formed to 'watch' the unfolding situation and it was agreed that a 'Declaration of Hostility' to the scheme should be sent to the Kendal Committee and the Central Committee in Carlisle.

No doubt the Kendal Committee was pleased to receive this declaration. There were even rumours that persons in Kendal were orchestrating some of this 'hostility'!

In Sedbergh and district the reaction was very different. A meeting was held at the King's Arms, in Sedbergh, on 16th February: 'for the purpose of expressing a decided opinion in favour of the proposed Line of Railway through the Vale of Lune'.

This meeting was also attended by a number of landowners as well as various others from Sedbergh, Garsdale and Dent. It was felt by those present that a railway would bring greater prosperity to the district and even went so far as to state:

> And whereas the town of Kendal already possesses peculiar advantages for the purposes of traffic; that, of the two competing Lines, the statistical properties are nearly balanced, and the engineering capabilities, and consequent expense of construction, much in favour of the Lune line ...

A 'Declaration of Support' was sent from the meeting to the various bodies involved in the promotion of the scheme.

Towards the end of the year the correspondence, once again, came thick and fast. No doubt the editors of the *Kendal Mercury* and the *Westmorland Gazette* had some difficulty deciding what to print and what to withhold as they tried to balance an impartial approach with a desire to champion the cause. The redoubtable Cornelius Nicholson seemed ready to take on all comers and, yet again, wrote at great length in support of the route which would result in the railway passing near to Kendal. On 22nd November he sat down to write a letter of what, by any standards, was of extraordinary length and this was published on 3rd December. It was headed:

CALEDONIAN RAILWAY
RELATIVE ADVANTAGES OF THE KENDAL LINE AND THE LUNE LINE AND THEIR JUNCTION AT BORROW BRIDGE CONSIDERED

It is addressed 'To the Committee appointed by the associated Railway Companies for the purpose of constructing the Caledonian Railway' and lays out in considerable detail the various arguments for the Kendal line when compared to the Lune line. In many ways it is a rerun of his earlier missives but he puts the case with even more vigour. He recognises that the two schemes are still 'in a rival position' and whilst he maintains he will take a dispassionate view in weighing up the two sets of proposals, he nevertheless makes it very clear from the outset what his position is on the issue. He goes back to the Commissioners' recommendation, the significance of Kendal in relation to the Lakes and possible tourism, where would be best served by a railway, in terms of population figures, the comparative costs of construction and the possible income generated.Nicholson believes there is now greater parity in the costs and even the possibility that the Kendal line could be cheaper; these results he attributes to a 'recent' survey by Locke. He cites other minor factors and signs the letter 'On behalf of the Kendal Railway Committee'.

There was, perhaps, something of a surprise when a further meeting was held at The Royal Hotel in Kirkby Lonsdale, on 8th December. The meeting, chaired by the vicar, The Reverend J.H. Fisher, was convened to support the scheme to route the railway through the Lune Valley. This was clearly at variance with the meeting held in February and concurred with the group meeting in Sedbergh on 16th February. Although there were those who remained apprehensive, not least Mr Wilson of Rigmaden, the arguments which were put forward were accepted by the meeting. These arguments, in favour of this route, included the assertions that it would be shorter, easier and cheaper to both build and maintain. It would also serve a population of some 20,000. Another point made was that the Lune line would not have to compete for one-third of its length with the 'well established' Lancaster & Kendal Canal as the Kendal line would have to do. The meeting was attended by representatives from Sedbergh and at the end of it a committee of 12 was set up and a declaration made:

> We, the Undersigned Landowners, Manufacturers and other Inhabitants of the Valley of the Lune and its Neighbourhood for the reasons set forth in a resolution unanimously

adopted at a Public Meeting held at The Royal Hotel, Kirkby Lonsdale, on 8th December 1842, do hereby declare our most decided and hearty assent to the projected Line of Railway by the Valley of the Lune and do pledge ourselves to forward the fulfilment of the same by every means in our power.

Listed amongst the 12 was Richard Atkinson Esq. Atkinson would later air his views on the matter under consideration, with the result that he would be the next individual to be the recipient of Cornelius Nicholson's derision.

On 10th December, the editor of the *Kendal Mercury* was upbraided for appearing to be biased in the newapaper's reporting of the two aspects of the debate and for clearly favouring the Kendal line. 'R.H.' of Howgill, near Sedbergh, went to some length to make the point which also included criticism of Cornelius Nicholson. The editor noted that he felt it necessary to print the letter in order to present both sides of the argument, even though he may not agree with the contents!

The flood gates now opened for more correspondence and once again it was Cornelius Nicholson who waded into the fray. In a letter written on 14th December he attacked Richard Atkinson's assessment of the situation regarding the Lune line, especially the population statistics. He was also critical of the remarks made by the Reverend J. Fisher. The gloves were coming off again as Nicholson demonstrated his determination to ensure the Kendal line would be the one selected.

As the year drew to a close, the matter of the route was still not resolved. At the end of December there was a public meeting in Carlisle and the prime issue, addressed by a Mr Swift, was the raising of money for the project and how this might be achieved. At the end of the meeting Mr Dixon asked whether any decision had been made concerning the route. The reply was that it had not yet been decided. Mr Swift did say:

Suppose it turned out that the Kendal route was the more practical of the two, and the most likely to furnish the largest amount of traffic, I presume it will be adopted, but if it is found that the gentlemen in that district grow cold shouldered it is scarcely to be expected that the company will adopt a line that is likely to be more expensive than the other. If, however, the Kendal gentlemen are ready to take on a due share in the burden of the undertaking, I personally have no doubt that the Kendal line will be adopted. However, the company at this time cannot pledge itself to either route.

So, the situation was still open and the match was still on.

1843 – Stop the press – A breakthrough ... and a threat from the canal company

On the 4th February a meeting of the Associated Committee was held in Liverpool. John Wakefield, William Whitwell and Cornelius Nicholson attended, representing the Kendal Committee. The editor of *The Kendal Mercury* stopped the press for the second edition of the newspaper. He stated:

We have stopped the press, to announce that the deputation which attended this day at Liverpool, from the Kendal Railway committee has just returned by mail (12 midnight-Friday) and have brought intelligence to the effect that the Associated Committee have decided with proceeding with their undertaking in their present session of Parliament provided the necessary funds from the district be forthcoming, within the space of, at the utmost, a fortnight or three weeks from the present date ...

The Kendal committee representatives had made their case well and the railway would pass close to Kendal.

However, from the Kendal Group's point of view, there was an alarming development on another front. In September 1842, the Lancaster Canal Company in effect took over the running of the Lancaster & Preston Railway with a view to leasing it. The railway was in parlous financial straits and this proposal to lease it had been approved by the shareholders in that month. Such a lease could have grave financial consequences for the Kendal cause. The canal company had proved more than a match for the railway in the way it had managed to carry goods and passengers. In addition, the canal company had offered £50,000 towards the construction of the railway north of Lancaster if it was built through the Lune Valley. This would clearly be in the interests of the canal company but certainly not in the interests of the Kendal group. Matters were coming to a head with the provision of a Bill. A well attended meeting was held in the town hall in Kendal on 25th February, 1843 to determine how these moves could be opposed. After a lengthy debate it was decided that John Wakefield, Thomas Harrison and Cornelius Nicholson should go to London to provide opposition to the Bill when it went before a Commons Committee in March. In the event this proved to be ineffective and the Act for the lease received the Royal Assent on 3rd April, 1843. Later the terms and conditions laid down were to be challenged by the Lancaster & Carlisle Railway ... but that is another story.

In conclusion

On 6th June, 1844 the Act for the construction of the railway from Lancaster to Carlisle was placed on the Statute Book. The line would take the Grayrigg route and so pass near to Kendal. No doubt there were those in the Kendal Group who had hoped, certainly during the initial discussions, that the line would actually pass right through the town of Kendal, such as it was in the 1830s and 1840s. Yet this was never really a practical proposition in the eyes of those who had the brief to plan the route. The terrain, in their view, was simply not suitable and not one of the schemes put forward, not even the Longsleddale line, took the railway through Kendal itself. Once the Kendal Committee realised this, it was then a matter of bringing the railway as close to the town as possible. The plans for both a coastal route and also the Kirkby Lonsdale route would have left Kendal in comparative isolation and were rightly strongly opposed by those for whom Kendal's interests were paramount. The resulting route for the Lancaster & Carlisle, therefore, offered a sort of compromise in that it passed through Oxenholme, just a 'stone's throw' away from the town. Nevertheless there were those still determined to provide the town of Kendal with a proper railway link. They were not ready to give up that aspiration at this stage and their desire would lead to new plans. These plans would give rise to further struggles, further controversy and a lot more rhetoric.

If the early hopes of those wanting a line through Kendal had actually been realized, the events which were about to follow may never have taken place.

Cornelius Nicholson in his latter years. This photograph forms the frontispiece of the book *A Life Well Lived* written by his daughter, Cornelia Nicholson.

Local Studies Section, Kendal Library

Chapter Two

Further Plans

Once the matter of the route for the section of the line to Scotland north of Lancaster had been settled, the Kendal Party regrouped and began to plan for a railway which would include Kendal. It came up with a proposal for a line from the Lancaster & Carlisle line at Oxenholme which would extend to Lake Windermere.

1844 – August to October

On 31st August, 1844, a notice appeared in the press. It carried the heading 'Railway from Kendal to Windermere' and informed readers that there would be a capital sum of £125,000 needed to build a line; to be raised by issuing 5,000 shares at £25 each. The consulting engineers would be J. Locke and J.E. Errington. Further, the solicitors would be Clay & Swift of Liverpool, together with Thomas Harrison of Kendal. A list of the names of 18 provisional Directors is given:

Edward Wilson Esq.	Abbot Hall
John Wakefield Esq.	Sedgewick House
G.B. Crewdson Esq.	Kendal
John Gandy Esq.	Kendal
W. Briggs Esq MD	Ambleside
John Braithwaite Esq.	Orrest Head Windermere
George Burrow Esq.	Lancaster
Giles Redmayne Esq.	Brathey Hall
John Davy Esq. MD FRS	Ambleside
Hornby Roughsedge Esq.	Fox Ghyll Ambleside
James Bryans Esq.	Bellfield Bowness
James Hewetson Wilson Esq.	Grange, Sussex
William Whitwell Esq.	Kendal
Isaac Braithwaite Esq.	Kendal
C.L. Braithwaite Esq.	Kendal
John Jowett Wilson Esq.	Kendal
John Harrison Esq.	Hundhow
Cornelius Nicholson Esq.	Cowan Head

Cornelius Nicholson, although last on the list (which appears to be in no special order, alphabetical or otherwise) is certainly by no means least. There was a proviso to add to the list if necessary. The notice sets out the advantages to be had if a railway is built from Kendal to Windermere. Nothing linguistically is spared in the description:

> The present Undertaking, extending from the Lancaster and Carlisle Railway at Kendal to the head of Windermere [it is the lake that is being referred to here] will complete a Railway communication between the District of the Lakes and every part of England and Scotland.

The latter part of this statement immediately sent shivers down the spines of some and such shivers were not those of excitement, as soon became clear. The statement continues,

> Preliminary Surveys are in the course of execution and have proceeded far enough to demonstrate that the line is peculiarly easy of construction ...

The next phrase was either intuitive or someone had already heard rumours,

> ... and happily takes a course which will not mar the natural beauty of the scene, skirting behind the woods of Rayrigg and Calgarth.

Not everyone, however, would be convinced by this claim. The statement goes on to explain how,

> The Railway will give the town of Kendal the advantage of a proximate station which the levels of the Trunk Line or Lancaster and Carlisle Line would not afford.

This is a rather curious statement in view of what had gone before but may well have been intended to defray any criticism that this was second best to what might have been.

The route is outlined next, with Burneside and Staveley mentioned. It is proposed that the line will end,

> ... within one mile of the much frequented village of Bowness and thence to the head of the 'Queen of the Lakes', Windermere, terminating a little below Low Wood at about one mile distance from Ambleside.

Once again, the last six words of this section almost certainly set the alarm bells ringing in some quarters and no doubt the question 'And where to next?' was being asked around the dining tables of some of the well to do of the district.

It is stated that 'a considerable number of landowners have already signified their consent to the line'. This statement would be challenged later. Then there is a brief account of the sort of returns such a venture might bring. With the anticipated cost being met, a dividend of 8 per cent might be realized. However, the hope is expressed that 'when Mr Locke shall have matured the Plans, that for a single line of Rails, the cost of Works may fall considerably within this amount' [£125,000]. A further aspiration is that if there was close working with the Lancaster & Carlisle Railway there may also be a reduction in the estimated working expenses.

At this stage the provisional committee had already subscribed over £50,000 of the capital and this information, it appears, was made public so that others would be encouraged to join forces. When the shares were offered, preference would be given to those having shares in the Lancaster & Carlisle and what is referred to as 'Parties locally interested'. Thereafter, shares would be allocated on a 'first come, first served' basis. Those making application were required to furnish 'respectable references' if they were 'strangers' and all successful applicants would be called upon to pay a deposit of 30 shillings per share. Applications were to be made in the form specified, to Cornelius Nicholson (as interim secretary), Foster and Braithwaite in London, H.C. Langton in Liverpool, George Carr in Manchester or

W. Welsh in Lancaster. Deposits were to be paid to Mastermann & Co. in London, Moss & Co. in Liverpool or Wakefield, and Crewdson & Co. in Kendal.

It was then announced that the share list would close on 14th September and anybody who had not received letters of appropriation within a week after that date was to assume they had been unsuccessful.

Opposition

In the 1830s, there had been the beginnings of what would, in hindsight, be referred to as the 'Railway Mania'. The collapse of certain projects and the ensuing loss of investors money on a large scale, had caused some curtailing of over ambitious speculation by the beginning of the 1840s. Even so, the major boom, which would see a further proliferation of schemes, was yet to come and this would subsequently also be the cause of a great deal of financial ruin in some cases, following a second spate of rash speculation. For those of a cautious nature, investing money in railway schemes was not necessarily seen as a wise move. That said, these were early days and the coming of the railways still generated mixed reactions. Some saw 'railways' as being essential to the way in which progress would be made and the means by which fortunes might still be realized. Others envisaged the social impact the railway system might bring. They were ready to welcome that development and included men like Cornelius Nicholson and those who assembled behind him, to push forward with the scheme to build a railway into the Lake District.

Nevertheless, few people, at this time, had actually seen a railway or a railway locomotive and rumours were in circulation, some of which were very florid. Railways, it was argued by some, could never succeed because they were not scriptural (in other words, not mentioned in the Bible). This view had been promoted when the London & Birmingham Railway was proposed. Horses, oxen, donkeys, camels and even water transport (which presumably covered canals) had scriptural support but certainly not railway locomotives. It will be seen later that there were those who introduced God into the debate about the wisdom (or lack of it) of proposing the building of the Kendal & Windermere Railway. Then there were those who held the view that travelling by rail at the sort of speeds anticipated, would almost certainly cause ill health or even death. Most significantly, perhaps, there were those who were vehemently opposed to the railway for more pragmatic reasons; those who owned land which would be needed for building a railway. They could be quick to object. They resented the prospect of land being taken 'by force' (compulsory purchase) and also to the invasion of their estates by what they perceived would be a noisy and smelly intruder. So it was that many landowners on the route between Kendal and Lake Windermere were quick to react. A group was formed to discuss a proposal to oppose the building of the line and a meeting was held at The Low Wood Inn on Wednesday 2nd October. Those attending included landowners 'in the neighbourhood of Ambleside and Bowness'. The meeting was chaired by Professor Wilson. A committee was formed with 12 members. Later another 11 were added to this number, including the Earl of Bradford. The solicitors acting for the group were R. & R. Moser. The public was informed in a notice in the *Kendal Mercury* that 'a subscription was immediately entered into for defraying the expenses of the Opposition'.

There were other points of view raised against the building of the line. One quite plausible one was voiced in a letter to the *Kendal Mercury*:

> The Kendal and Windermere Railway, which has recently been brought before the public to the surprise of the uninitiated appears to me to claim the serious attention of the inhabitants of this town [Kendal] and all who are interested in its welfare as it threatens to neutralize many of the advantages which Kendal ought to derive from the formation of the Lancaster and Carlisle Railway and to transfer them to Bowness, Ambleside &c. On the completion of the Lancaster and Carlisle Railway, Kendal will naturally become the pulse of departure for the lake tourists and consequently may benefit largely by the increased travelling : but if the Kendal and Windermere Railway is carried forward, passengers to the Lakes will be hurried away at once to the Low Wood terminus without spending a farthing to the direct benefit of the town.

The writer who signs himself or herself simply as 'A Friend to Kendal' goes on to express concern about the detrimental effect the line will have 'on the most beautiful scenery of the valley'. The writer does appear to believe there is one advantage that might be gained,

> ... to compensate for the loss of the Lake passengers and that is getting a station rather nearer the town; but this is a mere idea, the proposed station on the Windermere line being nearly as far from some parts of the town as the station in Peat Lane. We are told that the Peat Lane station will be inconvenient and difficult of access; but so far from this being the case it may easily be made perfectly accessible and commodious ... [In spite of this, the writer concludes] In short, as regards the welfare of Kendal, the Kendal and Windermere will not only be useless but extremely injurious and therefore is not entitled to the support of those who desire the prosperity of the town.

It would seem impossible to know what those who were so enthusiastic about the proposed railway really felt about this opposition to their plans. Perhaps they were rather bemused by it; the scheme seemed to them (or most of their number) to be such an obviously beneficial one that strong resistance could be hardly credible. Certainly they had been aware of the need to protect the beauty of the countryside and had said as much in their early statement. So why, they might have wondered, such disagreement? The length of the list of those landowners opposing the scheme also seemed to call into question the proposers' claim that most of the landowners along the route supported them. Had this been a speculative comment or was there reason to accept it as a fact? What is clear is that in spite of the opposition, the group was determined to press ahead undaunted. Yet more was to come and initially this was, perhaps, from an unexpected source.

Of the second group of 11 names, added later to the committee opposing the railway, the Earl of Bradford was not the only well known figure. There was another name which must have stood out. Unlike the more mundane opposition to the railway from local landowners, borne out, primarily, on the grounds of self interest, this opposition stemmed from an all together more aesthetic standpoint: opposition which, though possibly unique, was no less determined. Amongst the list of 11 was the name of the Poet Laureate, William Wordsworth ...

Chapter Three

William Wordsworth,
A poetic interlude

1844 – October to December

I wandered lonely as a cloud
That floats on high o'er vales and hills
When all at once I saw a crowd
A host of golden daffodils

These are the opening lines of what is possibly one of the best known of all William Wordsworth's poems. The original poem was written in 1804 (although modified later) not long after his return to the Lake District. The word 'lonely' may not be without significance in the light of later events, even though it is likely that Wordsworth was in the company of his sister, Dorothy, when he saw this yellow vision. It is clear that for him, solitude was to be desired. Wordsworth was born in Cockermouth in 1770. By 1783 he and his siblings were orphans and William was sent to Hawkshead Grammar School. He later went on to Cambridge and in 1796, after an eventful period in his life, he and Dorothy moved to Somerset. However, in 1799 they moved back to their native Westmorland, living first at Grasmere and then, in 1813, moving to Ambleside. Wordsworth had a great love for the peace and tranquillity of the Lake District. No doubt 'wandering lonely as a cloud' through these hills was his idea of bliss. In 1844, at the age of 74 and only six years before his death in 1850, he perceived a threat to this tranquillity. The proposal to build a railway from Kendal to the shores of Lake Windermere had been mooted. There was even rumour that there might eventually be an extension as far as Ambleside. Wordsworth set his face against such developments and, as mentioned previously, had put his name to the list of those ready to oppose the scheme. But in such circumstances what is a poet to do? Surely the response must be 'to write poetry' and that is precisely what he did!

A sonnet was published on 26th October, 1844 in the *Kendal Mercury* and elsewhere, which carried the heading 'On the Projected Kendal and Windermere Railway':

Is there no nook of English ground secure
From rash assault? Schemes of retirement sown
In youth and mid the busy world kept pace
As when the earliest flowers of hope were blown
Must perish: how can they this blight endure
And must he too his old delights disown
Who scorns a false utilitarian lure
'Mid his paternal fields at random thrown?
Baffle the threat bright scene from Orresthead
Given to passing travellers rapturous glance
Plead for thy peace thy beautiful romance
Of nature; and of human hearts be dead
Speak passing winds, ye torrents, with your strong
And constant voice protest against the wrong.

Bearing in mind that these were words penned by the Poet Laureate, there might well be those in high places who would take notice. Wordsworth added a rider to the poem as if to attempt to justify his argument on grounds other than those which may appear as simply emotional ones. He wrote:

> Let not the above be considered as merely a poetical effusion. A degree and kind of attachment which many of the yeomanry feel to their small inheritance can scarcely be overrated. Near the house of one of them stands a magnificent tree which the neighbour of the owner advised him to fell for profits sake. 'Fell it,' exclaimed the yeoman, 'I had rather fall on my knees and worship it.' It happens, I believe, that the intended railway would pass through this little property and I hope that an apology for the answer will not be thought necessary by one who enters into the strength of the feeling.

The poem sparked off quite a reaction and clearly moved others to be inspired by this particular Muse. This was not to support Wordsworth but rather give the counter argument.

The following appeared in *The Scotsman*:

REPLY TO WORDSWORTH
O thought unworthy of the poet sage
Can the most lovely of terrestrial scenes
Be marred when human science intervenes
To place the marvels of a recent age
By God's old grandeurs? What can so engage
And raise the mind as to behold the proud
Long-tameless elements of nature bowed
To turn to mortal good their governed rage
How grand to note the use of slightest things
Such formless vapours as the mountain lake
Give to the warming sun, serve, as man wills
To bear him mighty loads on thought-swift wings
At his call only earths fall glories wake
Or echo else were silent on the hills.

(Not attributed)

And, also, from the *Glasgow Citizen:*

Not all unworthy of the tuneful race
The wish to save from 'rash assault' the scene
To which affection clings as doth the green
That clasps it yearly in a fresh embrace
When the poor field mouse fled before the plough
Or meek-eyed daisy crushed and ruined lay –
The hand of culture held its onward way
Yet were poetic tear-drops wept as now
Art must pursue the triumphs of its might
As ever as some sweet sequestered nook
Blame not nor deem it neither weak or strange
That tho' the patriot's heart may own the right
The poet's feelings should bewail the change.

(Not attributed)

This poetic battle for the hearts and minds of those who opposed or supported the scheme to build the railway is probably unique. There had certainly been nothing quite like it before nor probably has been since. Later, for example, when the route for the Cockermouth, Keswick & Penrith Railway was planned to pass, in some people's opinion, right through the middle of the Lake District, there was a certain amount of grumbling but no bard of this standing came forward to oppose, so forcibly, what might have been viewed as desecration of the worst possible kind.

This was not the end, by any means, and Wordsworth now found himself being drawn into a heated debate in which he himself was, by inference, accused of a sort of hypocrisy. The *Kendal Mercury*, in the edition of 9th November, saw fit to reprint an item from the *Carlisle Journal*. In this the writer suggests surprise at Wordsworth's stance because at other times he has appeared to support progress of the sort he was now attacking. Wordsworth's sonnet 'Steamboats and Railways' is quoted:

Motions and means on land at sea at war
With old poetic feeling not for this
Shall ye, ye Poets be even judged amiss
No shall your presence howso'er it mar
The loveliness of nature prove a bar
To the minds gaining that prophetic sense
Of future change, that point of vision whence
May be discovered what in soul ye are
In spite of all that beauty may disown
In your harsh features. Nature doth embrace
Her lawful offering in man's art : and time
Pleased with your triumph o'er his brother space
Accepts from your bold hands the proffered crown
Of hope and smiles on you with clear sublime.

The writer of the article expresses the view that initially the assumption was that the sonnet, 'Is there no nook…' was a hoax and not a work penned by Wordsworth. This assumption, however, was not correct and consequently the writer goes on to accuse Wordsworth of being, what, in modern parlance is, a NIMBY (not in my back yard)! He writes,

> What a contrast between the generous sentiment of one sonnet and the petty selfishness of the other. 'Motions and Means' on land warred not with poetic feeling as long as Rydal Mount was 'secure from rash assault' and nature embraced 'her lawful offspring in men's heart' so long as the Lake District was not invaded by a railway.

Strong stuff! Yet there would be more salvos to come in this battle of words.

> We have no objection to Mr Wordsworth giving vent to his attachment to old associations in a sonnet heedless of reason as either the lover or the child … but it is monstrous that such a production, whatever its poetic merits, should be allowed to weigh with men … and that fourteen miles of railway which will enable thousands to enjoy the beauties of the lake district who never could otherwise have that opportunity, which should be stopped by fourteen lines of metre, claiming a monopoly for those beauties for Mr Wordsworth and his neighbour the yeoman, because the one has sown schemes of retirement and the other has a magnificent tree which must be felled if the railway be proceeded with!

There is a caustic final paragraph,

> We trust, therefore that his last sonnet was merely intended as a salvo to his conscience for having committed this offence against Apollo and the Muses, written as Laureate odes used to be of yore on a given occasion as a proof of allegiance and in which neither feeling nor reason were expected to enter.

There had also been an article in the *Morning Chronicle*.

Perhaps, in fairness, it should be pointed out that whilst there was concern expressed here about marauding hordes descending on the Lake District, some years after the opening of the London & Birmingham a similar sentiment was expressed in London about visitors from the north! An anonymous writer penned these lines:

> Oh, the Euston Station! What a botheration,
> And tribulation at the Christmas time;
> With the folks from Yorkshire, and the Pot'thry works sure,
> And the coves from Cork sure with their brogue sublime.
>
> Oh! the noise and clangour, and the Welsh from Bangor -
> Come up to London for to see the sights;
> And the stokers, and the cokers and the red-hot pokers -
> Like Crofton Croker's tales of fairy lights.

The railways were about to bring in a new era which would result in the movement of the population in a way that had never been possible before. Migration of the masses was about to begin and would prove to be unstoppable. Yorkshire puddings would be found alongside Bath buns and Pontefract cakes with Cheddar cheeses.

However, for the moment, it was perceived that all was not yet lost. When poetry seemed to have failed in making an impression on the way things were turning out, Wordsworth turned to prose. In the meantime there had been other reactions to Wordsworth's sentiments. A letter appeared in the *Kendal Mercury* on 23rd November. This had been written by Hartley Coleridge and in dealing with Wordsworth's stance he also introduced a religious element into the debate:

> Sir, I have no inclination to enter a protest against the threatened Windermere Railway. The powers that be are ordained of God and blind must be the man who does not see that steam and machinery are mighty powers that do exist and are ordained of God for mighty good. But I do protest against the calumny - calumny I hope of ignorance, not of malice which ascribes to Wordsworth the unworthy wish to makes the Lakes a cabinet curiosity, like a unique copy of a book - unique it may be because worse than worthless, to be shewn as a special favour to such of his admirers as come in their own carriages. If there be a man upon earth that has an interest in the *publication* of the Lakes, that man is Wordsworth, for they are his shrine; and will be when it has pleased God to call him to his reward, his hallowed sepulchre. The view from Orrest Head is his best commentator. There is not a rock which must be blasted, not a stone- bridged syke which the railway must consign to Stygian obscurity that does not realize some passage of his multifarious writing, which are to visible nature what Shakespeare's are to human nature and passion connecting sensation with perception, perception with thought and

> thought - most perilous and irreligious when it stops at itself - with that devotion which is all and alone sufficient to beget in man the image of his maker in which and for which he was made - in right whereof we call our God our Father.

Readers of this letter may have reacted in different ways. Some may have found it eloquent and felt it was prose which actually bordered on the poetic. Some, on the other hand, may have found difficulty in understanding what the writer was really getting at! Others may have had a reassuring feeling that the writer was bringing God into the matter. This was, after all, a period in which religion still played a prominent part in many peoples' lives. Yet whatever the view, perhaps many would need to remind themselves that what was at issue here was actually the proposal to build a railway line!

Hartley Coleridge continues his argument and manages to include Spenser, Milton, Pope, Gray and even Chaucer in the case he presents. In short what he is saying is that Wordsworth is not against the railway because it will bring 'a poorer class to see the Lakes' but rather on account of 'the good it will destroy'. He comments that 'the railroad will take away more honest bread than it will give', He concludes,

> I do not subscribe to all Mr Wordsworth's objections, but I believe that he objects not for himself but for nature and mankind. He knows well that we must submit to the necessities of time, and where trade requires a railway, there a railway must be. But is there any such necessity in the present case?

Mr Coleridge was a resident of Ambleside.

Religion had been brought into the debate and where religion is, theology is not far behind. The following week, on 30th November, the *Kendal Mercury* published another letter. It deals with both the poetic and religious objections in a very robust way:

> Mr Editor, I have read in your paper Mr Wordsworth's Sonnet, with its prose appendix and, last week, a letter from Mr Hartley Coleridge, in defence of Mr Wordsworth. Setting aside the question of *exclusiveness* with which the Poets may have been (I hope unjustly) charged, the aforesaid writings have, at least, suggested one important benefit which the Railway may confer. As a professor of the Gospel I feel alarmed at the *pseudo-poetic* religion which the Poets wish to establish in the Lake District and I hope that if the Railway makes no other 'inroad' it may, under God's blessing, make a successful inroad upon such worse than nonsense, and worse than mockery! I hope it will carry *missionary* preachers of the living Gospel into the spiritually benighted minds of the sentimentalists: and with this view and motive, I beg to subscribe myself.
>
> *A convert to the railway*

This may have almost seemed like a last word. Not a bit of it. The religious and poetic elements may have been silenced, even exhausted, for the moment, but there were still other views to be aired and by this time, if the correspondence is anything to go by, it would appear there was a majority against the building of a railway.

A letter signed simply 'W' (which may well have made readers wonder) was printed in the *Kendal Mercury* of 14th December:

Sir, I really should have thought that the facility of travelling to the Lakes was now so great that no one would have been found to desire for so small a gain the inconvenience of a railway. Even now, to go from Lancaster to Ambleside is only a journey of four or five hours and when the Carlisle railway is completed to Kendal, it will be about two hours at the most to get from there to Ambleside. A railway from Kendal to Bowness (which I believe is the proposed terminus) would save perhaps three quarters of an hour between Kendal and Ambleside. It is, then, for three quarters of an hour that this railway is to be made, a trifling advantage even in point time, and for the rest, I appeal to everyone whether a drive by the Whitehaven and Lancaster mail is not a pleasanter mode of conveyance to Ambleside than a broken journey, half of which you are shut up in a railway carriage and for the other half jolting in a chaise or fly or, perchance, an omnibus. It cannot be denied, Sir, that there is a *prima facie* case against a railway in the Lake country; all our associations and inclinations are averse to it. Are its advocates prepared to prove that there are advantages to be derived from it which will out weigh all these considerations?

Hoping, Sir, that you will exact your powerful influence against the Windermere Railway and the consequent nuisance of a Windermere steamer.

It would appear that 'W' had not been keeping up with the developments which had been reported in the newspapers. By the time this letter was written the proposed terminus referred to, as will be seen, had been changed. Another aspect of this letter which is significant is that it only addresses the issue of passenger traffic on the railway, with the times involved in the journeys outlined. Once again there is a clear message here about where the objection really lies. There is no consideration given to the passage of goods and how the railway will bring advantages in that respect. The mention of the steamer would seem to introduce a new dimension to the argument and one which thus far the opposition had not really made a issue.

With poetic remonstrations failing, Wordsworth turned to prose. He was certainly ready to fight on.

William Wordsworth (1770-1850). *Local Studies Section, Kendal Library*

Chapter Four

The Scheme Progresses

1844

This was by no means the last to be heard from the opposition but whilst all the rhetoric was being produced, the promoters of the scheme were pushing on with their plans. The shares which were available, readily sold and the subscription deed was placed in the Commercial Inn, in Kendal, on the 5th and 12th October between 11.00 am and 3.00 pm for the purpose of obtaining signatures and, in exchange for bankers receipts, scrip certificates would be issued.

A proposal to change the location of the northern terminus

On 5th November there was a special meeting of the proprietors to consider a recommendation by Errington (one of the consulting engineers) that the northern terminus of the line should be at Birthwaite, near Bowness and not at Low Wood. Edward Wilson was in the chair. Cornelius Nicholson proposed this recommendation and John Harrison seconded it. It was agreed. There were two other proposals, both of which were agreed, namely that Joseph Locke should be thanked for his work in making the initial preparations of the project and that Edward Wilson be thanked for his chairmanship. The first of these resolutions signalled a significant change of plan and this was put to a meeting of the shareholders which also met at The Commercial Hotel in Kendal on the same day. Edward Wilson read the resolution which had been passed at the meeting of the proprietors and which was now to be placed before the shareholders. He informed the meeting that it had been found that the last 3½ miles of the line presented 'such obstacles that the committee thought it desirable to come to the resolution which would be submitted to them for approval of making Birthwaite the terminus'. Whilst Wilson chose to leave Errington to explain the situation in detail, he did point out two aspects which he felt of significance. The first was that the route as originally planned would involve the building of a substantial viaduct at Troutbeck and secondly (and this must surely have raised some eyebrows) 'The property of Lord Bradford would be interfered with in a most unpleasant manner'. The surveyor, Job Bintley, had been instructed 'to avoid interfering with this [Lord Bradford's] property as much as possible'. Wilson expressed the view that all the original objectives could be met even though the terminus was transferred to Birthwaite. Errington then spoke at some length and in a very eloquent manner. He pointed out that the decision to be made really depended much more on a matter of commercial policy rather than engineering merits and felt those present were in a better position than he was to deal with the former. He attempted to analyze the comparative merits in terms of revenue from the traffic of each scheme. He informed his listeners that,

> The Bowness Traffic would have been secured at a station placed at Birthwaite on the way to Low Wood, and, of course, it would be equally secured by the Station at Birthwaite being made the terminus ... As to Ambleside, the proposed terminus at Low Wood would not have accommodated passengers to or from that place without the aid of Carriages, and terminating at Birthwaite only increases the distance by Turnpike Road 2½ miles. For as it happens that while between Kendal and Birthwaite the Railway is shorter than the Road, between Birthwaite and Ambleside, the Road is shorter than the proposed Line of Railway ...

He develops his argument and then makes the point which Wilson made, namely, that the works in the final section, as presently proposed, would be very heavy. A further consideration involves the price that would be asked by Lord Bradford and others in the same area for the land which would be needed. In any case any attempt to acquire this land would lead to opposition to a Bill. There was one other significant consideration. In Errington's opinion the present capital would not be sufficient to take the line through to Low Wood. This was, in part, because the scheme involved taking the line into Kendal and would therefore result in a longer length of line because of the gradients. Errington felt that money was better spent at that end of the line rather than going through to Low Wood. Cornelius Nicholson then pointed to the possible returns, commenting that the opponents had been circulating 'fallacious' views using, what he described, as 'elegant epithets' such as 'Bubble' and 'Bug Bear'. He said these were inaptly applied!

Although the term 'bug bear' is quite innocuous and one which is still fairly familiar today, the description 'bubble' had a potentially more disturbing and damaging implication. It was more than just a reference to a scheme that might 'burst' like a bubble. The South Sea Bubble in the early 18th century had given the word a rather more sinister meaning. It had the implication of 'fraud' attached to it. In this connotation it became a term applied to a certain type of railway scheme which lead to many of the problems caused by rash speculation and some of the losses in what became known as the Railway Mania of the mid-1840s. In a 'bubble', a railway scheme would be floated by a group, shares would be offered, and subscribers would pay a deposit and perhaps the first call. The scheme would eventually be abandoned; from the outset there would have been no hope or possible intention of carrying it through. The income was allegedly used up in expenses, although questionably so. Investors in such schemes would lose their money and although suspicions might arise about the original viability of the project, it was often virtually impossible to call the promoters to account. There were those who made fortunes by this fraudulent practice.

George Cruikshank, the famous satirist, wrote:

> As gudgeons hurry to their fate,
> To railway bubbles some incline,
> Forgetting that beneath the bait,
> A hook's the end of many a line.

This is what was being implied about the motives of the promoters of the Kendal and Windermere.

Nicholson went on to say that whilst a change in terminus might be seen as reducing a projected dividend from 8 to 7 per cent there were several factors which had not been taken into account because his 'care had been purposely to moderate and put the promised remuneration as low as possible'. He also saw fit to comment on the challenge made by some opponents about the statement that most of the landowners had consented to support the scheme when it appeared there was clearly a substantial number who did not. 'They were fully justified in using such language,' he asserted, adding that he had a list of landowners in his hand, drawn up by Mr Bintley, showing the consents, dissents and neuters and that 'nine tenths were of the latter class'. (Given that the word 'latter' should only used when referring to two groups or items, it is a rather misleading statement!) Trading in shares had gone very well, all deposits had been paid punctually, with no exceptions, and the company had benefited £1,200 from the profit of 300 shares which had been originally reserved. It had then been decided to sell these shares at a premium of £4 per share and there was satisfaction expressed that half of them had been bought by a member of the committee. (In the report of the meeting the word 'Cheers' in parentheses occurs at this point!)

There followed a great deal of discussion about the proposal to change the line's terminus to Birthwaite. Many of those present were not happy with the idea. 'What would be the cost of the last three miles?' Errington could not give a precise figure but was sure 'that it was considerably more than any other portion of the line.' 'It was desirable that the railway came as close to Ambleside as possible and therefore the original terminus would be preferred.' This view was supported by others. Errington again drew attention to the fact that the capital was insufficient to take the line further than Birthwaite. 'Why not create new shares to raise further capital?' It was felt Hawkshead would be disadvantaged by the change of terminus although not everyone agreed as 'Hawkshead traffic all passed by the ferry and set by the head of Windermere'. There were those who felt that the whole area should benefit from the facilities a railway would bring. However, as Mr Roughsedge pointed out, 'if they stopped at Birthwaite, Ambleside would not be satisfied and then Grasmere would want a railway.' Then again 'were the proprietors not keeping faith if they changed the original plan?' Dr Davy expressed the view that 'so far as the interest of Ambleside was concerned, it was very desirable that the railroad should come as near to that town as possible'. He went on to say that a railway to Ambleside 'would be a very great public good and he therefore wished that it should approach that town as nearly as possible'. This comment was greeted with cheers by some of those present. More discussion ensued about income and trade. Eventually the chairman decided there had been enough talking. He stated that he thought the reasons for stopping at Birthwaite were 'conclusive'. The capital would not allow them to go further and he remarked there were 'great objections to increasing the amount of their capital'. In view of this he moved the resolution and this was seconded. Messrs Clay and Roughsedge begged to differ. They proposed and seconded a motion that the line should go through to Low Wood, as originally planned. Following a vote, the chairman's resolution was carried. The line would terminate at Birthwaite.

This decision was, in some ways, a turning point for the project and the proposers must have realized this. Some of the more formidable land-owning opponents of the scheme would possibly be placated. The tide might begin to turn in this respect. It did, though not entirely.

Seeking Parliamentary approval – Vigorous exchanges

Having determined the position of the northern terminus, official notice was given the following day of the group's intention to make application to Parliament, in the following session, for an Act to build the railway. This may well have galvanized the opponents into further action. Some of the remarks made at the shareholders' meeting did not go down well with the opposition committee and over the following weeks there was a flurry of correspondence published. This ran parallel to the more general correspondence which was described in the previous section but was more specific in that it directly involved the promoters and the opposition group. Feelings were beginning to run high and towards the end of the year the exchanges between Cornelius Nicholson, for the Directors, and Roger Moser, for the opposition group, eventually flared up to the point where the issues became overlaid by the exchange of personal comments 'not' it was said,' befitting gentlemen'. The first round was fired in a letter by Roger Moser, writing on behalf of the opposition committee. Exception had been taken to some of the views expressed at the shareholders' meeting and it was felt necessary to set the record straight so that the public at large should be well informed about the 'real state of affairs'. In a letter to *The Westmorland Gazette* dated 13th November, and which was published on 16th November, both Mr Roughsedge and Dr Davy were singled out for allegedly making comments at the meeting which were refutable:

> Sir, Your paper of last week contains the report of a meeting of the shareholders in the Kendal and Windermere Railway at which Mr Davy is represented to have said, 'he believed that a railway to Ambleside would be a very great public good, and he was pretty confident that the general feeling of the inhabitants was in favour of bringing it as near as possible to that place' and Mr Roughsedge is represented to have said ' But with regard to stopping at Birthwaite he believed Ambleside would not be satisfied nor would Grasmere and there would be another railway projected to Grasmere almost a certainty'. The committee for conducting the opposition to this railway do not impute any improper motives to either of the above gentlemen in making these statements, nevertheless they think it proper that the mind of the public should be set right on the subject. They have taken considerable pains to ascertain the sentiments of the inhabitants and landowners in the Lake District respecting this railway and they authorise me to say that the inhabitants generally are opposed to it, and that *there are not twelve resident landowners in all Bowness, Ambleside and Grasmere who are not opposed to it.* The committee consider that the statements of Dr Davy and Mr Roughsedge like many others which are daily sent forth to the public were made without due investigation.

The matter certainly did not rest there. The pace of the exchanges gained momentum. Dr Davy was quick to respond and the following week, 23rd November, a very lengthy letter written by him was published in reply to Roger Moser's letter. There is an argument beginning to creep into the correspondence relating to who was actually presenting the facts correctly, and thereby telling the truth. In time this argument would escalate even further.

In his letter, Dr Davy made a number of points. He acknowledged that he had made the remarks quoted my Mr Moser. Davy is prepared to concede that the landowners involved are probably against the scheme but declares that he thinks Moser (and presumably the opposition committee for whom Moser speaks) is wrong in saying that the inhabitants are against it. Davy attempts to justify his point in what can only be described as a rather tenuous argument,

> When a party is formed and that party is composed of the majority of the land owners, it is difficult to learn what are the real sentiments of the people, most of whom, in a country district, are more or less under the influence of the landed proprietors and therefore on a subject such as this, in which they do not consider themselves (ignorantly, I believe) materially interested, will answer, when applied to, in a manner likely to be agreeable to the persons asking them.

At this point he decides to go on the offensive:

> But admitting that the committee are altogether right and that the inhabitants of this district as well as the proprietors of the land, are opposed to the railway, does it follow that there ought not to be a railway? We know that in many instances the opposition have become the advocates for the railway; that the same party who successfully rejected a railway fearing many evils from it, finding after certain experiences, they were in error, and having lost advantages, have exerted themselves to obtain one. Does this not prove that too much attention may be shown to local feelings? Ought not the merits of any particular line of railway to be considered apart from fleeting opinion, taking for data what is positive both of good and of evil and if the former preponderates, ought not the railway to be supported?

The letter goes on at length and Davy is at great pains to emphasize how beneficial the railway would be. He believes it will reduce the cost of important items such as coal and lime and all commodities 'brought from a distance'. As for the matter of the environment, he expresses the view that the beauties of the Lake District should be open to all and that the impact visitors will have is not something to be feared because it will not have the effect many think it will. He then makes the following statement, which may well have ruffled a few feathers:

> Is not stagnation, dullness, want of stirring interests, want of wholesome occupation more to be dreaded in country life and even in these beautiful valleys?

In reply to the notion that a railway will ruin the beauty of the scenery he argues that a railway could actually enhance it. He becomes very eloquent in making this point. As far as the building of new houses is concerned, he suggests that those who choose to build will be lovers of beauty and therefore any new housing will reflect this. The cry that 'the morals of the natives are likely to suffer from an increased influx of strangery [*sic*]' he also believes to be unfounded. Experience, he maintains, shows this is unlikely to happen. The letter concludes with further insistence that a railway will be of great advantage to the area.

The local newspapers were not the only stage where this drama was being played out. Articles were appearing in newspapers further afield. These were often published in the local press as it was realized that many local people would not have access to this wider press and so could not, therefore, read the originals.

The war of words reaches a climax

A letter appeared in the *Railway Times* on 7th December in which the writer was once again afforded anonymity, just signing 'A' at the end. The content was another attack on the scheme to build the railway. The *Westmorland Gazette* was very ready to reprint a copy of the letter Cornelius Nicholson had sent to the *Railway Times* in reply. In the edition of 14th December, it was pointed out:

> We have much pleasure in publishing the letter which follows from Mr Nicholson in defence of the Kendal and Windermere Railway. Anonymous slanderers are rarely worth the notice of gentlemen who have the conduct of these great public works but it may be very wise and salutary in the latter (as in an instance like the present) occasionally to act above 'silent contempt' and teach parties such as our contemporary's correspondent, that there is a limit to provocation.

The account goes on to extol the virtues of those involved in the project and declares, 'As to the imputation against them of being actuated by selfish motives *that* deserves only to be scattered to the winds'.

Again, it is quite clear where the sympathies of the *Westmorland Gazette* lie. There also follows a letter from Nicholson. It is manifest, by the wording of the opening paragraph, that feelings are beginning to run high:

> Sir,- In the *Railway Times* of Saturday last there appears a letter traducing the Kendal and Windermere Railway, which calls for some observations from me as one of the projectors of the line. The letter is signed 'A' which stands for *assassin* very appropriately, as from behind this significant incognito the assailant hurls his poisoned shafts. I have no concern with his declamatory abuse - my object is merely to defend the honour of the promoters in matters of fact ...

Nicholson answers the allegations made by 'A'. He points out that one-third of the land through which the line will pass is owned by members of his committee. He then suggests that,

> ... our accuser in this matter mistook *projectors* for *objectors* because it is a 'fact' and a truth that not a single gentleman whose name stands on the opposition committee owns *one inch of land* through which the line passes.

He acknowledges that those promoting the line have motives such as business interests or the enhancement of the value of land or improving communication or benefiting from a sound investment (what is wrong with any of these?) but there is also, 'a desire to open up the Switzerland of England to our countrymen generally'.

He even quotes Wordsworth when the latter said, 'The lake scenery is a national property to which every man has a right who has an eye to see and a heart to feel'. On the second matter, Nicholson is of the opinion that the financial returns from the line may well be higher than had been estimated. He then asserts that he has in his possession letters from Lord Brougham, the Honourable Colonel Lowther and Mr Alderman Thompson informing him that they are willing to undertake the conduct of the Bill.

21st December

The next edition of the *Westmorland Gazette* (21st December) carried a number of letters. The matters under scrutiny had become whether the men that Nicholson had said were ready to see the Bill through the House had agreed to do so, whether the claims about members of the committee and ownership of land could be substantiated and whether some of those listed as committee members had actually consented to be on the list at all. In addition to these matters, Wordsworth had a letter published in the *Morning Post* on 11th December and this was reprinted on the same date in the edition of the *Westmorland Gazette*. The first letter is the one from Wordsworth which is followed by a reply from Dr Davy. The third letter is from Roger Moser on behalf of the opposition and appears to carry some surprising, if not alarming revelations. Moser writes as follows:

> The committee for conducting the opposition to this railway having had the letter of Mr Cornelius Nicholson, which appeared in your last week's paper, brought before them, request me to state that, according to their directions, I applied by letter, some time ago, to both the members for the county, enquiring if they had consented to carry the Kendal and Windermere Railway Bill through the House of Commons, and that I received the following replies, subsequent to the announcement in the WESTMORLAND GAZETTE of the 12th of October last 'that the Hon. Col. Lowther and Mr Alderman Thompson would conduct it through the Commons, having both signified their pleasure herein':
>
> *Lowther October 26, 1844*
>
> Sir,- I know nothing of the Kendal and Windermere Railway except what has appeared in the public prints, nor have I been applied to by any one to give the bill alluded to my support.
> I remain, sir, your obedient servant,
> H.C. Lowther
>
> *Underley Hall, Kirkby Lonsdale, 28th October 1844*
>
> *Messrs R. & R. Moser*
> Dear Sirs- In answer to your letter of the date of 25th inst, I have to inform you that all I know about the Kendal and Windermere Railway is this. Application was made to me to introduce the bill, which I have consented to do as I conceive it to be my duty to afford a *locus standi* in the House of Commons to any local measure which a respectable body of my constituents may require of me, but I have not been asked to give any pledge to carry the bill through and had such a request been made to me it would have been refused, because I never have or will commit to support or oppose a measure respecting which there is a difference of opinion among my constituents, whether it would prove beneficial or otherwise for their interests. I therefore need hardly say that I am in the position to hear the merits of this project discussed before a committee of the House of Commons free from any predilection whatsoever. I have not the smallest pecuniary interest in the railway. I have been told that the line will pass through my land at Kendal, but I have not given as yet my consent thereto.
> I am, dear sirs, yours respectfully,
> *W.M. Thompson*

This did not seem to put Nicholson in a good light and Moser challenges Nicholson 'to reconcile his statement with these letters'. The next observation in Moser's letter is a very telling one and possibly begs the reader to 'read between the lines'.

With respect to the inuendo [*sic*] that there is not a single gentleman on the opposition committee who owns an inch of railway through which the railway will pass, I cannot help observing that the committee were owners through which the railway *was intended to pass* for upwards of two miles so long as Low Wood was the terminus, but when the promoters determined to excise three miles from the length of the line the committee ceased to be landowners on the line, *because* their estates were within the portion cut off.

Whilst it may have been felt that this might have settled the matter for those whose land had seemed under threat from the line, there were still other issues to address.

So, Moser had thrown down the gauntlet; Nicholson was only too ready to pick it up, as the following week would show.

In the meantime, in the same edition of the *Westmorland Gazette*, Dr Davy dealt with a letter from William Wordsworth. Wordsworth's letter appeared alongside the letter from Davy but the former, written on the 9th December, had originally been published in the *Morning Post* on 11th December. The letter was a follow up to the sonnet about the railway, also published in that newspaper. Such a letter, like the sonnet, would no doubt have been sympathetically received at the *Morning Post* because when David Stuart took over the newspaper in 1795, it was flagging. He had enlisted writers such as Coleridge and Wordsworth to increase its status. In spite of the decision relating to the northern terminus, Wordsworth was not prepared to give up yet. At times, the arguments in Wordsworth's letter are very tenuous and some may have seen them as little more than the ramblings of an old man who was greatly prejudiced. The following extracts give an indication of the case presented:

Sir, Some little time ago you did me the favour of inserting a sonnet expressive of the regret and indignation which, in common with others all over these Islands, I felt at the proposal of a railway to extend from Kendal to Low Wood, near the head of Windermere. The project was so offensive to a large majority of proprietors through whose lands the line, after it came in view of the Lake, was to pass, that, for this reason, and the avowed one of the heavy expense without which the difficulties in the way could not be overcome, it has partially abandoned, and the terminus is now fixed at a spot within a mile of Bowness.

The projectors have induced many to favour their schemes by declaring that one of their main objects is to place the beauties of the Lake district within easier reach of those who cannot afford to pay for ordinary conveyances. Look at the facts. Railways are completed, which, joined with others in rapid progress, will bring travellers who prefer approaching by Ullswater to within three miles of that lake. The Lancaster and Carlisle Railway will pass the town of Kendal, about six or seven miles from eminences that command the whole vale of Windermere. The Lakes are therefore at present of very easy access for all persons; but if they be not made still more so, the poor it is said will be wronged. Before this be admitted let the question be fairly looked into.

And I have no hesitation in saying that the good is not to be obtained by transferring at once uneducated persons in large bodies to particular spots, where the combination of natural objects as such as would afford the greatest pleasure to those who have been in the habit of observing and studying the peculiar character of such scenes, and how they differ from one another. Instead, therefore, of tempting artisans and labourers, and the humbler classes of shopkeepers, to ramble to a distance, let us rather look with lively sympathy upon persons in that condition, when, upon a holiday, or, on the Sunday, after having attended their parish church, they make little excursions with their wives and children among neighbouring fields, whither the whole of each family might stroll, or be conveyed at much less cost than would be required to take a single individual of the number to the shores of Windermere by the cheapest conveyance.

What can, in truth, be more absurd than that either rich or poor should be spared the trouble of travelling by the high roads over so short a space, according to their respective means, if the unavoidable consequence must be a great disturbance of the retirement, and in many places a destruction of the beauty of the country, which the parties are come in search of?

The wide-spread waters of these regions are in their nature peaceful; so are the steep mountains and the rocky glens; nor can they be profitably enjoyed but by a mind disposed to peace. Go to a pantomime, a farce or a puppet show, if you want noisy pleasure - the crowd of spectators who partake your enjoyment will, by their presence and acclamations, enhance it; but may those who have given proof that they prefer other gratifications continue to be safe from the molestation of cheap trains pouring out their hundreds at a time along the shores of Windermere.

Today there may be some wry smiles or even indignation, when reading this letter. Smiles in view of the sort of sentiments being expressed and the reasons being set out but also because there are those who would say that in some aspects, Wordsworth might be seen as something of a prophet in his analysis of what would happen if the railway arrived!

Davy wrote a long letter in reply. This extract conveys something of his feelings on Wordsworth's statement:

Mr Wordsworth, in a letter with which he has favoured the public, inserted in the *Morning Post* of the 11th instant, has taken a view of the proposed line of railway, of a very unfavourable kind, considering it as no wise required in relation to the public wants, and likely to be evil in its consequences.

So, Wordsworth had made his case. In fact, the decision to make the terminus at Birthwaite would result, if not in a more positive attitude, then in a less hostile one by some of the landowners, from whom land might have been needed. In effect this would leave Wordsworth somewhat out on a limb because much of the opposition would melt away. Even so, he did write another lengthy letter which was reprinted in the next edition of the *Westmorland Gazette*.

Private correspondence between Cornelius Nicholson and Roger Moser

Following the letter from Moser, published in the *Westmorland Gazette* of 21st December, Nicholson wrote privately to Moser that day. In his letter, Nicholson expresses 'great surprise' relating to the allegation that there was no authority from the county members that they would see the Bill through Parliament and states:

According to my notions of the etiquette of correspondence, one has no right to publish the letters of another without the sanction of the writer and I therefore enclose to you the original letters Lord Brougham, Hon. Col. Lowther and Mr Alderman Thompson ...

Nicholson challenges Moser to 'peruse' the letters and when he returns them, to make it clear whether he was justified or not in saying what he had said. Nicholson points out that the other matters can be dealt with without recourse to private correspondence and he concludes:

And you must excuse me for expressing a regret that you could not discharge your professional duties without provoking a personal altercation, and requiring the vindication of my credit and veracity. *21st December*

There is a 'P.S.' which carries something of a sting! 'You will understand that I propose to publish a copy of this note with your reply to it'.

Two days later, on 23rd December, Moser sent a reply informing Nicholson that copies had been made of the three letters. Although the opposition committee would have an opportunity to read them and make their own decisions, he (Moser) felt that whilst Nicholson might have been justified in asserting what he did, even so, the committee was in order to request Nicholson publicly reconciled what he had said, with what was in the letters. This seems a rather strange thing to say but, clearly, there is a struggle going on here for the moral high ground. Now it is the turn of Moser to go on the defensive:

I did not accuse you of making mis-representations. For the rest of my letter I am alone personally responsible. You made a public attack on the opposition committee, leaving to be inferred that they had not been owners of the land on the intended line, and I deemed it my duty to bring the circumstances before the public. The committee feel assured that if an act can be obtained to carry the railway to Birthwaite, attempts will soon be made to extend it, and they therefore continue their opposition.

There follows a personal comment which is surely likely to fan the flames of this exchange:

Of course you are at liberty to deal with this letter as you think proper; I cannot however refrain from expressing my surprise at the tone of your letter to me (which appears to have been written to me in a hasty spirit) and my regret that you should consider my letter 'as provoking a personal altercation requiring the vindication of your credit and veracity'.

Moser then describes a situation when he attended a meeting concerning the Lancaster & Carlisle Railway, following which he was taken to task by an anonymous writer to verify certain statements he had made:

Did I consider my 'credit and veracity impeached'? Not I, indeed; neither did Dr Davy nor Mr Roughsedge consider theirs to be impeached, when some of their statements respecting this railway were publicly impugned. You surely do not mean to say that each time an individual is called on to explain or reconcile any statement he has made, that he is thereby impliedly charged with a want of veracity.

The ball was now back in Nicholson's court. There was no hesitation in returning it.

On 24th December Nicholson wrote back. By this point, however, in his mind the railway becomes almost a secondary issue, if indeed, for the moment, an issue at all. It seems that it is not a plan to build a line into the Lake District which is paramount but rather a matter of his honour which is perceived to be at stake.

Dear Sir, I have yours of yesterday with its enclosures, and as you are surprised at the tenor of my last letter, 'written in a hasty spirit', I think it right privately to inform you why that tone and spirit pervaded it. I should reckon myself deficient in self-respect if I could have sat quietly for a moment under the aspect of such an impeachment. The inference which I drew from your letter and which many of my friends - our mutual friends, I may say, drew - (as they expressed themselves to me on Saturday) were, that I was accused of having misrepresented or belied sundry facts. I admit that no such terms as 'false' or 'untrue' stand as part of the indictment, but the *animus* of the letter appeared to convict, or labour to convict, me of misrepresentation. I agree that any persons publishing statements by pen or tongue is fairly open to criticism upon them; but the difference between being called upon to reconcile matters of opinion and matters of *fact* - vouched for as fact - is very manifest, and I do not admit to the cases you now cite to be parallel or relevant to the matter at issue. As, however, I desire to avoid personal enmity with you, for whom I would rather encourage feelings of unmixed regard, I give you the opportunity, before I communicate with the newspapers, of explicitly disclaiming any intention to impeach my credit. I shall substantiate my statements, but the application of my remarks may take their direction from the tenor of your reply to this, and I shall be obliged for an answer by to-morrow morning's post.

I am, your obedient servant,

Cornelius Nicholson

It is now Roger Moser who was in the position of picking up the gauntlet. At the season of 'good will to all men', he puts pen to paper. He was not going to acquiesce yet! It was time for counter-measures:

Dear Sir, - I have just received yours of today. I have consulted friends and they agree with me that my published letter does not bear the construction you have put upon it. You first impute motives to me, and then you ask me to disclaim them, and you conclude your last letter with what I read to be a threat. I beg, therefore, respectfully to say that I consider my letter of yesterday to be sufficient answer to yours of today, and I can only repeat that you are at liberty to make such observations on my letter and conduct as you may deem proper. I leave the public to decide between us. I have no objection to your publishing your letter of today and this reply.

Yours truly,

Roger Moser

28th December

The festive season is brought to an abrupt end; at least for some, The *Westmorland Gazette* of 28th December carries more letters. There is another lengthy one from Wordsworth. The main thrust of the letter is much as before. However, at the end, Wordsworth has this to say:

I have now done with the subject. The time of life at which I have arrived may, I trust, if nothing else will, guard me from the temptations of having written from any selfish interests, or from fear of disturbance which a railway might cause to myself. If gratitude for what repose and quiet have done for me through the course of a long life and hope that others might be benefited in the same manner, and in the same country, be selfish, then, indeed, but not otherwise, I plead guilty to the charge.

In conclusion he makes an observation which some might say has a vaguely familiar ring about it, even in this 21st century:

> We have too much hurrying about in these islands; much for idle pleasure, and more for over-activity in the acquisition of wealth. It might be added that this habit is too apt to degenerate into the love of gain, pursued without regard to the real good or happiness of others.

It was, however, a letter from Nicholson that really caused a stir. From the outset there is no mincing of words:

> Sir, Your last week's paper brings me a challenge from Mr Roger Moser to substantiate sundry statements which I made in a letter of the 21 inst on the Kendal and Windermere Railway. I accept the challenge with no other regret than for the damage I must needs inflict on Mr Moser in the exposure of a species of chicanery which is totally unworthy of his private or professional character.

Nicholson says that he will try to be as brief as possible and continues,

> There is, everywhere, as far as I can ascertain, only one impression left on the minds of the reader's of Mr Moser's accusatory letter, viz, that I was thereby charged with having *falsified* certain facts. We shall see as I reply to his questionings, and examine his language closely, whether it bears this construction. He now says that he did not 'accuse me of making mis-statements', and that he is not guilty 'of provoking a personal altercation'. After this I despair of forming any judgement as to what is a personality or what is an impeachment of one's veracity.

Nicholson goes on to list the four issues over which his integrity is apparently called into question, namely:

> *First.* Whether it was correct in me to say that I had letters from the county members, that they would take charge of the bill.
>
> *Second.* Whether I was justified in asserting that 'the railway committee are owners of land for nearly one third of the distance'.
>
> *Third.* Whether I was quite right in stating that 'the opposition committee do not own one inch of the land through which the line passes'.
>
> *Fourth.* Whether as Mr Moser says, I advertised the names of two gentlemen, as committee men, without their consent.

If Roger Moser thought he might be calling Nicholson's bluff in stating that the correspondence could be published, he was mistaken. In what was seen by some as a rather un-gentlemanly act, Nicholson goes on to include all the letters written by the two of them between the 21st December and the current edition of the *Westmorland Gazette*. Nicholson then goes on at length to vindicate his position in what becomes a scathing attack, concluding the letter with the words:

> Supposing Mr Moser to have had some regard for my credit in this particular, he had in one case, the means of information within a hundred yards of his own door - he had the easiest mode of ascertaining the accuracy, or otherwise, of this scandal; but studiously eschewing all enquiry he choose rather not 'in a hasty spirit' (that's my fault) but in cold blood he preferred to affix this calumny upon me on such slender grounds. How, then, I ask, should this conduct be described? Those of the public who adjudge most leniently will declare that he is guilty of 'taking up the reproach against his neighbour' and his practice - to say the least of it - must be classed among 'the deceits of the world'.
>
> I am your obedient servant
>
> *Cornelius Nicholson*
>
> *Cowan Head, Kendal, Dec 26, 1844*

1845

The two letters written by William Wordsworth to the *Morning Post* would seem to have been in demand because on 8th January an advertisement appeared in the *Westmorland Gazette* informing readers that reprints (revised and with additions!) could be purchased for 4*d*.

In a final attempt to claim the moral high ground, Roger Moser did have a short letter published in the *Westmorland Gazette* on 4th January:

> Sir, Mr Nicholson's letter which appeared in your last week's paper, is of too abusive a character to be worthy of a reply.

Even so, he was going to give one!

> Before dismissing the subject I ask such of your readers as may be interested in it dispassionately to peruse the whole correspondence and not to form their judgement on the letter above mentioned. Let them bear in mind that neither Mr Edward Wilson nor Mr Cornelius Nicholson is an owner or reputed owner of lands mentioned in the book of reference deposited with the Clerk of the Peace which contain the names of all persons who are, not of those who *will* be owners of lands which may be required by the railway and that neither Mr James Gandy and Mr Thomas Harrison is a member of the committee printed in the *Kendal Mercury* of the 7th September last. I beg to say most distinctly that I have such evidence in my possession as justified in me writing my letter of the 18th last that I only allow the matter to remain in its present state because I am not at liberty to mention the names of third parties.

This brought to a conclusion the exchange of letters between Nicholson and Moser although other writers were to come forward. In the same edition of the *Westmorland Gazette* there was a letter from someone signing simply as 'A Resident'. It throws a light on the prevailing attitudes of some in that period. The writer made a plea that philanthropic persons should come forward, as they had done in other places, to provide 'spiritual instruction and the performance of divine worship' for those working on the line, given that 'the men usually employed on works of the above description [that is, the railway] are often persons very ignorant, reckless and taking no thought for the morrow and that very often they are the perpetrators of numerable mischiefs and promoters of disturbances and offences in districts otherwise peaceable and orderly'. Further the writer expressed the hope that 'the Windermere Railway may not be unattended by efforts to remove the spiritual darkness too often found among "navvies"'.

In the meantime progress was being made by the Bill which it was hoped would lead to an Act. On Wednesday 19th February, the line was reported to the House of Commons and the Bill was ordered to be brought in by Colonel Lowther, Alderman Thompson and Mr Warburton. The following day, in the evening, it had its first reading.

The opposition suffers a blow

A blow for the opponents of the scheme came in April when the Railway Department for the Board of Trade issued a report on 16th of the month. The report related to its stance as far as the line was concerned. It made its views very clear when it dealt with some of the perceived motives for opposing the scheme.

It reads as follows, with the opening section being fairly pedestrian:

> The KENDAL and WINDERMERE proposed line leaves the Lancaster and Carlisle Railway at Oxenholme and, curving round by Staveley, terminates near Bowness: the length is Ten Miles Twenty-three Chains, and it is to be worked by the Lancaster and Carlisle Railway Company. This project is not of an expensive character, and may expect to command a remunerative traffic, and will afford a very desirable outlet to the Lakes from the manufacturing districts; nor are we aware of any objection except one that has been strongly urged viz, that in the event of the railway being made, the privacy of the locality will be invaded and the comforts of the residents in the neighbourhood will be materially diminished.

It was the next section that no doubt set pulses racing either with dismay or anger,

> We are precluded from taking into consideration the private interests of Individuals, but where a general local feeling, made up of the feelings of individuals who are personally, though privately, interested exists, it is right to notice it. We must therefore state that an argument which goes to deprive the artisan of the offered means of occasionally changing his narrow abode, his crowded streets, his wearisome task and unwholesome toil, for the fresh air, and the healthful holiday which sends him back to his work refreshed and invigorated - simply that individuals who object on the grounds above stated may retain to themselves the exclusive enjoyment of scenes which should be open alike to all; provided the enjoyment of them shall not involve the infringement of private rights, appears to us to be an argument wholly untenable; and we are of opinion that there are no public grounds which ought to be decisive against the Kendal and Windermere proposed railway receiving the sanction of Parliament.

The statement is signed by Dalhousie, C.W. Pasley, D. O'Brian and G.R. Porter.

On Tuesday 22nd May, Nicholson and Errington attended a Railway Committee at the House of Commons. The Kendal & Windermere scheme was listed under Group II and the committee was chaired by Viscount Barrington. The Bill was listed as unopposed and the project was examined under such headings as the preamble, the curves and gradients. It was noted that considerable passenger traffic was expected 'because of its approximation to the Lakes, an object of attraction to the pleasure seekers of the vicinity'. The clauses of the Bill were read through and as there was nothing 'objectionable' the Bill received the assent of the committee. This signified that another hurdle had been successfully negotiated.

The third and final reading took place on Monday 2nd June and the Bill was passed. The Act for building the Kendal & Windermere Railway (Act 8 & 9 Victoria I, c. xxxii) was placed on the statute book on 9th June. The battle was over; the railway company had triumphed.

The ceremony of cutting the first sod or, as the *Westmorland Gazette* preferred to describe it, 'breaking ground' became, over the years for many railway companies, an event accompanied by great festivities. However, although it was observed by 'a considerable concourse of spectators', on this occasion, it seems, it was a fairly low profile affair. The action, as may be guessed, was undertaken by Cornelius Nicholson in the company of gentlemen 'interested in the formation [of the line]'. The date was Wednesday 16th July. The 'navvies' present gave three hearty cheers and 'success to the Windermere Railway'. The local press made very little of it.

An unusual letter

Although it could be assumed that matters had now been settled in favour of the railway being built, on 20th September, there appeared in the *Kendal Mercury* what may have been assumed at first sight to be a letter. It was printed under the title 'Railway Memoranda' and had the heading 'Reasons against Railroads in the Lake District' It read as follows:

> We the undersigned are determined to 'withhold our consent' from any Railroads coming through this district for the following reasons.
>
> *First.* Because our 'consent' has never been solicited and is not likely to be and we have no idea of anybody making railroads without asking our leave.
>
> *Second.* Because a railroad would spoil the scenery, which is OURS notwithstanding what the BOARD OF TRADE may say to the contrary. And we do not believe the doctrine that God made these beauties for any sort of 'common observers'.
>
> *Third.* Because it would make coal cheap and break down the distinction between the fires of the rich and poor. We like the smell of peat and like to see the small column of blue smoke rising from an occasional cottage but railroad prices will raise a cloud of black coal smoke from every house alike which is horrible to think of. Blazing fires were never intended for poor people.
>
> *Fourth.* Because it will bring tons upon tons of sea fish and they will be selling at a penny per pound as they do in Manchester and *Cod's Heads and Shoulders* will no longer be a luxury.
>
> *Fifth.* Because all our farmers round about will be rearing all their poultry and butter and eggs to what we called the great 'hives of industry'. We hate industry and all that belongs to it and we won't be contaminated.
>
> *Sixth.* Because it will raise the rate of wages and will make our servants dissatisfied with their places which they have no right to be. Servants will be running away to manufacturing towns and all grades of people will be riding off to see their relations so that the relations of society will be completely destroyed.
>
> *Seventh and Lastly.* Because it will bring crowds of vulgar people to jostle against us and disturb our charm of solitude and eat up everything that is edible in this country and because our Hotels are throng enough already and we don't want more customers; and finally because we won't have a railroad and that's enough.
>
> *Signed* *Thomas Mala Growler* *Miss Anne Thrope* *James Cynic*
> *Simon Snarl* *Anty Progress* *&c &c*

It is only when the list of signatories is consulted that this remarkable offering is seen in its true light.

There is a footnote 'From our own correspondent'. In much later years such a document would be seen as a satirical comment but, for the period, it is not really easy to see into the mind of whoever wrote it. Perhaps it was intended to be an attack on those who opposed the railway rather than for the amusement of the readers. Whatever the intention it is a very perceptive piece of writing and must have stirred many to realise just how reactionary some of those opposing the project were being.

The first General Meeting

The first general meeting of the proprietors was held on Tuesday 23rd September. Edward Wilson was Chairman. He informed the meeting that there were several resolutions to deal with at the meeting. The first was that the seal which had been produced should be the seal of the company and authorized for appropriate use. This was agreed. This seal (now kept at the National Railway Museum in York) has, in some ways, a rather rough and ready design. It is circular and depicts what is presumably Kendal Castle. Round the edge the words 'Kendal & Windermere Railway Company. Incorporated 1845' are inscribed.

Once this seal had been approved, Mr T. Harrison then read a report and said he was pleased to be able to inform the shareholders that the Act of Incorporation had been obtained without opposition and further, at a cost which was considerably lower than that paid by some other companies. An astute move had been made in the purchase of rails. The previous January there had been an indication that the price of iron would rise quite steeply and so a contract had been agreed to purchase the rails and chairs needed. This resulted in buying these at a price which was some 30 per cent lower than the price at the time of the meeting. The contractors for the scheme, Brassey, McKensie and Stephenson had agreed a price of £97,065 8*s.* 10*d.*, which the company's Engineer found to be 'reasonable and satisfactory'. The contractors would carry out all the work needed except building the stations at the termini and it was felt the project would be carried through within the estimate. It was then announced that Errington had decided to stand down as the company's Engineer. This was 'in consequence of a connection which he had formed with the Ulverstone and Milnthorpe Railway'. (Put very delicately!) The Directors had accepted his decision and had appointed John Harris to replace him. By this stage, one-third of the land required to build the line had been acquired and work was moving forward on these sections 'with energy'. Concern had been expressed regarding the site of the station in Kendal and this issue was one which it was felt had to be addressed. A survey had been carried out and it was reckoned a cost of £10,000 would be needed to change the route from the one originally sanctioned (and referred to as the parliamentary line) to the one involving a deviation. The Directors felt that the issue must be decided by the shareholders and a lengthy discussion ensued. In the end a vote was taken; there were seven votes for the 'parliamentary line' and six for the newly proposed deviation. This was clearly an issue which was by no means cut and dried.

At the meeting optimism was expressed about a scheme to build a line from Cockermouth to Windermere which would pass through Keswick and Ambleside. This project, which went under the name of The Furness and Windermere Railway, would, it was anticipated, be of considerable benefit to the Kendal & Windermere in opening up a considerable portion of the Lake District and thereby being a potential source of considerable revenue. In the event, the optimism was not justified. The plan to build a section of line from Keswick through to Ambleside would prove to be prohibitively expensive, given the difficulty of the terrain. It would be another scheme which would link

Cockermouth to Keswick and this would go forward to Penrith with no connection to the Kendal & Windermere Railway.

There was considerable dissatisfaction with the decision to retain the location of Kendal station as originally proposed. This was expressed in a letter to the *Kendal Mercury* and appeared in the edition of 4th October. Once again it is attributed to 'A Friend of Kendal':

> It appears from a report contained in your last paper, of a meeting of The Kendal and Windermere Railway Company that it was resolved not to bring the line through the town although the Directors were fully aware that many of the most influential inhabitants were extremely anxious to have a central station. Thus the company has thrown away the only chance of making some amends to the town for the injury that the line will certainly do. In our aspect of the case and keeping out of view the standing of the parties who took the most prominent part in opposing the wishes of the public the result is perhaps more vexatious than surprising because this railway is not the offspring of public opinion or public necessity either local or national. It professes to supply a want which nobody felt and consequently is altogether a private affair. But on the other hand, the public of Kendal reasonably demanded that their interest should not be left altogether out of the question but that the line should be brought in such a direction as to compensate, in some measure, for the injury inflicted in the town by diverting from it the lake traffic. This object would have been answered by the simple process of making the railway straight but by a perverse ingenuity it is now made to avoid the town by a long curve. There is no doubt that the company, by the course which they have adopted may save a few thousand pounds but it is somewhat difficult to reconcile such paltry and rigid economy with the confidence they profess to the brilliant prospects of this 'Gem of Railways'. In fact The Kendal and Windermere Railway or the line now resolved upon so far from being of any service to Kendal will be an unmitigated nuisance.

It might be argued that this letter was just a case of 'use any stick to beat a dog' and that the writer was simply using the issue of the location of the station as a means of heaping more criticism on the whole project. However, the very close vote which resulted from discussion of the matter at the previous meeting may well indicate that the writer had raised a point which many shared. This is borne out to some extent in a further letter which appeared on 25th October. Again the writer wished to conceal his or her identity signing with a flourish as 'A Well-wisher to the Railway, Our Good Old Town, and No Enemy to the Corporation'. The tenor of the letter was rather more constructive,

> Sir, Through the medium of your paper, will you allow me to enquire whether the practicality of making Peat Lane the junction of the two above named Railways, by some such plan as the following, has ever been suggested? Say, to make a direct line from the Lancaster and Carlisle, on the Sedbergh Road, to about the Organist's Close and from thence two forks, one to the Canal Warehouse, for goods, coals &c, and another to Far Cross Bank, Sandy's Close, or Black Hall Croft for passengers: of course to work those, a stationary engine would be requisite, but as it would save the making of from a mile to a mile and a half of railway (say from Peat Lane to Oxenholme) with the cost of land &c also a vast amount of cartage (if not in omnibus fares also) annually, would not these items far more than counterbalance the cost and wear and tear of engine?

This radical proposal would fall on deaf ears!

A further change in the plans was proposed in October, when an Extraordinary General Meeting was called. This was held at 2.00 pm on Wednesday 22nd of the month and the matter under consideration on this occasion was that of making a double line of rails instead of just a single one. This was agreed. At the meeting it was also proposed that there should be an additional Director appointed. This was also carried. John Whitwell was appointed and in the first instance he would hold the office until July 1846. There was good news as well; the proprietors were informed that the work was 'progressing rapidly'.

1846

On Wednesday 28th January there was a half-yearly meeting of the proprietors. On this occasion, John Gandy was in the chair. He displayed a real sense of optimism. By this time almost all the land required for the project had been acquired and, in addition, the proposal to lay down two sets of rails rather than having just a single line, agreed in the previous October, had been actioned and the contractors informed. In addition arrangements had been made with the Grand Junction Railway to provide locomotives and carriages, these to be 'in conjunction with the working of the Lancaster and Carlisle line'. Such arrangements were expected to be 'economical and advantageous'. The work had progressed satisfactorily and there was every expectation that the line would be able to open when the Lancaster & Carlisle opened. There was more news. A sum of £200 had been voted towards a survey of the proposed 'Lake District Railway' and this was on a par with a similar amount being made by the Directors of the Cockermouth & Workington Railway. In the event only the monies from the Cockermouth & Workington were called upon at that stage, namely that for a line as far as Keswick, referred to as the 'Cockermouth and Workington Extension'. In fact this scheme was not realized, at least in this form. Even so, at this stage, it was recognized such a link (and, later, possibly others) would enhance the standing of 'The Kendal and Windermere'.

At this stage there had been receipts totalling £24,451 5*s*. 6*d*. These were made up of the deposits and calls on shares and the profit on the 300 shares sold at £4.

Under 'disembursements' were the following:

	£	*s.*	*d.*
Preliminary and Parliamentary Expenses	2,097	10	4
Engineering	294	12	6
Land and Compensation	5,943	17	0
Police	36	0	0
Works	10,000	0	0
Rails and Chairs	5,623	3	7
Salaries	88	6	8
Misc.	46	17	0
Interest and Commission	57	13	8
Lake District Survey on Account	36	4	0
Office Furniture	15	0	9
Direction and Audit	212	0	0

John Harris, the Engineer, was able to report that the previous day he had examined the works and that they were proceeding satisfactorily. Work was being carried out on almost every part of the line, several of the bridges had been erected and the heavy part of the rock cutting near the Windermere end of the terminus was nearly completed. He was confident the line would be able to open simultaneously with the Lancaster & Carlisle.

The next half-yearly meeting was held on Wednesday 28th July. John Gandy was in the chair and it was noted that the attendance was 'very small'. In the Directors report it was stated that,

> ... if the Lancaster and Carlisle Railway had been completed in time for the Lake traffic of this season, it would have been of the greatest importance to this company to open for the whole distance at the same time; but since the former company are not likely to complete their line before the Lake season is nearly over, it will not be of so much importance to your interest that the opening of this line to Windermere be deferred until the ensuing spring.

However, it was possible to say that the line from Oxenholme would be opened together with the opening of the Lancaster & Carlisle. It was noted that John Gandy would be standing down as a Director, along with two others, but all would be eligible for re-election; they were. In his report, John Harris was able to be very positive about the progress being made. Some 200,000 cubic yards of earthworks and rock had been excavated and carried into embankments or spoil and this left about 220,000 cubic yards to be dealt with. The viaduct at Long Pool (near Kendal) had been completed and two other viaducts, one over the River Kent and one on adjoining meadowland were well advanced. As far as the 30 bridges, which included cattle ways and occupation roads, were concerned, 12 had been completed and nine were under construction; the rest, many farm crossings, had yet to be started. It was possible to report that the delivery of permanent way materials was keeping pace with requirements. Harris was able to confirm that the railway would be ready to open along with the Lancaster & Carlisle but only as far as Kendal. It was reported that to date the expenditures of £66,891 12*s*. 8*d*. and £9,910 0*s*. 11*d*. had been borrowed from Wakefield's Bank. J.T. Clay had resigned as a Director and been replaced by G.B. Crewdson, who had been the auditor, and Samuel Marshall was elected to replace him in that capacity.

The first locomotive in the Kendal area

On Wednesday 26th August there was a great deal of excitement in the Kendal area. Crowds of eager sightseers gathered at Oxenholme and Birklands. News had been passed around that at some time during the day a locomotive with carriages would be passing. Most of those who gathered had never seen such a sight before and so they waited in anticipation, not knowing at what time this event would take place. They were not disappointed. The engine *Medusa*, pulling two carriages, arrived from Lancaster at about five o'clock in the afternoon. It may be hard to imagine what sort of impact such a sighting might have made but there was certainly a lot of cheering when, as one report described it, the 'monster' arrived after giving 'a noisy token of its approach'. The locomotive, which had been used when ballasting work was carried out near Carnforth, belonged to the contractors for the line; the carriages belonged to the North Union Railway Company. A group of the Lancaster & Carlisle Railway Directors was on board for an inspection visit and they were conveyed further north over Docker viaduct, after which they travelled by 'lurry' to meet a group which had come from Penrith 'with another engine'. *Medusa* remained in the district to assist with further ballasting work but was damaged beyond repair in an incident which occurred at a later date on the Lancaster & Carlisle line north of Oxenholme.

By the middle of September, the work on what might be described as the first stage, namely that between Lancaster and Kendal, was virtually complete. There had been no set-backs or hold-ups, as there would be in later schemes in the area, when engineers were frequently pleading lack of progress was the result of inclement weather. There had been no major obstacles to overcome.

So, on Thursday 17th September, with the work as far as Kendal completed, Messrs Mould and Worthington, together with others, made a trip along the whole length of the line. The journey from Lancaster to Oxenholme took 55 minutes, including three stops, and from there to Long Pool (Kendal) station took a further 10 minutes. All was ready for the formal inspection of the line.

The inspection

In the edition of 19th September, the *Kendal Mercury* was able to report that General Pasley, the Inspector General of Railways, had gone over the line from Lancaster to Kendal the previous day, Friday 18th September. He had found the work to be of a satisfactory standard and was able to issue a certificate, so enabling the line to be opened. There had been one aspect which had caused the inspector to ask for further work to be carried out. This was near Lancaster. He had noticed a number of loose rails and felt they were not safe. Two hours work had rectified the problem.

So with everything ready to open the lines as far as Kendal, it was time for the party to begin. And begin, it certainly did.

This sketch of a locomotive and carriage was used a number of times in connection with the Kendal and Windermere Railway, both in the press and elsewhere. It would suggest that the artist had not seen the locomotives likely to be used on the railway and so the result is a rather stylised subject. However, the locomotive does have the correct number of wheels!

Chapter Five

The Line Opens in Two Stages

21st September, 1846 to 20th April, 1847

When it came to the matter of motive power and rolling stock, the small, emerging railway companies of this period had a number of options to choose from. The first possible way forward was simply to purchase outright whatever was needed. A second way was to enter into an agreement with a larger company, if such there were in the same region, and get it to take over the running of the line. A third choice was to lease from a larger company and run the line but still retaining complete control over it without capital outlay. Option one needed capital and it also needed the back-up facilities to maintain locomotives and stock; the second could be an attractive option. The Cockermouth, Keswick & Penrith Railway Directors struck such a deal with the London & North Western which operated passenger traffic and the North Eastern to deal with freight. The Kendal & Windermere plumped for what was, in effect, something between the second and third arrangements; leasing with operating crews from the London & North Western Railway.

An agreement was drawn up in 1846, before the railway opened. It is some 17 pages (approximating to modern A4 size) long and written in fine copperplate handwriting. The document covers more than just the arrangement regarding locomotives and stock. As far as these were concerned, the London & North Western Railway (LNWR) agreed to supply engines, tenders, carriages, trucks, waggons and 'all necessary for the official working of the railway'. Also included were horse boxes and cattle waggons. The LNWR would keep these items in good working order by maintaining them, cleaning them and greasing them and renewing them when necessary. It would provide the men for such purposes at 'the two extremities' [of the line] and at the intermediate stations and the standard maintained would 'be equivalent to that ordinarily performed on the railways between London and Liverpool'. For its part, the Kendal & Windermere company was required to deal with waggons and similar items in a proper manner 'taking care of them as if they were their own property'.

The agreement then considers others matters. The maximum number of carriages and other 'conveyances' attached to any one engine would not exceed 11 or 130 tons. This latter figure would not include the engine and tender. If these were exceeded an additional expense would be incurred.

If a second engine was needed (at the option of the Grand Junction Railway*) double mileage would be charged. On the other hand if a 'pilot' engine was required 'in other circumstances' no charge would be made. The maximum speed for 'mail express passenger trains' would, 'in the first instance' be 30 mph over the whole of the Kendal & Windermere line and for other passenger trains, 22 mph. For 'merchandise' trains it would be 12 mph. Stoppages at stations

* At this stage the GJR was in effect a subdivision of the LNWR and provided some locomotives.

would be 'five minutes at a first class station and three minutes at a second class station'. There was a qualification for what were described as 'trains with special dispatches'. These would not be limited to these speeds and the speed could be increased according to the importance of the dispatches.

The agreement then deals with the late arrival of trains. There would be no penalties for late arrivals up to a quarter of an hour unless more than one-third of the trains were so affected, in which case there would be a fine of 10*s*. for more than 10 minutes. (This fine would, clearly, be paid by the LNWR.) If a train was more than 15 minutes late but less than 30 minutes late, the fine would be 15*s*.; more than 30 minutes but less than 45, the fine would be 40*s*.; more than 45 but less than one hour, the fine would be 60*s*. If the train was more than one hour late, the LNWR would forfeit the whole cost of the train and have no right to any payment.

There was a qualification that the LNWR must take all precautions to ensure proper timing and (possibly with the climate of the area in mind) 'even to the extent of the weather'. If there were any irregularities or complaints, these could be dealt with by the Kendal & Windermere Railway with some recourse to the LNWR company.

Further, it was agreed that a reasonable number of spare carriages and similar items would be made available. The Kendal & Windermere company had to provide sufficient engine sheds, workshops and 'fixed materials' and the LNWR would, for its part, provide all tools and moveable objects for repair work. The Kendal & Windermere company was obliged to meet the costs of the engine sheds and other provisions. The LNWR agreed to meet the cost of all coke and similar materials, needed to work the engines and there would be free passage for those persons carrying out the work. The Kendal & Windermere could dismiss those whom it felt were failing to meet the terms of the agreement but the LNWR had, first, to be notified of this intention whereupon arbitration could be invoked.

Finally there was the all important matter of rates. These would be 1*s*. 3*d*. per mile for the engine; first and second class carriages would be three farthings per mile with third class and trucks (possibly an indication of the quality of third class travel!) a halfpenny per mile. Distances would be rounded up to quarter miles. This agreement was initially for three years from the time the Kendal & Windermere actually started operating.

Later, there would be some misgivings about having entered into this agreement, but at the outset it seemed to be the best way forward. The Lancaster & Carlisle had also initially decided to follow this course of action and it was the LNWR which had the availability of stock enabling it to set up such an agreement.

At the time when locomotives were needed, the LNWR had been formed (on 16th July, 1846) from other companies and these included the Grand Junction Railway. Three years previously, in 1843, this company had set up a works at Crewe and it was from this department that the Kendal & Windermere Railway would draw locomotives, along with the Lancaster & Carlisle Railway. Francis Trevithick (son of Richard) was, in effect, managing the works and on offer were the so-called Crewe-Allen (or Trevithick-Allen) locomotive types. These were of the 2-2-2 arrangement for passenger work (a picture of this type is depicted at the top of the invitation to the opening ceremony) and a 2-4-0 type for goods. The Kendal & Windermere initially had four locomotives.

1846 – The first opening ceremony

In spite of the fact that the Lancaster & Carlisle Railway had yet to reach Carlisle and the Kendal & Windermere had, thus far, not reached Windermere, it was decided that an important stage in the progress of the two lines had been realized and therefore celebrations were in order. When it came to marking momentous events, such as the opening of a new railway, the Victorians were second to none in the lengths to which they were prepared to go in order to effect what has often been referred to as ' a truly memorable occasion'. Both the *Kendal Mercury* and the *Westmorland Gazette* carried extensive coverage of the events which formed part of the opening ceremony.

The *Westmorland Gazette* coverage starts with a flourish,

> Monday last was a day that will be memorable in the annals of Kendal. Never, perhaps, since the opening of the Lancaster and Kendal Canal, twenty-seven years ago, was the town such a scene of excitement and hilarity.

There follows a brief résumé of the developing links between the two places; the old packet boats taking seven hours and then the new ones taking less than four; the rapid coaches for the better off, bringing the time down to two and now the railway reducing it to an hour.

The day had been declared a general holiday, thereby giving everybody the opportunity to be involved in the festivities. Flags were flown on the town hall and on the ruined towers of the castle. The original plan had been for a party of Directors to leave Kendal at 11 o'clock, journey to Lancaster and join the celebrations there. However, there was concern that a large number of people from Kendal would not be able join the trip and so it was decided to bring further carriages from Lancaster to accommodate a greater following. This change in the arrangements resulted in the departure time being put back over an hour. For those who were waiting, there was the opportunity to listen to a band, provided to jolly up the day.

The train arrived at Kendal being pulled by the locomotive *Dalemain*, named after the residence of the Chairman of the Lancaster & Carlisle Railway, E.W. Hasell. Again there were flags adorning the train in order to create, further, the sense of festivity. There may well have been gasps of surprise and admiration at the beautifully turned out coaches (built at Crewe by the LNWR) with their fine maroon-liveried exterior and luxuriously-cushioned interior. The reporter commented that they 'were the roomiest we ever observed on a narrow guage [*sic*] line'. (Had the writer recently visited the Great Western Railway and felt *that* gauge was the norm?) The second class coaches were lined with imitation oak and the third class ('considering the fares') were similar to the second class but the doors had wooden slides instead of glass. With everyone on board, the train of eight carriages left the 'temporary station at Longpool' at half past noon. Off they went with G.B. Worthington Esq., Engineer, at the controls. How exhilarating to be travelling for the first time in this new mode of transport which promised speeds never experienced before (albeit, on this occasion, not much in excess of 20 mph and sometimes considerably less). No wonder the ladies, in their fine crinolines, chattered in an animated fashion; perhaps some a little anxiously but being reassured by the gentlemen present that it was all quite safe.

Up the incline (an almost alarming 1 in 80!) to Oxenholme station (still under construction, as, we are told 'were all the stations on the line') stopping at Sedgwick to pick up several other people, thence to Milnthorpe, Burton and Holme and eventually to Carnforth. The penultimate station was Hest Bank and so to Lancaster, arriving 52 minutes after leaving Kendal. After a 20 minute wait, the train left for the return journey, this time with no less than 14 carriages. It would seem that most of the local populace turned out to watch the train pass and positioned themselves anywhere where they could get a good view.

The heavier load of the train on the return trip increased the time of the journey by a few minutes and it took 'a minute or two over the hour'. The writer of the report in the *Westmorland Gazette* informs the readers that 'the slopes of the Castle hills were black with human figures and both sides of the line from thence to the station were occupied with many thousands of spectators including, as is natural in all matters of sight-seeing, a very large proportion of the fairer portion of creation'.

Once the passengers had alighted it was time to go over to the Whitehall Assembly Rooms where the junketing, a feature so often connected with significant events in this period, formed an important part. It was three o'clock by the time the 130 guests were seated and ready to partake of what was described as a sumptious meal. ('Dejeuner' was the term actually used.) Those who tucked in to the cold collation provided by Mr Fisher of the Commercial Hotel included Cornelius Nicholson, who assumed the role of Chairman and was mayor of Kendal at the time, E.W. Hasell, the Member of Parliament, W. Thompson, John Wakefield and J.E. Errington.

The speechmaking and toasts which followed were legion, even for an event such as this, and suggest that an enormous sense of euphoria pervaded the whole experience. Nicholson was clearly acting in a dual role. On the one hand he was the mayor but on the other he was deputizing for John Gandy, the Chairman of the Kendal & Windermere Railway, who was unable to be present. Nicholson opened with a surprising comment. He pointed out that in effect they would have to get a move on because they were expected back in Lancaster at seven o'clock that evening for dinner! He suggested that the speed of eating and drinking might be suited to the opening of a railway. This was greeted by shouts of 'Hear, Hear' and laughter. So the event moved on apace. 'Welcomes' and then the Queen, Prince Albert and all the royal family were 'honoured'. Next there followed toasts to the health of the Lord Lieutenant of the County, Lord Lonsdale. An accolade of praise was poured upon him, as indeed so it was on Colonel Lowther in the toasting of the County. It was, perhaps, Alderman Thompson who was given the greatest ovation and in replying to the toast, although he noted the Chairman's wishes to keep matters brief, did go on at some length, extolling the merits of the railway and placing great emphasis on how there would be considerable advantages in the way important commodities (butter was specified in particular) would become cheaper. He regretted that Kendal had not made the sort of progress it might have done in relation to the woollen trade because there was no effective outlet but he hoped that would now change. 'At risk', he said, 'of trespassing on their time', he felt he must honour not only those who built and planned the line but also the advancement of science that had made it possible.

Next on the list was E.W. Hasell, whose health was proposed by the Chairman. In so doing, he said what many others would say on similar occasions, namely that the railway they had was the best engineered in the kingdom. Locke and Errington were lauded for their part. Hasell replied, again making the point that there was a need for brevity. Reflecting perhaps on what Elizabeth I had once said about speeches being best when they were over, he observed that long speeches were evil in themselves 'and were especially so in the present situation'. He commented that much of what should be said had been said by the Chairman (Nicholson) and Alderman Thompson and so he added a laudum about his fellow Directors of the Lancaster & Carlisle and about Locke and Errington and their part in the contribution they had made in advancing the objective of bringing a railway from London into Scotland. 'These were,' he said,' no mean efforts and they might be thankful to the Almighty if they were able to effectuate that great work in a manner satisfactory to themselves and to those who so kindly appreciated their efforts.' At this point there were cheers. Hasell later apologized for having broken his promise to be brief but he did continue at some length.

It may be difficult to appreciate some 160 years after the event what a remarkable achievement it was to be able to travel between Kendal and Lancaster in less than an hour and to do so in comparative comfort. Hasell made great play on the fact that travel had entered a new era and it is not really surprising that he did so. He was optimistic that the project would be completed in six to eight weeks as far as reaching Carlisle was concerned. He then turned to the subject of 'that pretty little railway which his friend on the left (Cornelius Nicholson) had, in a speech which he had read a short time ago in the papers, called the gem of railways'. Hasell then waxed eloquent. Turning to a group of the ladies present he remarked 'And I hope it will be the means of introducing a great many gems like those from the south'. At this there were cheers and laughter. He went on 'I hope it will turn out a glittering gem , and, not only so but be so productive of gold and silver as to remunerate the proprietors' He then had further words of praise for Nicholson 'No man had been more diligent and more earnest in promoting the Lancaster and Carlisle line'. He had also been the connecting link between the two schemes being celebrated and Hasell much regretted that Nicholson had decided to stand down as the Vice-Chairman of the Lancaster & Carlisle. In reply, Nicholson said that in spite of the fact that others seemed not to have taken heed regarding the request for short speeches, he would not be tempted to follow their example but in spite of this he did speak at some length, once more emphasizing the merits, as he saw them, of the railway. There would be benefits, he believed, greater than they had yet expected; that it would confer on the inhabitants of the most populace districts the signal benefit of drawing them from haunts of vice and intemperance; by exhibiting to them the works of nature; opening their minds in a way that only the works of nature could do ('Hear, Hear' at this point). He then indulged in some self praise in pointing out that he had been one of the first to suggest the scheme to the Directors of the

LANCASTER & CARLISLE RAILWAY.

OPENING TO KENDAL.

TIME AND FARE TABLE,

On and after the 22nd SEPTEMBER, 1846.

Kendal & Lancaster to Liverpool, Manchester, Birmingham, and London.	1	2	3	4	5	6
	Mail, 1st Class.	1st and 2nd Class.	1st and 2nd Class.	1st, 2d, and 3d Class.	1st and 2nd Class.	Mail, 1st & 2d Class.
Leave	a.m.	a.m.	a.m.	a.m.	p.m.	p.m.
KENDAL	2 0	—	8 0	11 0	—	5 30
Kendal Junc.	3 7	—	8 6	11 8	—	5 38
Milnthorpe	—	—	8 22	11 25	—	5 55
Burton and Holme	—	—	8 30	11 35	—	6 5
Carnforth	—	—	8 40	11 45	—	6 15
Hest Bank	—	—	8 50	11 55	—	6 25
				p.m.		
Lancaster	4 5	6 50	9 5	12 30	2 30	6 45
Preston	5 10	8 0	10 20	1 30	3 30	7 53
Arrive at				p.m.		
LIVERPOOL	6 45	9 45	11 50	3 20	5 30	9 45
Manchester	6 35	9 35	11 45	3 5	5 20	9 25
			p.m.			a.m.
Birmingham	9 15	—	3 20	7 35	—	12 36
	p.m.					
LONDON	1 0	—	8 45	11 0	—	5 32

London, Birmingham, Liverpool, and Manchester to Lancaster and Kendal.	1	2	3	4	5	6
	1st & 3d Class. Mail.	1st and 2nd Class.	1st, 2d, and 3d Class.	1st and 2nd Class.	1st & 3d Class, Mail.	1st and 2nd Class.
Leave	p.m.	a.m.	a.m.	a.m.	a.m.	p.m.
LONDON	8 45	—	—	6 15	*10 0	—
	a.m.				p.m.	
Birmingham	1 25	—	6 0	11 15	1 45	—
				p.m.		
Liverpool	—	8 0	10 15	1 30	3 35	6 0
Manchester	—	8 15	10 30	1 45	3 50	6 15
Preston	5 35	9 40	11 55	3 40	5 35	7 40
			p.m.			
Lancaster	6 29	10 30	12 50	4 30	6 40	8 40
Hest Bank	—	—	1 0	4 42	6 50	—
Carnforth	—	—	1 10	4 53	7 0	—
Burton and Holme	7 0	—	1 25	5 3	7 10	—
Milnthorpe	7 10	—	1 35	5 15	7 20	—
Kendal Junc.	7 30	—	2 0	5 40	7 40	—
Arrive at KENDAL	7 40	—	2 10	5 50	7 50	—

FARES between Lancaster and Kendal — First Class, 4s.; Second Class, 2s. 9d.; Third Class, 1s. 8d. Between Lancaster and Kendal — First Class, 4s. 8d. Second Class, 3s.; Third Class, 1s. 9d.

On SUNDAYS the Mail Trains only will run.

The Mails and other Coaches from the North arrive at Kendal in ample time for Passengers to proceed to the South, by the Mail Trains, and Passengers from the South arrive at Kendal in ample time for the Mails and Coaches to the North.

Lancaster & Carlisle. That said, he then proposed the toast to his 'old friend the vicar of Kendal'. In a pointed remark Nicholson commented that the vicar was 'not one of those who had abbreviated scripture into scrip like some of his brethren had done'. Cheers followed. The vicar replied, then came the Vice-Chairman who suggested they had so far been remiss in not proposing the health of the ladies and to this Hasell said he wanted to add the lady mayoress.

Still more oration followed, with the Chairman now proposing the health of the engineers Locke and Errington. Errington replied, comparatively briefly, thanking the people of Kendal for their help and kindness and then praising Nicholson for his part in bringing the scheme to fruition. Locke, it transpired, was not present because he was opening a new railway in France. It appears things started to be get a little out of hand at this point. (Perhaps the fine wines were beginning to have an effect!) The Chairman, it would seem, attempted to rise and dismiss the 'merits' laid on him by Errington. At the same time, however, the Vice-Chairman cut in again to propose the toast to the contractors Mould and Stephenson. Then Hasell was on his feet again to apologize for this omission. He praised the contractors highly and was immediately followed by Errington who wished to do the same. Stephenson briefly thanked them for their words and said he hoped the line would be open throughout in six to eight weeks. There must have been those present who were beginning to wonder whether they would ever get away to Lancaster but after a further toast to Mr Garnett, who was present and representing the London & Birmingham Railway, and proposing a vote of thanks to Mr Wakefield, the festivities concluded.

The train for Lancaster left at approximately six o'clock and was driven by Errington. The group arrived at seven o' clock and by half past seven they were all sitting down to 'a superb dinner' at the King's Arms, given by the Directors of the Lancaster & Carlisle. What can be described as a rerun of the afternoon's activities took place.

All this and both railways had yet to be completed! There was more celebrating to follow at a later date.

With the railway at the brink of opening, the following notice, dated 21st September, had appeared in the press and related to travelling south without changing at Preston:

OPENING OF THE LANCASTER AND CARLISLE RAILWAY AS FAR AS KENDAL
NOTICE TO THE PUBLIC

On and after Tuesday, the 22nd inst, passengers desirous of proceeding from the north by Railway to places beyond Preston in the same carriage, and of payment of the one fare through, MUST GET BOOKED at the Railway Station, Kendal, the LANCASTER AND CARLISLE RAILWAY COMPANY'S STATION, Meeting-house Lane, LANCASTER, or any other Station on their Line, in order to secure themselves against exchanging at Preston, and NO TICKETS but their's will pass parties beyond Preston south. The Lancaster and Carlisle Company's fare between Lancaster and Preston is *only 4s. First Class, and 2s. 9d. Second Class.*

The timetable is shown opposite.

There is then a notice about the Kendal departures which was issued at Kendal Station on 24th September, 1846:

RAILWAY
KENDAL TO LANCASTER &c &c

The trains start punctually from the Kendal Station as follows:

At	3 0	*am*	First Class
At	8 0	*am*	First and Second Class
At	11 0	*am*	First, Second and Third Class
At	5 30	*pm*	First and Second Class

ON SUNDAYS

At	3 0	*am*	First Class
At	5 30	*pm*	First, Second and Third Class

The trains arrive at KENDAL as follows:

At 7.40 *am* 2.10 *pm* 5.50 *pm* 7.50 *pm*

ON SUNDAYS

At 7.40 *am* 7.50 *pm*

FARES

				First class	*Second class*	*Third class*
From	Kendal	to	Lancaster	4*s*. 6*d*.	3*s*. 0*d*.	1*s*. 9*d*.
	"		Preston	8*s*. 6*d*.	5*s*. 9*d*.	3*s*. 5*d*.
	"		Liverpool	14*s*. 6*d*.	9*s*. 9*d*.	
	"		Manchester	14*s*. 6*d*.	9*s*. 9*d*.	
	"		Birmingham	27*s*. 6*d*.	20*s*. 3*d*.	
	"		London	47*s*. 6*d*.	34*s*. 3*d*.	

SHORT FARES

From	Kendal	to	Oxenholme	0*s*. 6*d*.	0*s*. 4*d*.	
	"		Milnthorpe	1*s*. 6*d*.	1*s*. 0*d*.	0*s*. 8*d*.
	"		Burton	2*s*. 3*d*.	1*s*. 6*d*.	0*s*. 10*d*.
	"		Carnforth	3*s*. 0*d*.	2*s*. 0*d*.	1*s*. 3*d*.
	"		Hest Bank	3*s*. 9*d*.	2*s*. 6*d*.	1*s*. 6*d*.

Passengers, Parcels, Carriages and Horses, &c can be booked through WITHOUT CHANGING CARRIAGES, from this Company's Station and from the Lancaster and Carlisle Company's station at Lancaster.

Sheep on the line

Within a short time after the railway opened, there were complaints being made by some farmers in the locality that sheep were able to get onto the line. A fence had been erected, together with what was described as a quickset hedge. The latter, however, did not appear to be growing quickly enough and sheep were able to get under the lower rail of the fence. One observer, no doubt tongue in cheek, commented that if trains were running it might result in a whole flock being converted into mutton chops in one fell swoop. During November, in one exchange, apparently of a particularly vehement nature, between one farmer and a person described as an agent of the railway, the owner of the sheep had berated the agent and said that the company had to do something to prevent the sheep getting onto the track. The agent, described as 'a lively and irascible native of the emerald isle', eventually reached the end of his tether and in a manner described as anything but benedictory told the farmer that he should buy bigger sheep!

Progress continues

During the rest of the year, steady progress was made in completing the line to Birthwaite. The work was not without incidents. In the last week of November there was a fatal accident near Staveley where the line traversed the Middlefair Bank estate. A man of 19, who was working in a gang employed by Mr Underhill, the sub-contractor for the section, was killed when a piece of rock fell on him and he was crushed. Several other workers were injured on the same occasion.

Cornelius Nicholson found himself in the press again early in December, this time in connection with the East Lancashire Railway. His resignation as Managing Director from what was described as a less than harmonious Board had been reported in the *Westmorland Gazette* on 5th December and it would seem that he was not very satisfied with certain inferences being made. In his usual manner he was quick to respond and in a letter published in the same paper, the following week, he was at pains to make it clear why he had decided to resign and did so by including with his correspondence the letter he had sent to the East Lancashire Board. What is notable is that as well as stating, in effect, that he wished to spend more time with his family, he also refers to what he describes as the 'precarious' state of his health. The effort he had put into promoting the cause of the Kendal & Windermere Railway against the tide of opposition and his other commitments may well have started to take its toll.

As the end of the year approached, there was another fatal accident. On Friday 18th December, Joseph Parker, of Captain French Lane, died at the works on Bowstone Cutting, Strickland Kettle. It would seem the accident was caused essentially by the very frosty weather. A huge mass of earth had fallen and buried the victim who was aged 51, was a former miner from Coniston and who was working with his son at the time. In warmer conditions there would usually be a warning that a fall was about to occur by the opening up of the soil above but the conditions resulted in no such warning and there was no time to get out of the way of the falling earth. A widow and eight fatherless children was the outcome. A high price one family paid during the construction of the line.

The Lancaster & Carlisle Railway opens throughout

There was, however, good news on another front. On Tuesday 16th December, the Lancaster & Carlisle railway opened the remaining section and reached Carlisle. Although this was a significant step in the quest to create a link between London and Scotland, reports indicate that it was not an event celebrated in Kendal. It seems a few people went to Oxenholme to see the first train pass and a number boarded it. The attention in Kendal was no doubt focused on the Birthwaite link. Although the key route for the Lancaster & Carlisle was the section between the places named in the company's title, the service from Kendal to the south was maintained. In the same way as had occurred elsewhere and with other publishers, Scott and Benson produced a sixpenny guide to coincide with the opening. The public was informed that the guide was in 'a portable shape'!

At the end of the year the Kendal & Windermere company took the step of calling in a further £3 per share and this had to be paid by Thursday 7th January, 1847 with a 5 per cent per annum penalty for unpaid calls after that date. This was the fifth call.

1847 – Goods and mail

In the middle of January the public was 'respectfully informed' that goods trains left for the north on Tuesdays, Thursdays and Saturdays and for the south on Mondays, Wednesdays, Fridays and Saturdays. Further information could be had from the superintendent of the goods station, George Chamley.

The 1st February saw a significant development in railway facilities. For the first time mail was taken from Kendal to Carlisle by train. The Kendal & Windermere Railway had the contract for the section from Kendal to Oxenholme and the Lancaster & Carlisle took it on from there. A contemporary writer made the following observation:

> ... 'the twanging horn o'er yonder bridge' and the lively and picturesque arrivals and departures of the four-horsed mails and other coaches, will be numbered among the sights of olden time. A two-horsed mail to Keswick and the old Leeds coach will be the only coaches passing through Kendal.

From the outset, the opportunity to carry the mail must have been a great source of pride and satisfaction for the company. This was another piece of history in the making for Kendal and district and although carrying the mail had never been a significant part, if, indeed, a part at all, of the argument for building the railway, it was further vindication for the decision to do so. At the same time it was announced there would be a reduction in the rates for carrying goods from Kendal.

The timetable for trains to the south, issued at this stage, is similar to the earlier timetable, although the 3.00 am has been removed both during the week and on Sundays. The 11.00 am departure has been retimed to leave at 10.55 am The 5.30 pm is now designated 'Mail Train' and there is a note that passengers by this train cannot book at Carnforth or Hest Bank. The schedule for northbound trains reads as follows:

TO PENRITH, CARLISLE &c NORTH

At	7.30 *am*	(Mail) First and Second Class
"	10.55 *am*	First, Second and Third Class
"	7.15 *pm*	(Mail) First and Second Class

ON SUNDAYS

At	7.30 *am*	(Mail) First, Second and Third Class
"	7.15 *pm*	(Mail) First and Second Class

The note for this section of the timetable stated that passengers by the 7.30 am mail train can only book to Shap, Penrith and Carlisle and those by the 7.15 pm mail train could only book to Tebay, Shap, Penrith and Carlisle. There is also a note about arrivals at Kendal. From the south, on weekdays, these were at 7.45 (mail), 11.45 am, 5.50 and 7.40 pm (mail) and on Sundays at 7.45 am (mail) and 7.40 pm (mail). From the north; weekdays at 3.15 (mail), 11.15 am and 6.00 pm (mail) and on Sundays at 3.15 am (mail) and 6.00 pm (mail).

The first half-yearly meeting of the company, in 1847, took place on Wednesday 27th January. John Gandy was in the chair. His report was brief. Passenger traffic had been brisk and there had been an improvement since the Lancaster & Carlisle had opened to Carlisle. John Harris, the Engineer, sent a report informing the meeting that he had recently heard from Mr Mould, representing John Stephenson and Co., and he had been promised that the line would be ready for a private opening on 1st April. Although this was in the hands of the contractors, Mould said he had every reason to believe this would be the case. There was a statement of accounts showing that to date receipts had been £108,171 5*s.* 9*d.* Amongst the disembursements £59,587 19*s.* 9*d.* had been spent on the works, £27,456 17*s.* 9*d.* on rails and chairs and £286 3*s.* 8*d.* on salaries. A balance of nearly £17,000 was recorded. The accounts had been audited by Samuel Marshall and John Steele.

Poor weather – A navvies strike – A spectacular explosion

Mr Mould may have felt later that his projection concerning the date of completion had been a little premature. During the following weeks, the area experienced a spell of extremely cold weather with heavy frosts and temperatures reckoned to be 16 degrees below freezing (although, almost certainly, on the Fahrenheit rather than the Celsius Scale). At one stage, on 9th February, there had been a violent thunderstorm and high winds and these had been followed by snow. The work must have been severely hampered by these conditions. Whether these adverse circumstances undermined the morale and prompted dissatisfaction among the workers it is not easy to say, but at the beginning of March they staged a strike following pay-day the week before. It is thought, according to reports, that they were asking for three pence a day more. The choice of time was a bad one and their efforts were in vain. The building of the line was now so far advanced that the loss of any disenchanted workers would make little or no difference. Their services were no longer essential and if they were not happy they could leave. In the end, work was resumed without any increase in pay being awarded. Shortly after this incident, it was felt that the work was far enough advanced to give the necessary month's notice to the government inspector, Captain Coddington, informing him the company was hoping that before long it would be ready to open the line. It was anticipated that the double line of track would be ready as far as Staveley by the opening (already it had been laid for three-quarters of the distance between Kendal and Staveley) but that the doubling of the track from Staveley to Birthwaite would take a further six to eight weeks. At this stage there was still a considerable amount of work to do at the hill near Ings and also at the Bowstone Cutting. At the latter, there had been some vigorous blasting taking place in order to make rapid progress. The workmen proved to be so enthusiastic that on one occasion the charge went off with such force that not only was a shower of rocks thrown high into the air but the reverberation shattered the windows of a nearby farmhouse.

Amidst all this activity the company announced a change in the timetable, whereby from Monday 15th March the 10.55 am train from Kendal would be discontinued and, instead, a train with third class carriages would leave at 1.25 pm. This would get passengers to London by 11.00 pm. There would also be an additional train to the north at 5. 30 pm and this would stop at all stations.

A letter appeared in the *Westmorland Gazette* on 13th March, just before this change came into force. It was a complaint from an aggrieved traveller:

> Sir, The eleven o'clock train from Kendal this day took at least ten passengers for Carlisle. They waited at Oxenholme thirty minutes. At this station is a small room and over the door is written 'for passengers only'. Into this room when admission was sought by some of the shivering passengers, it was found filled with railway labourers, who took care to keep the fire to themselves, and thus virtually exclude the passengers from the shelter of this little room. Surely the directors of the two companies ought so far to consider their passengers as to prevent the change of carriages and consequent detention of passengers at Oxenholme. Is it not somewhat scandalous that every passenger going to and from Kendal by this and some other trains is obliged to change carriages; and each day when for the north, by the eleven o'clock train they are detained in the uncomfortable way alluded to?
>
> I am, sir, yours obediently,
>
> *A Passenger*

It may seem remarkable that after the initial excitement, brought by this new, greatly improved, mode of travel, it was not long before complaints were being made!

The beginning of April saw more snow and although it was not to stay for long, icy winds swept the district, no doubt, yet again, making for unpleasant conditions for those working to complete the line.

Another inspection

On Monday 13th April the line was deemed to be ready for what the press described as an 'experimental' opening but although Mr Mould, along with a group of Directors had initially intended to travel along to Birthwaite and back, this trip was postponed so that final preparations could be made for an official inspection the following day. It was Captain Simmons, deputizing for Captain Coddington, who came along to carry out the inspection. First the captain was given luncheon by a small group of Directors and then he set out on foot to begin his work. At 1.30 pm he boarded a train which consisted of a locomotive and three carriages and took his position on the tender which preceded the engine and he was joined by, among others, Mr Harris, the engineer and Mr Trevethick, of the LNWR. The other members of the party travelled inside or (we are informed) on the top of the carriages. The train 'proceeded at a moderate pace, stopping at any bridge by which the railway crossed a road but merely proceeding slowly under bridges that spanned the railway, giving the inspector time for a glance at the structure.' The journey proved to be a smooth one, a reflection, it was suggested, of the high quality of work that had been carried out. The train returned to Kendal after a wait of about half an hour. It was noted that the terminus at Birthwaite was 'in a state of great chaotic confusion'. This was because blasting was still taking place to make a road from the railway to the hotel which was being built. There were piles of stone and timber strewn around and it was felt a lot of work would have to be done in readiness for the tourists arriving. It was also observed that all the stations along the line were a long way from completion. Nevertheless the line received the official approval and was ready for use.

A tragic accident

The day before the second opening ceremony, there was a serious fatal accident on the line which led to a coroner's inquest. This was held at The Bowl Alley Inn, Over Staveley, on 20th April. On Monday 19th April, William Constable had met his death whilst working on the railway. The evidence given to the coroner by various witnesses is not altogether consistent. According to Alan Dodd, who had been with William Constable at the time, the two of them were working about a mile from Staveley. It was between 7.00 and 8.00 am and the two men were making their way along the line to deal with some wagons carrying ballast. Alan Dodd's evidence is not too clear but it would appear that the two men went to unload these wagons whilst other wagons were being brought up by an engine. William Constable was walking on the line on which the engine and wagons were travelling; Alan Dodd was walking on the other line. The train was approaching them from behind and moving at an estimated 11 or 12 mph. When it was within three yards of William Constable, Alan Dodd called to him and warned him to get out of the way. It seems the driver of the engine blew the whistle but the locomotive struck William Constable. The resulting injuries, as described by Alan Dodd, were horrific. However, William

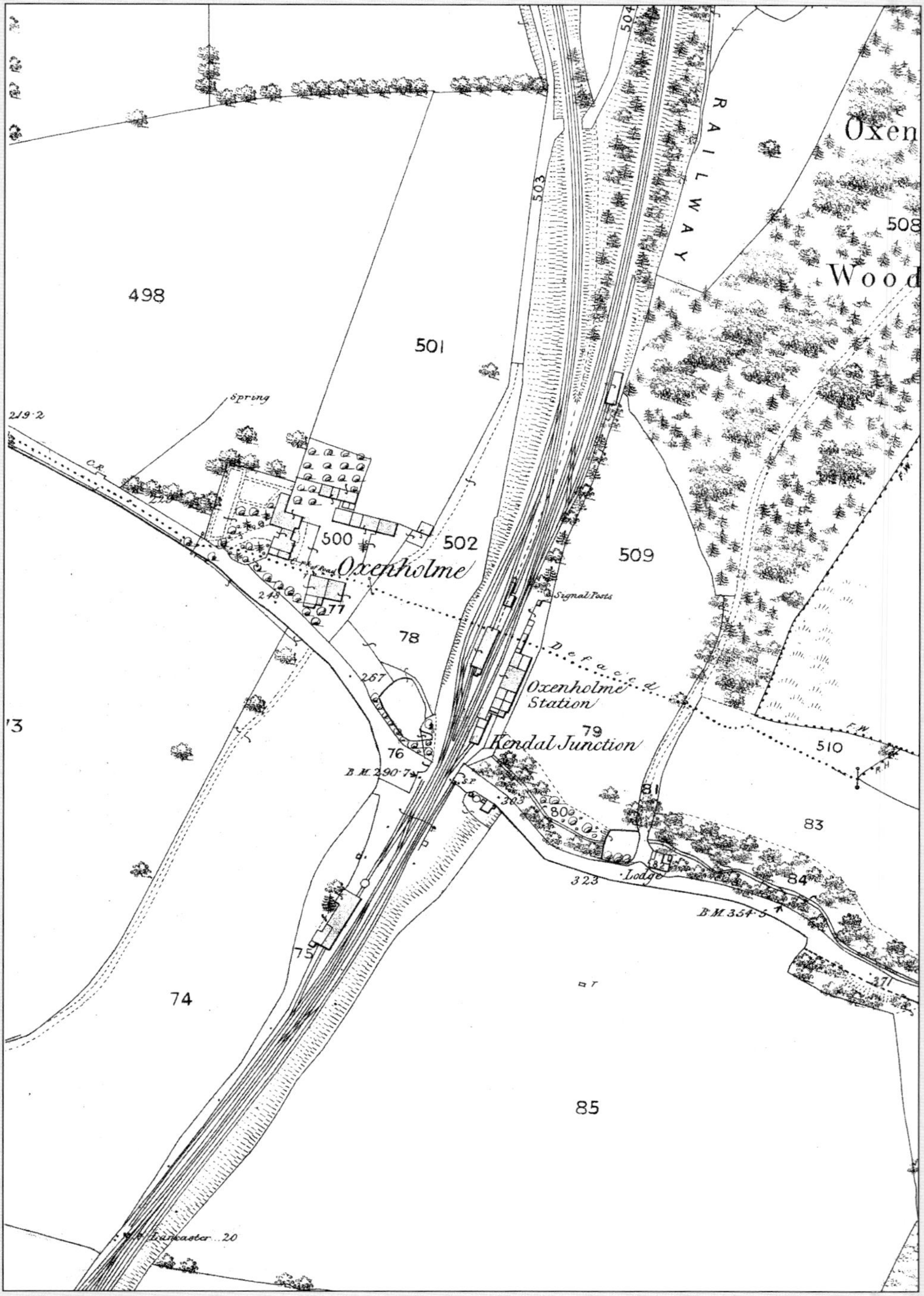

Oxenholme station. *Reproduced from the 25″ First Edition Ordnance Survey Map*

Constable was not killed and was taken to Richard Beetham's house in Over Staveley where he later died. In the interim, William Constable had been able to tell those with him that he thought the engine had been on the other line and that he did not blame the driver of the engine for what had happened. The engine driver, John Wilson, of Burneside, told the coroner that he did not see William Constable until the engine was about to hit him. He did point out that on previous trips the engine had been travelling on the 'other' line and speculated that perhaps William Constable had assumed that would be the case on this occasion. This notion had already been confirmed by the evidence given by Mr Brocklebank, of Staveley, who said that the injured man had told him he was walking up the line on which the engine had previously been driven and expecting it to come up that line he stepped off it and upon the other line without looking towards the engine and was immediately run over. A verdict of accidental death was recorded.

The line opens to Birthwaite (Windermere)

The unfortunate situation of having a coroner's inquiry on the same day as the second opening ceremony, did not, in the event, detract from the celebrations which took place later that day, when the line was opened to Birthwaite. Both the *Kendal Mercury* and the *Westmorland Gazette* carried very full coverage of the event. Pictures of local landmarks were included in both accounts and the *Kendal Mercury* carried a version which was embellished with florid descriptions which in some ways tended to mask the factual account. 'The honours of its paternity we believe belong' asserted *The Gazette* 'to C. Nicholson Esq. ...' There was a background history of the project given by both newspapers.

The celebrations began with two trains leaving Kendal station for Birthwaite. The first moved off at 10.00 am. It was made up of 16 carriages, suitably adorned with flags, and was hauled by three locomotives. The second departed two hours later and this one was made up of 18 carriages and this was also hauled by three locomotives. These carriages had been provided by the LNWR. Tickets had been 'liberally distributed' and it was estimated that upwards of 800 people travelled. The proceedings were enhanced by music provided by the Kendal Teetotal Band. No doubt encouraged by the fine weather, many people came to view the trains and there was much cheering as they passed. The people in Staveley and Ings turned out in force with flags and banners which prompted one writer to comment that although 'Mr Wordsworth resents the railroad, the residents in these retired villages regard it with most friendly feelings'. In view of the size of the trains, progress was maintained at a steady pace and Birthwaite was reached in just under 30 minutes. Shortly after 2.00 pm about 37 guests went to luncheon (or dejeuner) at the Royal Hotel. John Gandy, Chairman of the Board, was 'in the chair'. After what seems to have been a splendid lunch it was once again time for the toasts and speeches. Much of what was said echoed that which had been stated on the previous occasion of the initial opening ceremony. Here, though, there was no sharing of the accolades with a significant number of Directors from another company. The toast 'The

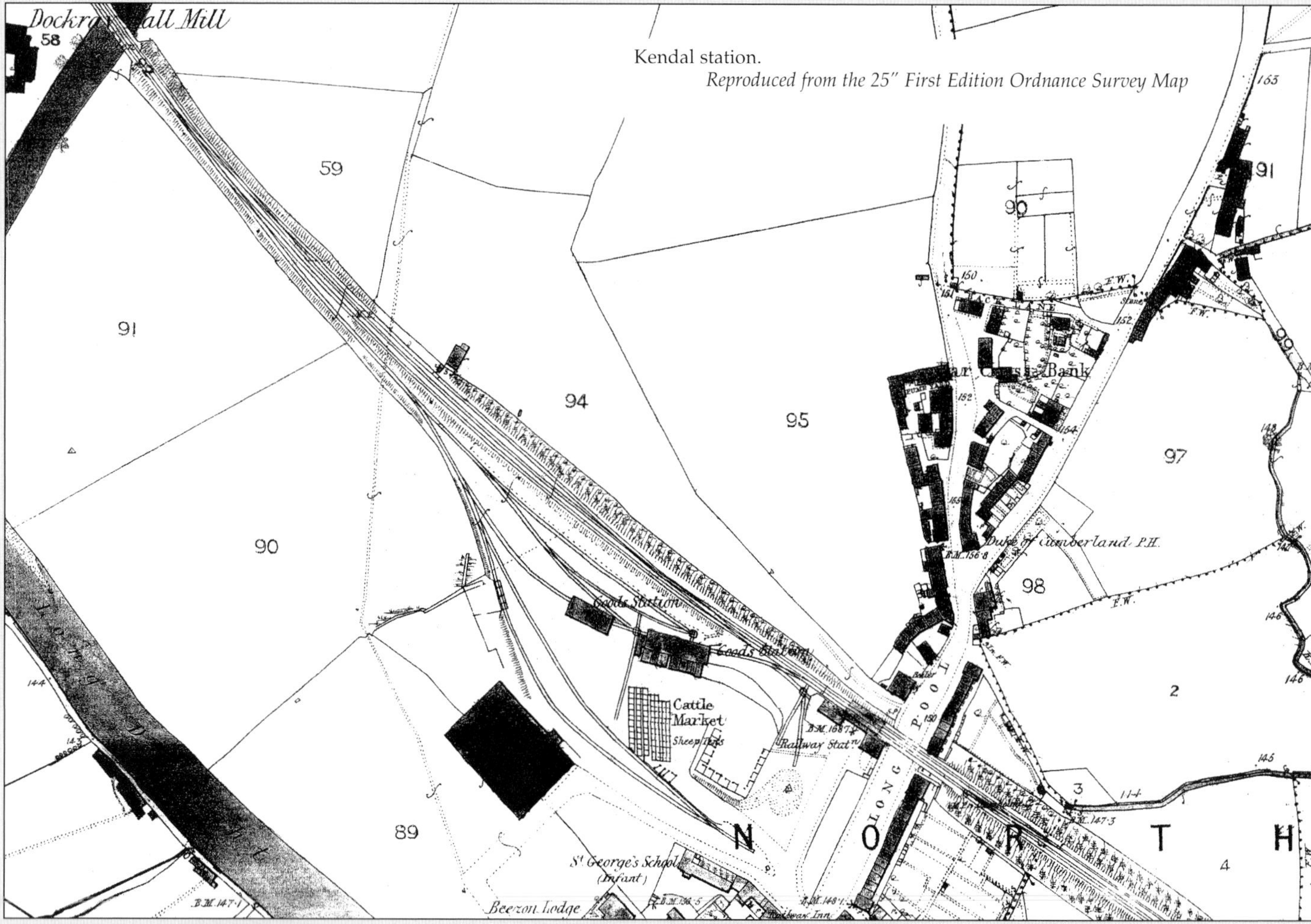

Kendal station.
Reproduced from the 25" First Edition Ordnance Survey Map

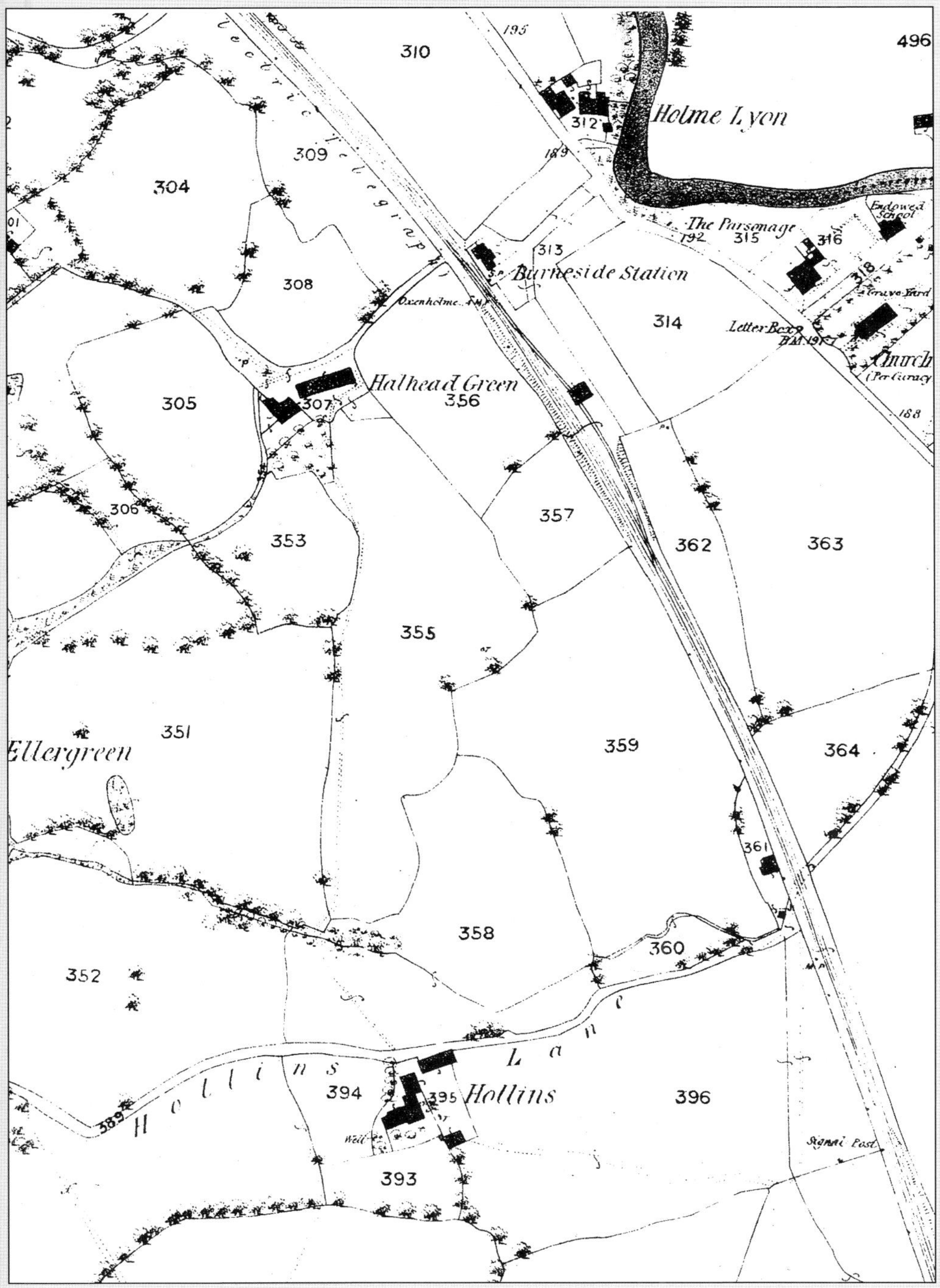

Burneside station and Hollins crossing.

Reproduced from the 25″ First Edition Ordnance Survey Map

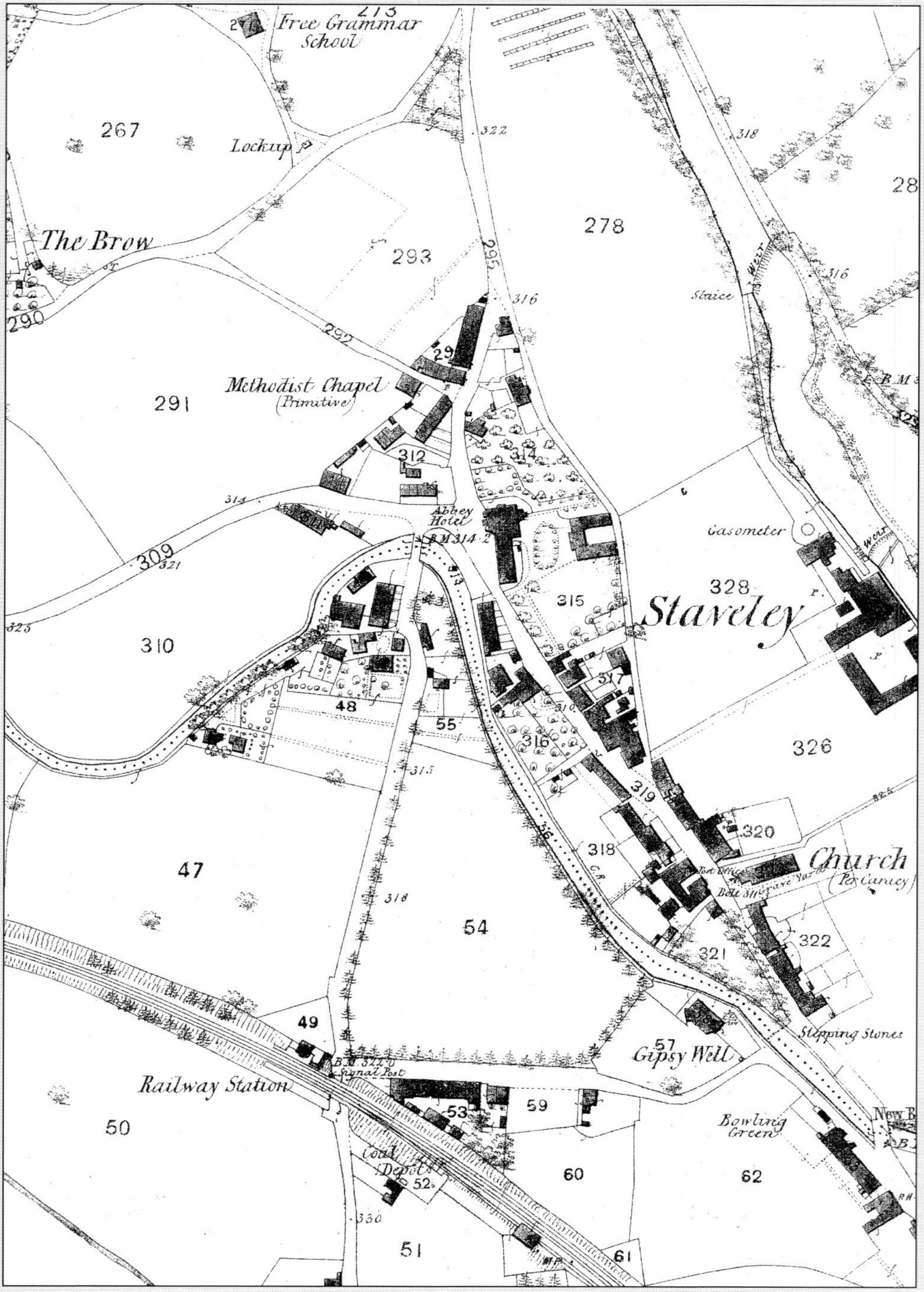

Staveley station. *Reproduced from the 25" First Edition Ordnance Survey Map*

Kendal and Windermere Railway' came from the chair and those present drank it using bumpers. Cornelius Nicholson responded and although the *Kendal Mercury* reports him as introducing his speech by saying quite simply that it was not inappropriate for the Vice-Chairman to respond, the *Westmorland Gazette* goes further and quotes him as adding that because in some sort he had been responsible for the undertaking. Cornelius Nicholson was clearly not a man to risk hiding his light under a bushel! The speeches had to be brief because there was another feast in preparation for 4.00 pm.

It might have been thought this would be back in Kendal but not so. The dinner, which, as things turned out, did not begin until 5.00 pm was given under the auspices of Watson, the assistant engineer of the line, and was held at the Crown Hotel in Bowness. There were 18 gentlemen present. This time it was Cornelius Nicholson who presided and again he praised the undertaking very much in the sort of terms he had used before. There were several other toasts, a lot of self congratulatory remarks and several bumpers were 'downed' before the party broke up at 8.00 pm and the group was conveyed back on a special train.

This second opening ceremony seems to lack the excitement of the first, perhaps because it *was* the second and had lost the novelty associated with the initial event. In spite of the lengthy coverage by the press there is a considerable amount of background information in the reports and the speeches, lengthy though they are, have a strongly repetitive quality. Presumably the people of the district had already witnessed the coming of a railway and although this was a significant happening, it had lost that novelty. In addition the opening was not marked with a holiday and that may well have affected the numbers turning out.

A very lengthy poem was composed to coincide with the opening event. It opens with these lines

'Baffle the Rail, bright scene from Orrest Head'
Somewhere in Wordsworth I this line have read;
Who calls on winds and torrents fierce and strong
In sound and fury to forbid the wrong
They heard the call in vain,-on English Ground
No 'sacred nook' has ever yet been found
To scare the deed when enterprise could throw
A fair surmise that 'flowers of hope' may grow.

It makes a point with these lines,

And for the Bard - (as Offring for our crimes)
We'll give the world to appreciate his rhymes
The mind will surely place his beauties higher
When read 'mid scenes that did the thoughts inspire
We'll spread his fame:- what more can he require?

With the railway now open throughout, a comprehensive timetable was published in the press. This timetable would take effect from 1st May:

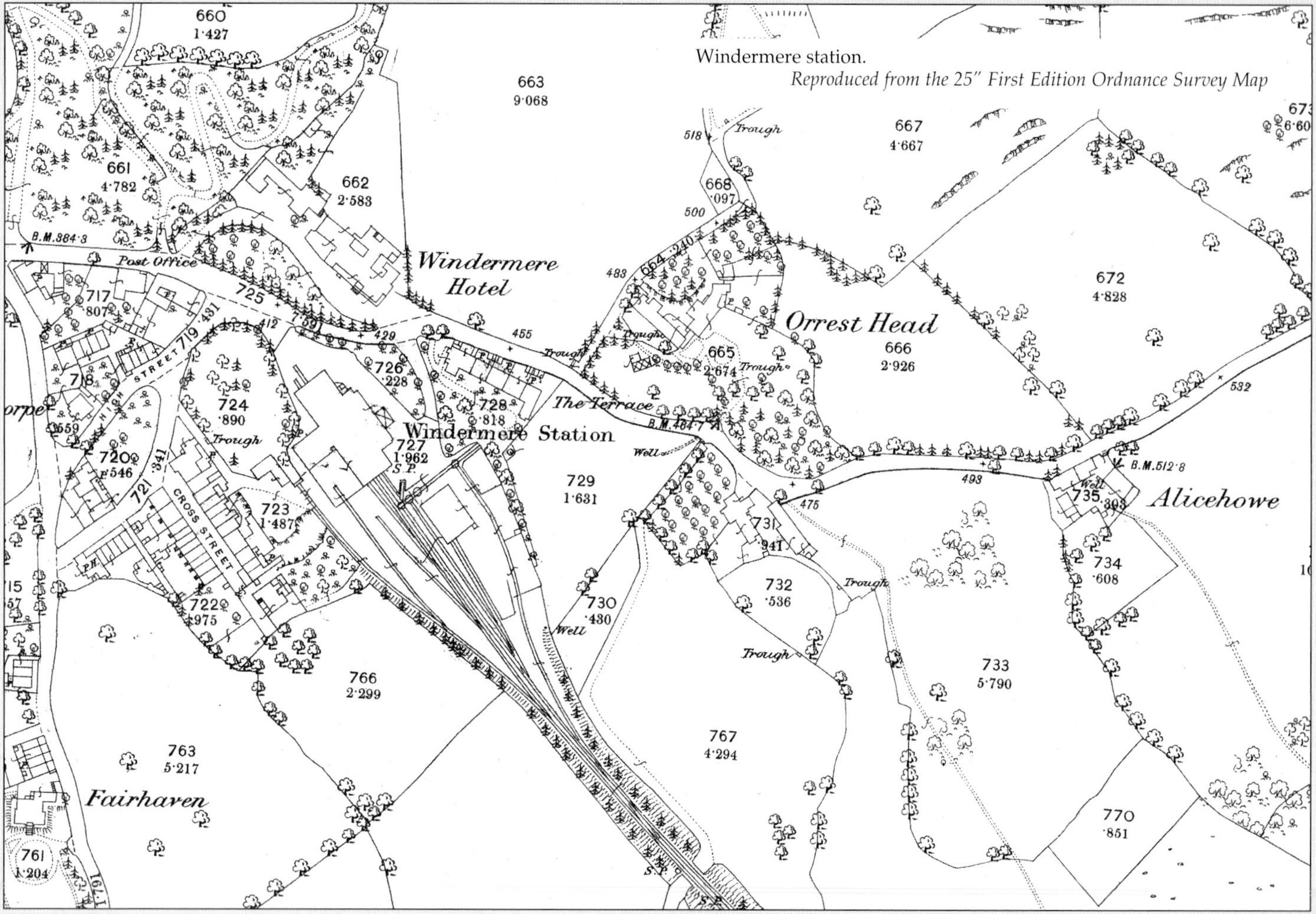

Windermere station.
Reproduced from the 25″ First Edition Ordnance Survey Map

Up trains	1 *1st, 2nd & 3rd class**	2 *1st, 2nd & 3rd class*	3 *1st, 2nd & 3rd class†*	4 *1st & 2nd class*	5 *1st & 2nd class*	6 *1st, 2nd & 3rd class*
Leave	*am*	*am*	*pm*	*pm*	*pm*	*pm*
Windermere	7.00	11.00	12.45	4.50	–	8.30
Staveley	7.10	11.10	12.55	5.00	–	8.35
Burneside	7.15	11.15	1.05	5.10	–	8.45
Kendal for North	7.30	11.30	–	5.30	7.15	8.55
South	8.10	–	1.25	5.30	–	–
Kendal Junc.						
North	7.38	11.44	–	5.37	7.29	–
South	8.20	–	1.39	5.49	–	–
Lancaster	9.30	–	2.50	6.53	–	–
Preston	10.30	–	3.50	7.53	–	–
	pm					
Liverpool abt	12.20	–	5.45	9.45	–	–
Manchester						
Salford St	12.20	–	5.55	9.45	–	–
Victoria St	12.10	–	5.35	–	–	–
				am		
Birmingham	3.20	–	7.35	12.36	–	–
London	8.45	–	11.00	5.32	–	–
	am	*pm*		*pm*		
Carlisle	10.04	2.15	–	8.10	9.55	–

* This train is 3rd class to Kendal only. † Express only to London and Birmingham. Passengers arriving at Kendal at 7.30 am from Windermere for the *South,* and at 7.45 am. from the South *for Windermere* will have half an hour for refreshment at the Kendal Station.

Down trains	1 *1st, 2nd & 3rd class*	2 *1st, & 2nd class*	3 *1st, 2nd & 3rd class*	4 *1st 2nd & 3rd class*	5 *1st, 2nd & 3rd class*	6 *1st & 2nd class*
Leave	*am*	*am*	*am*	*am*	*pm*	*pm*
Carlisle	–	6.00	–	11.00	3.28	–
		pm			*am*	(8.30)
London		8.45	–	–	6.15	(10.00)
		am				*pm*
Birmingham	–	1.25	–	–	11.15	(1.00)
Manchester					*pm*	(1.45)
Salford St	–	–	7.15	–	2.00	3.50
Victoria St	–	–	7.40	–	1.40	4.00
Liverpool	–	–	7.30	–	1.30	3.50
Preston	–	5.50	9.35	–	3.40	5.35
Lancaster	–	6.39	10.38	–	4.40	6. 30
				pm		
Kendal Junc.	–	7.38	11.45	1.39	5.50	7.29
Kendal	5.30	8.30	12.00	1.45	6.00	7.45
Burneside	5.35	8.35	12.05	1.50	–	7.50
Staveley	5.45	8.45	12.15	2.00	–	7.55
Windermere	6.00	9.00	12.30	2.15	–	8.15

Return tickets between Kendal and Windermere are granted. Those granted on Saturdays are available to return on the Monday following. No trains West of Kendal on Sundays at present.

Already the terminus at Birthwaite was being referred to 'unofficially' as 'Windermere'. Sadly, the very next day, on Wednesday 21st April, there was yet another accident. This involved William Hutton, from Kendal. It is reported that he was working as a 'breaksman' [*sic*] in the employment of Mr Ross who had the responsibility of finishing off the line near the station at Windermere. William Hutton was running a wagon down the incline near the station 'with rather too much speed'. He slipped and fell on the rail and the wagon passed over his foot, a part of which had to be amputated (Mr Longmuir carrying out the operation). He was said to be recovering from the ordeal.

In spite of the unfortunate mishaps, the line was now open throughout its length. All the shareholders needed to do next was to sit back and wait for the generous dividends that the Directors had so optimistically promised.

There were others with aspirations as well. On 24th April, the following letter appeared in the *Westmorland Gazette* and was signed by 'H',

> Now that the Kendal and Windermere rail-road has been opened to the public, the inhabitants of this neighbourhood are anxiously looking forward to a great reduction in price of many of the common necessities of life, which have long been and must continue to be conveyed hither by land-carriage.The consumption of coal in the Lake District is very extensive; and hitherto that most necessary article has, in consequence of the distance to Kendal, and the charges at the Ferry and Turnpike, being chiefly supplied from Newby Bridge and Greenodd the expense of carriage, even from those places being very considerable and the article often being of very inferior quality. In order to remedy this great evil, it is suggested to the proprietors of coal mines, to establish three depots for good coals from Newcastle or Wigan in the neighbourhood of Windermere - one at Bowness, one near the Ferry and a third at Ambleside. Such an arrangement would doubtless prove of great advantage both to the merchant and the consumer.
>
> Hoping this suggestion may be speedily acted upon.

The shareholders would be set for some disappointments but 'H', at least in part, would see some of the 'evil' he alluded to, being rectified.

In the meantime the hotel planned by the railway for Windermere was completed and opened in May. Abraham Pattinson was the builder and the cost was £1,327 7*s*. 6½*d*. The first tenant was Mr Richard Rigg.

Abraham Pattinson (1817-1871) was responsible for building the first station at Windermere. He went on to do other work for the railway and then carried out extensive building projects around Windermere.

Diana Matthews

Chapter Six

The Initial Years: 1847-1860

May 1847

An idea of how well or badly a railway was doing during this period is reflected to a large extent in the reports of the half-yearly meetings. The oscillating to and fro of the company's fortunes and the challenges faced are echoed in these brief but often informative sessions. Before the first meeting after the opening, which was held in July, some indication was given when the figures were released for the week ending 3rd July. In this period 511 first class passengers, 1,729 second class and 1,170 third class had been carried. The receipts for these amounted to £177 12*s*. 1*d*. Already the tourists were on their way. On Saturday 10th July, an excursion train left Leeds (at 6.00 am) and there were arrangements for people from Bradford, Wakefield, Huddersfield, Preston and Lancaster to join the train en route for Windermere. The participants would stay over and leave Windermere on Monday afternoon. It was anticipated that 'a very numerous assemblage will avail them of the facility' even though the weather was not as good as might have been expected for the time of year. Also, by this time, Sunday trains had been introduced when the railway started to carry the mails. From Sunday 30th May, trains left Kendal at 8.50 am (first and second class) and 1.30 pm (first, second and third class) and from Windermere at 9.25 am (first and second class) and 4.30 pm (first, second and third class). There was some further dissatisfaction among passengers who still felt that connections at Oxenholme were not arranged well. The waiting time was considered to be too long. This misgiving was voiced in a letter written to the *Kendal Mercury* on 10th July and signed by 'A Traveller'. Improvements were called for.

The first half-yearly meeting to be held after the railway opened along the whole of its length, took place at the company's offices in Kendal on 27th July. John Gandy was in the chair and the general tenor of the event was encouraging. It was reported that traffic had increased steadily since the opening and had matched the expectation of the Directors. Up to 30th June, 53,830 passengers had been carried and it was hoped that in the near future coal, slate, lime and 'other goods' would be carried over the whole line. Stephenson, Brassey & Co. had been given the maintenance contract for one year and it was hoped that thereafter the maintenance would be light. The accounts were presented and included expenses of £846 paid to the LNWR for the hire of locomotive power and various items of rolling stock. The Chairman proposed that the accounts be adopted and Cornelius Nicholson, in seconding this, as was his wont, did not miss the opportunity of saying 'a few words'. There was a good deal of self praise as he outlined his own involvement in the scheme and how he had enabled it to move forward successfully. There was praise for his fellow Directors and also for the LNWR, not least the Manager, Captain Huish, who had been so helpful. There followed further discussion involving Mr Tinker, who claimed he was speaking on behalf of the many shareholders who could not be present, and who expressed satisfaction at the progress being made. He accepted that the 75 per cent of the revenue being swallowed up in expenses, although high, would diminish with increase in revenue. One significant item of information, given by Cornelius Nicholson, was that 'a Reverend gentleman' who had property in the neighbourhood had made a submission to the Bishop, which had been approved, to build a church nearby and he (Cornelius Nicholson) felt this would encourage gentlemen to come to the area and build 'elegant mansions'. All seemed to augur well.

In September it was possible to inform the public that arrangements had been made to forward goods to Tebay station for Kirkby Stephen, Appleby, Brough, Barnard Castle and beyond at 7.30 am on Wednesdays and Saturdays, with goods being collected the previous day. This information was circulated by James Relton, the superintendent at the Kendal goods warehouse.

1848 – The railway is a victim of a depression

From 1837 to 1842 the country had been gripped by a serious financial depression which had resulted in manufacturing and commerce being badly affected and almost brought to a standstill. There had been resulting high levels of unemployment and these various factors, in consequence, had an impact on the railway companies, with receipts dropping. In 1841, Prime Minister, Sir Robert Peel, had been moved to remark, 'Can there be a more lamentable picture than that of a Chancellor seated on an empty chest by a pool of bottomless deficiency, fishing for a budget?' After 1842 there had been something of a recovery but in 1848 another downturn started to manifest itself and there may well have been fears that this, the second depression of the early 19th century, might last as long as the previous one. Fortunately any such fears were unfounded and this later slump lasted for only about a year. It was, however, with this prevailing condition in the background that the first half-yearly meeting of the Kendal & Windermere took place in 1848. It was held on Tuesday 25th January. In some respects, understandably, it was rather more subdued than the previous one and the absence of Cornelius Nicholson meant there was no rousing speech to urge the members on. There was an attempt to put on a brave face for what had been something of a downturn. It was the Secretary, Thomas Hudson, who was called upon by the Chairman, John Gandy, to read the Directors report. The opening paragraph sets the tone:

> Gentlemen – In laying before you the Capital Account of this Company and the Revenue Account for the first half year, your Directors would express a hope, that all circumstances being duly considered, the result can by no means be held to be unfavourable.

At the meeting, it was possible to report that in spite of these problems, since the last half-yearly report, 81,860 passengers had travelled on the line. The meeting was also informed that the Directors had made representation to Parliament in order to raise additional capital to meet the cost of laying the double line which had originally been proposed in August 1845 and also agreed in October that year. The estimated cost of rails, chairs and the works for this development had been £45,000.

There was very little discussion when the Chairman opened the meeting for questions and comments but one issue which did arise concerned the expenses being charged by the LNWR for operating the line. These amounted to some 48 per cent of the receipts and this was considered to be high by some of those present. The level was defended by the Secretary although he was quick to point out that he was not responsible for the traffic arrangements (as might have been expected) and that the Directors had taken that matter 'into their own hands'. Towards the end of the meeting, the Chairman pointed out that before the meeting Thomas Hudson had tendered his resignation. This was accepted and laudable remarks were made about the work he had done. He was replaced by William Watson, who had been the resident engineer under Harris. Watson's salary would be £175 per annum and he would also act as Engineer to the company. Immediately following this meeting there was a special meeting at which it was agreed a Bill should go forward for the purpose of raising £50,000 in shares and £10,000 in loans.

Cornelius Nicholson did surface again on 19th February when a letter written by him (from Stand Lodge in Manchester) was published in the *Kendal Mercury*. In the letter he refuted an assertion which had been made that he had become a Director of the Cockermouth and Keswick Railway. He also made it clear that he certainly had not purchased shares. Later events, it might be argued, would show that he would be destined to go on to greater things.

During the months which followed, the Lancaster & Carlisle made various changes to its timetables and the Kendal & Windermere, on occasions, had to keep up with these by making alterations which would maintain what was felt to be reasonable, if not always good, connections. At times there seemed to be little or no consultation about timings which meant the Kendal & Windermere was left somewhat lagging behind the company operating the main line. During this period there was inconsistency when referring to the place where the branch left the main line. From the outset, the Kendal & Windermere, on the timetable, referred to it as 'Oxenholme' but the Lancaster & Carlisle used the name 'Kendal Junction'. There are also references, less frequently, to 'Oxenholme Junction' as well. There seemed to be no significant rationale for this and, in fact, there were occasions, when issuing notices, that the Kendal & Windermere used the title 'Kendal Junction'.

On 1st May, the Kendal & Windermere published a comprehensive timetable. This provided the traveller not only with times of trains on the branch but also the schedules for journeys further afield. There were five trains leaving Windermere on weekdays, with one going only as far as Kendal, and two on Sundays. In addition there were four trains starting at Kendal for Oxenholme and two on Sundays. There were five trains through from Oxenholme to Windermere on weekdays, with one on Sundays. There were also three trains from Oxenholme which terminated at Kendal on weekdays and on Sundays there were two such, with a further train which went from Kendal to Oxenholme. At this stage the Lancaster & Carlisle was still operating trains from Kendal to Lancaster.

Coincidentally with the introduction of this timetable, on 1st May, the Lancaster & Carlisle changed the time of one of its up trains. The train leaving Carlisle and reaching 'Kendal Junction' at 11.30 am was discontinued and the replacement now reached 'Kendal Junction' at 8.46 am; not an insignificant variation.

What must have seemed an enormous leap forward came with the announcement that an excursion was planned for the Whitsuntide Holiday, which would enable the participants to go for a trip to London. Departure from Kendal would be on Saturday 10th June at 2 am (a very early start) and return would be on Monday 19th June in the evening. The cost would be 30 shillings (a point which was followed by three exclamation marks in the advertisement) and the travellers would be in *closed carriages*!

At the same time the Lancaster & Carlisle made another change to the time table. After 15th May the up express would stop at 'Kendal Junction' at 2.52 pm.

On 26th May, the Kendal & Windermere also announced a change in the timetable. On 1st June and thereafter, the 8.00 am from Kendal would be retimed to 7.45 am and the 2.40 pm, also from Kendal, was rescheduled to leave at 3.00 pm. In addition the 8.15 am from Windermere would be changed to 8.10 am.

More bad news

In a notice issued on 11th July it was announced that as well as the half-yearly meeting, which would be held on Monday 31st July, there would be a special and extraordinary meeting. On the face of it this special meeting would be to decide on resolutions which would be proposed for raising £50,000; the amount authorized by 'The Kendal and Windermere Railway Act Amendment Bill'. (Local and Personal Act 11 & 12 Victoria I, c.xxvi).

It turned out that there was also something of a hidden agenda in the Directors' minds for this special meeting.

At the meeting, on 31st July, John Gandy was in the Chair, again. The news was bleak. He expressed the view that he regretted not being able to present a more favourable picture as far as profits were concerned but the first year of operation had not seen the success for which they had optimistically hoped. He did draw attention to 'the disastrous state of commercial affairs' which was 'discouraging' traffic and referred to the parlous state the country was in. What he did not say, explicitly, was that members should not really have been surprised. The country was yet to emerge from the depression it was in and the Kendal & Windermere was no exception in suffering as a result of these hard times. What *was* clear was that the railway had to make all possible economies. There had been no acceptable quotation for a maintenance contract for the line and so because the line was reckoned to be in a good condition no significant action would be taken. The good news was that since the last report, 59,293 passengers had been carried without a single accident; the company had been involved in the building of a new hotel at Windermere (the name John Gandy choose to use) and approval had been given for raising further capital.

Ticket sales figures had, in fact, been showing a steady increase latterly,

	First class	*Second class*	*Third class*	*Total*	*Amount* £	*s.*	*d.*
Week ending 13th May	306	1,064	754	2,124	99	9	6
3rd June	347	1,012	650	2,009	109	13	5
24th June	524	1,472	959	2,955	152	16	0

The meeting was followed by the extraordinary meeting at which the matter of raising the £50,000 was to be discussed. However, when the press was excluded from the meeting, there seemed to be more afoot. The *Westmorland Gazette* did not seem to feel particularly snubbed by this exclusion but the *Kendal Mercury* took exception to it. It acknowledged that the meeting had the power to exclude all but shareholders but suggested that the press had an almost undisputed right to be there and lamented the fact that this was the first time such an exclusion had been exercised. The writer then proceeded to speculate on the reasons, possibly having had a tip off from someone who had been present. There had been, it was alleged, 'loud complaints' from some of the shareholders from 'a distance' that the working expenses, at 67 per cent of receipts, were too high. There had been a 'stormy discussion'. Perhaps more significant was the suggestion that there had been a discussion about the possibility of leasing the line to the Lancaster & Carlisle company. A committee had been formed to look into various matters and in the light of this, it had been agreed to adjourn the meeting until 28th August.

The special meeting, however, did not take place until 11th September. The Directors in the meantime had been very busy with negotiations. This time the press was allowed in. All could now be revealed. The committee which had been appointed had been in talks with the Lancaster & Carlisle about the possibility of that company leasing the Kendal & Windermere. Presumably this was seen by the Directors of the Kendal & Windermere as a way out of their difficulties; but the talks had not achieved anything other than an expression of goodwill and support by the Lancaster & Carlisle. John Gandy, in the Chair, was clearly disappointed by this outcome but assured the shareholders that every effort would be made to reduce expenditure further. He did comment that, in effect, he could see no real solution to the problems until the general economy of the country picked up again and it came out of the depression:

> Their [the Directors] recent close investigation into the situation and prospects of the line, have given them renewed confidence that nothing but a return to the general prosperity of the country is required to place your line in a very different position to that which it now occupies.

It was then agreed to raise the £50,000 by issuing preference shares at £10 each with these bearing interest of 6 per cent but without further participation in the profits or advantages of the company in preference to the dividends payable on the existing or ordinary shares. This business might have concluded the meeting. However, there were other matters raised.

Job Bintley has an idea

Presumably the Directors knew what was coming when Job Bintley had a proposal to make. He mooted that their line should be extended down to the lake by using an incline at Miller Ground. It is reported there was an 'animated conversation' about this proposal but in the end it was felt it would be unwise to take any steps to further the idea. Bintley also brought to the attention of the Directors the plans being made by the (so-called 'Little') North Western to bring a line over from the West Riding and felt there should be discussions with that company's Directors with a view to persuading them to route it onto the Lancaster & Carlisle at Sedgwick or Crooklands rather than Lancaster, as this would considerably shorten the distance from the West Riding to Scotland. Although the North Western did produce plans to include a link near Sedgwick, the company was destined to have problems of its own and such a connection was not made (see *The Ingleton Branch 'A Lost Route to Scotland'*, Oakwood Press, 1985).

It was at a short general meeting immediately following this one, that Cornelius Nicholson's resignation as a Director was announced. Mr J.J. Wilson was made Vice-Chairman in his stead.

The refusal by the Lancaster & Carlisle to take on a lease of the Kendal & Windermere may have been a disappointment for the Directors of the latter but should not really have come as a surprise. The Lancaster & Carlisle was in no way indebted to the Kendal & Windermere; either morally or financially. In spite of the *bonhomie* at the first opening ceremony, when Directors of both companies had celebrated together, much of the initiative had come from the Kendal camp and it could be argued (not least by Locke) that the line had only taken the route it did take because of the importunity of the Kendal Committee. The main line was starting to be financially viable and looked like becoming more so. At the half-yearly meeting which had been held on 9th February, 1848, the Chairman of the Lancaster & Carlisle, E.W.Hasell, had announced an interim dividend of 4 per cent which he was convinced would hold up. He was optimistic that the Caledonian Railway (the term was now being used to describe the line northwards from Carlisle), which was about to be opened, would further increase the fortunes of the Lancaster & Carlisle. Everything (apart, perhaps, from dealings with the Lancaster Canal Co.) was to the satisfaction of the Directors, including the arrangement with the LNWR regarding the use of locomotives and rolling stock. There was, also, harmony on the Board. In the light, therefore, of this success and with the prevailing economic climate, the Lancaster & Carlisle would be wary of taking on a company that was far from buoyant and could well become a liability. The proffering of 'goodwill' was all very well but it did not greatly help the Kendal & Windermere. A season would follow when the two companies would have a rather brittle relationship and the Lancaster & Carlisle would tend to hold the Kendal & Windermere 'at arm's length'. There would be friction at times and the matter of rates for operating the line would lead to a different solution being sought.

An issue was raised by Mr Braithwaite, at that February meeting. It concerned the poor connections at Oxenholme when passengers had to alight from the carriages if they were going from the main line to Kendal and beyond. Why was it not possible to detach and attach carriages to make life easier, not least because those (especially the first class passengers) who were heading for the Lakes usually had large amounts of luggage. Waiting times of up to half-an-hour were sometimes experienced. The Chairman felt it should be possible for the Kendal & Windermere to take passengers straight on to Kendal and should meet the trains arriving on the main line. There was also the issue of accommodation for passengers at Oxenholme. Hasell conceded that as the main line operator, the Lancaster & Carlisle should provide suitable accommodation but it had been expected that the Kendal & Windermere would do something towards this. There had, as yet, he pointed out, been no satisfactory resolution of this situation.

In the background, whilst all this was going on, visitors continued to flock to the Lakes. For example, on 10th August, there had been a trip from Preston which had been organized for the benefit of schoolchildren, who were on holiday. Six trains with approximately 20 carriages each and carrying some 2,000 people had enjoyed the outing on a fine day. The 8.00 am train from Kendal on that day was especially busy as people from Kendal travelled to Birthwaite to meet friends and relatives who came up from Preston. What a boon the railway was proving to be.

In the meantime, it would seem that the London excursions had been a success and others followed. It was announced that the last of these for the season and entitled 'Autumnal Trips to London and Back' would take place on Saturday 30th September (returning Friday 6th October) and Monday 2nd October (returning Monday 16th October). These trips were certainly breaking new ground as those who probably never even dreamed of being able to visit their capital, or might only do so in a manner that involved a great deal of time and inconvenience, were now able to make the journey with comparative ease. The population of Westmorland, as in so many other places, was on the move.

There was more good news at the beginning of September, brought about by the facilities created by the railway and one which had been anticipated when the railway was first proposed; the price of coal started to fall. The Blenkinsopp Coal Co., which was associated with the Newcastle & Carlisle Railway, opened a yard at Kendal railway station. It was Thomas Hudson who became the accountant and commission agent. Payment had to be made in cash and the cost was 10*d*. per cwt. An arrangement was made for carriers to place orders and it was made clear that if, as was anticipated, the tolls levied by the railway came down, the cost of coal would be reduced further. This happened by the end of September and as a result the price fell by 1*d*. per cwt; in other words by 10 per cent, not an insignificant sum. In October, the Hartleburn Coals Co., which leased the Earl of Carlisle's colliery, followed the Blenkinsopp Co. This company opened a yard near the station and for those collecting coal there, the cost was 8½*d*. per cwt with a cost of 9*d*. delivered. This undercut the cost charged by the Blenkinsopp company and the competitive element, now possible, was clearly having the sort of impact those who had been responsible for building the railway had envisaged.

1849

The first half-yearly meeting, held at the company's office, on Saturday 20th January, with John Gandy in the chair, did not provide an opportunity for presenting encouraging news for the shareholders. Even though the country was beginning to emerge from the recession, the effects of this move in economic change was yet to make a real impact. John Gandy made the point that with prevailing conditions there had been less demand for rail travel but the transportation of goods had seen an improvement by some 50 per cent compared with the same period in the previous year and this was especially so in the carrying of coal. Once again the cost of running the line as far as locomotive power was concerned had been high and the Chairman expressed the hope that improvements in locomotive design might lead to more efficient machines, burning less fuel and also more suited to their type of line. Much of the profit had been used in the payment of interest and although the capital account had yet to be closed it was hoped that what payments remained outstanding might be met by the conversion to share capital by the issue of preferential shares. The bottom line was a balance for the half-year of £134 3*s*. 3*d*. Although this brought the surplus fund to £2,300 John Gandy informed the meeting that the Directors felt this amount should remain in place for possible contingencies. The matter of the line being leased to the Lancaster & Carlisle was raised again and the Chairman said there had been no development in this direction. In spite of there being no dividend, there were signs of optimism and a feeling things would get better.

A terse announcement by the Lancaster & Carlisle informed the public that, from 1st February, the 11.00 am train from Kendal to the south would be withdrawn. No reason was given but it was probably no surprise because Kendal was now looked upon as being on a branch line rather than the main line system. However, there was a quick response from the Kendal & Windermere with the information that in view of this decision the 10.35 am from Windermere would go to 'Oxenholme Junction' [*sic*] with passengers for the north only.

The second half-yearly meeting was held at the company's offices on Monday 30th July. Matters were noticeably improving and a greater confidence was apparent. An improvement in the country's economic position was beginning to tell and as well as this, the company had taken a number of steps to strengthen its position. In his report John Gandy (who was actually absent through illness) was able to inform the shareholders that there had been a significant reduction in expenses latterly, the real effect of which would make itself more apparent in the next few months. In addition, the cost of construction had been liquefied by the preference shares and, very importantly, the income had risen substantially. This may well have seemed to augur well for a dividend but the Chairman, no doubt anticipating this, commented 'they [the Directors] would express not an unreasonable expectation of paying a dividend on the original shares at no distant period'. The future was looking brighter (if not bright) and there seemed to be a dividend in the offing at last! There was also optimism expressed about the arrival of the North Western Railway and it was anticipated (correctly as events would later show) this line would open up Windermere to the West Riding as people from places such as Leeds came on tours. In connection with the North Western, Job Bintley reiterated his belief that it would be an advantage to them if a junction was made with the Lancaster & Carlisle somewhere in the vicinity of Milnthorpe.

In August yet another fall in the price of coal was announced, this time by the Kendal Coal Co. 'Great' reductions would be made in the price of 'King Coal' and 'The Best Common Coal' at 'Kendal, Staveley and Birthwaite'. Prices did vary, with, for example, the price of 'King Coal' at Birthwaite being 2*s*. 6*d*. more per ton than the 13*s*. 4*d*. at Kendal.

Also at the beginning of August a boost to tourism was planned in the launching of a new company with a new steamer on Windermere. All was being prepared for a noon launch on 1st August when it was discovered that a vital piece of 'machinery' had been 'unaccountably detained' at the railway station in Kendal. This was something of a black mark for the railway because the parts were essential if the launch was to take place. The sections eventually arrived and were fitted but it was nearly 7.30 pm before the guests could make their way to the Ferry Inn for a reception.

The railway had also come in for some criticism from local people, in particular residents in Kendal, because it was alleged that whilst the railway was providing cheap excursions to Windermere for people coming from a distance, no such facilities had been made available to local residents. Whether this plea was heeded or whether it was by coincidence, cheap trips from Kendal were arranged during August and September with, for example, on Wednesday 29th August, trains leaving Kendal at 7.00 am and noon with a return train at 8.30 pm. What may seem quite remarkable is that whilst children would normally travel at a cheaper rate than adults, for these outings there was also a distinction made in some cases in the pricing for men and women.

	Males	*Females*	*Children under 12*
Kendal to Windermere and back	1s.	8*d*.	6*d*.
Burneside	10*d*.	8*d*.	6*d*.
Staveley	6*d*.	6*d*.	4*d*.

It was noted that the 'The Lord of the Isles' steam yacht would 'ply the whole of the day at reduced rates'.

September saw another significant drop in the price of coal when the Ince Hall Coal Co. announced that 'King Coal' at Kendal would cost 8*d*. per cwt and at Birthwaite 9½*d*. per cwt. Other qualities were also reduced in price, with Pemberton coal being as little as 6½*d*. for a cwt. This was no doubt welcome news with the winter months not very far ahead.

A further reduction in services was also announced this month when travellers were informed that from 1st September the 10.20 am from Windermere would be withdrawn; the 1.05 pm would be retimed to leave at 12.50 pm. There were yet more changes in November. The trains leaving Kendal at 7.00 pm and Windermere at 8.30 pm would be withdrawn. There were changes to the times as far as other services were concerned. Later in the month the train leaving Kendal at 12 noon and Windermere at 12.50 pm would only run on Mondays, Wednesdays and Saturdays (until further notice).

1850

The first half-yearly meeting of 1850 took place on Thursday 24th January. John Gandy was in the Chair. At first sight it seemed things were looking up. He felt able to congratulate the shareholders 'on the improved aspect of the affairs of the railway'. Traffic receipts had increased by just over £787 and there had been a saving on motive power of just over £111. With savings on passenger and general charges and costs of the permanent way, the total came to a saving of over £1,000. Against this there had been an increase in expenses of only just over £52 which meant on the face of it a very healthy position. Hopes might have been high that the Directors would declare a dividend at last. Not so. Once again the recommendation was for the monies to be added to the previous balance. When questions started to be asked, it transpired that things were not quite what they appeared to be. James Gandy pointed out that taking into account the whole picture over a longer period of time rather than just the previous half-year, the realistic profit figure was £584 and it was this last figure which would be available for a dividend. James Thompson, whilst being happy with the way in which the line was being run, did not appear too happy with this analysis. He worked out that over the previous two years there had been a profit of £1,838; so why no dividend? He declared that he was puzzled how James Gandy had reached the figure of £584 but felt whatever the profit was in reality, it should yield a dividend and to that end he proposed an amendment to that effect. James Thompson was undeterred by the rationale that James Gandy proceeded to give and pointed to the fact that the North Western was expected to bring more business to the line; also that a gentleman had purchased an estate in Bowness scheduled for building purposes and this would bring in more people. Considerable debate followed about the extent to which a reserve might be needed and in the end James Thompson proposed that the Directors' report be accepted with the exception of the clause relating to dividends and that a dividend of 2*s.* for each ordinary share in the company should be divided among the shareholders out of the net profits. This was passed. One matter which was raised during the discussion was whether the LNWR had intimated that they no longer wished to work the line. The Chairman informed the meeting that no such intention had been made.

Not everybody approved of the move to give the dividend agreed at the meeting. The following week a writer who simply signed the letter 'O' complained that such a decision had been made on the strength of fare increases and that it was the 'Windermere Company' which was 'pocketing the majority of this increased income'. It is noted that for second class:

Preston to Kendal	7*s.* 3*d.*	Preston to Oxenholme	6*s.* 6*d.*
		Oxenholme to Kendal	4*d.*
		Total	6*s.* 10*d.*

The writer complains that, in effect, the traveller is being charged 5*d.* for booking once and not twice! Obviously to guard against this 'gross imposition', as the writer describes it, travellers to or from Kendal are advised to book first to Oxenholme and then re-book at Oxenholme to Kendal or the other destination and 'by this means they effectively guard against this wrong'.

As the year progressed, the effects of the general recession faded and this began to be apparent in the company's fortunes. By the second half-yearly meeting, which was held on Friday 26th July, the situation was looking more encouraging and John Gandy was able to report that there had been an increase in traffic and it was anticipated there would be more to come. He noted that for the six months ending June 1848 income had been £3,656 18*s.*; for the same period in 1849, £3,916 12*s.* 8*d.*; and for 1850, £4,524 17*s.* 10*d.* The profit from June 1849 to June 1850 had been £1,220 7*s.* 1*d.* and after the agreed dividend had been deducted, the remaining amount was £773 11*s.* 1*d.* In the light of this a second dividend of 2*s.* was proposed. This was agreed and would be paid on 5th August.

The other piece of news was that the company had decided to cancel the contract it had with the LNWR to work the line. Certainly, there had been uneasiness among certain shareholders regarding the apparently high proportion of income being expended in this department. The LNWR seemed relatively unconcerned about this development and had waived the requirement for a 12 month period of notice to three months instead. The Kendal & Windermere decided, as the alternative, to enter into an agreement with E.B. Wilson & Co. of Leeds. At around this time Wilson's were building a 2-2-2 tank engine and also a 2-4-0 type with inside cylinders.

Mid-August saw the introduction of a further train on the line. This would be first class only and leave Kendal for Windermere following the arrival of the 'North Express' at about 3.05 pm. It would stop at Staveley. At least this decision went some way to meeting the criticisms of the Lancaster & Carlisle regarding proper connecting services.

In spite of the up-turn in business, the Directors decided to call a special meeting on Thursday 29th August. The purpose was to authorize the borrowing of such sums of money which might be needed but not exceeding £16,000; this to be done under the Kendal and Windermere Act Amendment Act, 1848.

The people of Kendal were able to take advantage of a cheap day return trip to Manchester on 24th August, this being organized by the Lancaster & Carlisle. Those who went had to be up early as the train left Kendal at 5.00 am. Return could be on the same day (leaving Manchester at 6. 00 pm) or the following day. The cost would be first class, 8*s*. 6*d*. or third class, 4*s*. 4*d*. For an extra 2*s*. it was possible to stay until Monday or Tuesday when there was a choice of return times on morning trains. Again, the point was made that covered carriages would be used. For something completely different, on 16th September the company put on cheap excursions for the people of Kendal and district to go to Windermere for 'the Nutting Season'. First class cost 2*s*. 6*d*., second class, 2*s*. 0*d*. and third class, 1*s*. 0*d*. These tickets could be used on the 6. 30 am or 12.15 pm trains out and the 1.50 pm or 5.45 pm back.

1851

The first half-yearly meeting of 1851 brought even better news for the Kendal & Windermere. At a national level there was a feeling that there were better days ahead and a grand exhibition of industrial achievements was planned which would be held in London. In Kendal, J.J. Wilson, as Vice-Chairman of the company and standing in for John Gandy when the meeting was held on Tuesday 28th January, was able to report to those present that traffic receipts were up 12 per cent on the corresponding period in the previous year; not only that, there had been a small decrease in expenditure with an even greater decrease anticipated for the following half. The Chairman pointed out that,

> ... after a period of great difficulty - owing in some pressure to the universal depreciation of railway property - this company finds its position secure and satisfactory.

The position certainly looked healthy. Most of the bonds bearing 5 per cent interest had been paid off or liquidated and the company had acquired a loan at what was considered to be a satisfactory rate of 4 per cent per annum. Then came the announcement that might well have given the shareholders the feeling of a warm glow inside; namely that as a result of the £1,512 17*s*. 7*d*. profit of the last half, a dividend of 5*s*. (being at the rate of 10 per cent per annum) was proposed and approved. This would still allow for a balance of £395 17*s*. 7*d*. to be carried forward. The company had continued to sell land for building purposes which it was hoped would result indirectly in bettering trade. It was noted that £22 10*s*. had been paid to provide a veranda for the Windermere Hotel! There had been some teething troubles, it seemed, over the new arrangements with Wilson's of Leeds but Mr Wilson had agreed to come over and sort out the problems. Savings to the company from the new arrangement had amounted to between 1*s*. and 1*s*. 3*d*. per mile. Everybody seemed happy. The Directors were highly praised for their work in making such a success of the undertaking and although thus far they had received no remuneration it was felt this was an unsatisfactory state of affairs and consideration should be given in future to rectifying this. Such was the ethos of the era; when men often saw it as a privilege to promote such an undertaking for the benefit it would bring rather than for the wealth they might personally make.

The Great Exhibition

The exhibition of 1851, the Great Exhibition, as it became known, was without doubt a huge success. Prince Albert had certainly been inspired when he came up with the idea and the Crystal Palace was a remarkable structure which many wished to see. The Lancaster & Carlisle organized excursions to London for an advertised return fare of 30 shillings (this was actually the second class fare from Lancaster) and these ran every Saturday from and including 21st June. It was possible to stay for either seven or 14 days. Passengers joining the train at Oxenholme boarded the 1 am from Carlisle at 2.15 am and paid 50*s*. for a first class ticket, 33*s*. second class and 26*s*. third class. The return from London was on Fridays at 8 .00 pm.

However, it was felt that the popular appeal of the exhibition had an adverse effect on the Kendal & Windermere because fewer people chose to visit the Lake District during the summer of 1851. This was a point raised at the half-yearly meeting which was held on Thursday 24th July. John Gandy was in the chair and informed the meeting that the profits for the previous half-year were down by just over £20. The outlook up to May had been very promising but thereafter the level of profit dropped sharply and this was attributed to the people visiting the Great Exhibition rather than coming to the Lakes. However, there was more encouraging news as far as the expenses of the company were concerned. Nearly £244 had been saved and in addition to this there had been a decrease of £192 in the interest and other charges since the last half. The overall effect of this was a resulting profit of £596 against one of just over £70 in the corresponding period of the previous year. On reflection there had been, over the years, a very significant reduction in operating costs. In June 1848, these had been 68 per cent of total costs, in December,

56 per cent, in June 1849, 57 per cent, in December, 43 per cent, in June 1850, 50 per cent, in December, 40 per cent and in June 1851 the expenses had been 42 per cent. All in all this dip in income was seen to be easily explained and there was confidence that things would be better once the exhibition was over.

There were other factors which seemed to augur well. The population numbers for Windermere were steadily rising, a situation which it was felt could be directly associated with the advent of the railway and, in turn, mean the likehood of more prosperity for the latter. Yet there were issues which had to be addressed. At the meeting Mr Foxcroft had a number of matters to raise. A butcher from Manchester had complained that cattle had been kept too long in the pens at Kendal before being dispatched and this had resulted in injury and loss of revenue. The butchers who had come to do business had been delayed and as a result of this, a special train had to be hired to get them back. It was alleged that the 'hostilities' between the Lancaster & Carlisle and the Kendal & Windermere meant that there was a charge of 5*s*. per mile; a sum considered excessive. The butchers involved were considering doing business in Milnthorpe in future, obviously to the detriment of the Kendal & Windermere. The Secretary, Harrison, said that this matter had been misunderstood. There had been a problem with a rail which had caused the delay and this was a matter beyond their control although everything had been done to sort out the problem. He was at pains to point out there was no hostility between the two companies. The outcome had been a demand made through a lawyer for recompense of £10.

There were also misgivings (Mr Foxcroft alleged) about the level of fares on the Kendal & Windermere line with a suggestion that if the fares were lowered, more people would travel and receipts would increase. Mr Foxcroft also enquired about the possibility of cheap excursions for schools and it was pointed out that a rate of 2*d*. per mile for schools had been used but it would not be feasible to drop below this. After a certain amount of banter, Mr Foxcroft was assured that if he arranged for 3,000 children to travel, not only would the railway carry them cheaply but they could go from Oxenholme to Windermere and have a trip round the lake on a steamer for 7*d*. This remark prompted laughter!

1852

When the first half-yearly meeting took place on Saturday 3rd February, the Great Exhibition was still being seen as the cause of the company's falling returns. The whole issue was clearly a matter of considerable concern.

A summary of the returns is shown below:

	1st January to 7th May (before exhibition opened)			*14th May 16th October (while exhibition was open)*			*23rd October to 31st December (exhibition closed)*		
	£	*s.*	*d.*	*£*	*s.*	*d.*	*£*	*s.*	*d.*
1848	2,116	19	4	4,824	19	7	1,274	0	6
1849	2,383	16	3	5,578	8	6	1,496	11	7
1850	2,560	16	9	6,385	8	3	1,618	3	0
1851	2,878	16	8	5,638	16	10	1,874	1	9

Nevertheless, as the cause of the loss in revenue appeared to be easily explained and was down to transient circumstances, there was optimism that this fall would be a passing one. Confidence was high enough for the suggestion made at the last meeting that the Directors should be remunerated to become a proposal and £200, whilst being seen as not really adequate for all the work that had been done, was agreed. This, it was also suggested, should be divided between the six Directors in accordance with their attendance record at the meetings.

There were two other matters of note. Wilson's had made a decision to discontinue working the line. In consequence, the company had arranged to purchase some of the locomotives and carriages and anticipated this step might result in further savings. It would seem that there had been rumours in various places that a merger of the Kendal & Windermere with the Lancaster & Carlisle was under consideration. The Directors did not deny this but pointed out that if there were tangible steps taken, the shareholders would be informed.

By the second half-yearly meeting on Thursday 22nd July (when there were only Directors present) the situation did seem to be improving. The Great Exhibition was over and the locomotives and other stock purchased were in use. Receipts were up £514 10*s.* 9*d.* on the same period in the previous year and costs on the operating side were down. Even so there had been a considerable outlay made on this stock with the result that the sort of saving which might be made had still to be determined. It was also noted that since the company had taken over the running of the line, the punctuality of the services had been improved. A dividend of 5*s.* per share was agreed and this would take up £1,117 of the £1,237 19*s.* 1*d.* which was available. The balance was to be added to the accumulated profits of previous years which gave a total of £1,521 5*s.* 3*d.*

1853

At the beginning of the year this is how the services looked:

Weekdays - Up Trains

5.30 am	*dep.*	Kendal	1st, 2nd, 3rd class (mail). For North.
9.15 am	*dep.*	Windermere	1st, 2nd, 3rd class (1*d.* per mile). For South.
		9.25 am Staveley	
		9.35 am Burneside	
		9.40 am Kendal	
11.30 am	*dep.*	Kendal	1st, 2nd class. For North.
2.30 pm	*dep.*	Windermere	1st, 2nd class. For North; Express South.
		2.40 pm Staveley	
		2.45 pm Burneside	
		2.50 pm Kendal	
4.20 pm	*dep.*	Kendal	1st, 2nd class. For South; Express North.
5.50 pm	*dep.*	Windermere	1st, 2nd class (mail). For North and South.
		5.58 pm Staveley	
		6.03 pm Burneside	
		6.10 pm Kendal	

Weekdays - Down Trains

6.50 am	*dep.*	Kendal	1st, 2nd, 3rd class (mail) (1*d*. per mile).
		6.57 am Burneside	
		7.07 am Staveley	
	arr.	7.25 am Windermere	
10.05 am	*arr.*	Kendal	1st, 2nd class.
12.15 pm	*dep.*	Kendal	1st, 2nd class.
		12.20 pm Burneside	
		12.25 pm Staveley	
	arr.	12.35 pm Windermere	
3.30 pm	*arr.*	Kendal	1st class (express).
4.00 pm	*dep.*	Kendal	1st, 2nd class.
		4.10 pm Staveley	
	arr.	4.20 pm Windermere	
5.00 pm	*dep.*	Kendal	1st class (express).
		5.15 pm Staveley	
	arr.	5.25 pm Windermere	
6.40 pm	*arr.*	Kendal	1st, 2nd class (mail).

On Saturdays there was also a market train leaving Kendal for Windermere at 3.15 pm, stopping at Staveley.

Sundays - Up Trains

5.30 am	*dep.*	Kendal	1st, 2nd, 3rd class (mail). For North.
9.00 am	*dep.*	Windermere	1st, 2nd, 3rd class.
		9.10 am Staveley	
		9.15 am Burneside	
		9.20 am Kendal	
5.50 pm	*dep.*	Windermere	1st, 2nd class (mail).
		5. 58 pm Staveley	
		6. 03 pm Burneside	
		6. 10 pm Kendal	

Sundays - Down Trains

6.50 am	*dep.*	Kendal	1st, 2nd, 3rd class (mail).
		6.57 am Burneside	
		7.07 am Staveley	
	arr.	7.25 am Windermere	
5.00 pm	*dep.*	Kendal	1st, 2nd class.
		5.05 pm Burneside	
		5.10 pm Staveley	
	arr.	5.20 pm Windermere	
7.00 pm	*arr.*	Kendal	1st, 2nd class (mail).

A number of (stage) coaches operated in conjunction with these services to provide connections to and from other places. A mail coach for Keswick and Cockermouth left Windermere at 8.00 am. It was scheduled to reach Keswick at 11.00 am and Cockermouth in time to catch the 2.00 pm train to Whitehaven and Carlisle. In the other direction, a mail coach left Cockermouth after the arrival of the train at 12.00 noon, Keswick at 2.00 pm and was scheduled to arrive in Windermere for travellers to catch the 5.50 pm train. The 'Wonder Coach' left Windermere at 5.45 pm for Rydal and Grasmere. Coaches left Ambleside for

Windermere at 8.20 am 12.00 noon and 4.20 pm. An omnibus for Low Wood met every train and there were also 'conveyances' to and from Bowness to meet all the trains. A basic transport network was beginning to develop.

The optimism in the previous year, which followed the closure of the Great Exhibition, was echoed again in the first half-yearly meeting. The Directors were quite clearly pleased with the returns which had been made and once again were quick to point out that the Great Exhibition had been the cause of what was perceived as a temporary downturn. Mr Hunt, who was now the inspector of the company's locomotives and stock, had reported that they were in good working order and the view was expressed that much of the equipment was now in better condition than a year ago. No expense had been spared, it was claimed, in achieving this state of affairs. In addition, a saving in the region of 50 per cent had been effected by the company using its own stock. The meeting approved a dividend of 7*s*. 6*d*. per share.

The houses at Windermere – A.W.N. Pugin?

It was at this meeting, held on 27th January, 1853, that the Directors announced they had decided to sell Birthwaite House and some eight acres of land for £3,300 to the Reverend Addison for the purpose of setting up a 'collegiate institution' for boys. This left 16 acres of the 31 they had originally purchased. In addition it had been decided to use part of the land the company owned near the station at Windermere, for the purpose of building five houses, in the form of a terrace, and a contract, involving £3,000 for the cost, had been made, presumably since the previous meeting in July 1852. Perhaps surprisingly,the projected cost was over double that for building the Windermere Hotel, possibly because there were ornate fittings which included elaborate fireplaces. The decision to undertake this building work, which the Directors were confident would be approved by the shareholders, had been taken, they pointed out, because it appeared that the amount of housing being built in Bowness, Windermere and Ambleside, whilst substantial, was not keeping up with the market. Property being built was being let out before completion. There was some discussion about the advisability of taking this step from a legal point of view and whether there might be complaints from shareholders about the use of company's money for this sort of project. Mr Harrison, for example, doubted whether it was a good policy and felt such a step should not be taken. However, the consensus appeared to be that because the land would not be saleable for other purposes there would not be a problem. Perhaps that was just as well because there was a certain *fait accompli* about the whole business and it was agreed the scheme should go ahead.

There has been speculation that the renowned architect A.W.N. Pugin designed these houses. Pugin became well known for his love of the Gothic style and these houses, which still remain today, certainly do have a rather Puginesque appearance. However, Pugin died in September 1852 aged only 40, before or around the time when the Directors decided to have these houses built. Before his death, at home in Ramsgate, Pugin had been committed to an asylum (Bedlam -

the Bethlem Hospital, now the Imperial War Museum), having had a complete mental breakdown, possibly following the enormous pressure he was under, given the workload he had undertaken. A convert to Catholicism, Pugin had designed many fine churches, in the Gothic style, a considerable number of very prestigious large houses and played a key role in designing the interiors of the new Houses of Parliament after the previous Houses had been destroyed by fire in 1834. He spent the final year or so of his life in a state that would indicate he was not in a position to execute commissions. So, great churches, stately homes, Houses of Parliament - then cottages at Windermere? It would seem unlikely! Some architects of his day did produce 'off the shelf' designs which could be purchased for use and if Pugin did so (which seems unlikely) there is a possibility that one of these might have been used for the houses at Windermere. Edward, Pugin's son, did continue his father's work and did design a building in Workington, but there was a whole 'school' of architects out there designing in the style of Victorian Gothic. On the other hand they sometimes used as guides the illustrations in the books depicting Pugin's work, rather like those who cook these days use recipe books! What is known for certain is that once again the company employed Pattinsons as the builders.

These houses built at Windermere were not for sale. In July 1855 it was reported in the minutes of a Directors' meeting that the houses had been built, the tenants were in and rents were being collected.

In spite of the exchanges which had taken place between the Kendal & Windermere and the Lancaster & Carlisle companies, on 4th March E.W. Hasell felt able, when reporting to the proprietors of the latter, to state 'The Directors are happy to report that they continue on the most friendly terms with all the other railway companies with whom it is requisite to interchange traffic'. Such a remark may well have raised one or two wry smiles in certain quarters and it so happened that towards the end of the year another dispute arose between the two companies. This time it was about demurrage (the rate or amount payable for failure to unload wagons in an agreeable time). The Lancaster company had made the claim for demurrage over a period of several years and the Kendal & Windermere Directors had contested it, arguing that their company was exonerated by the arrangement made for wagons from the opening of the line. The Kendal & Windermere Directors decided to appeal to the Railway Clearing House for a judgement and in a statement issued on 14th December, the decision given was that the claim could not be sustained.

On 21st May, a notice appeared in the press. It was issued by the Directors of the Kendal & Windermere Railway, who 'begged to express their thanks to the inhabitants of Bowness, Windermere and Kendal for the promptitude with which they rendered their services at the fire on Sunday last, which was soon subdued and the greater portion of the station and other properties saved'. The whole event, on Sunday 15th, proved to be a very dramatic one. The fire had started in Mr Harrison's joinery shop, which was situated to the west of Windermere station and was one of the properties, in this area, being let out by the railway to various businesses. When the up train left the station there was no obvious signs of a fire but by 11.00 am, the blaze had become very apparent. The alarm was raised and local people turned up to try and put the fire out. In spite of all their efforts, they could not prevent the fire spreading and in no time Mr Mitchell's blacksmith's shop, next door, was also ablaze. Next to that were stables, belonging to Mr Sheldon. Fortunately it was possible to get the horses out before the roof caught fire. It was reported that the heat of the fire could be felt a quarter of a mile away and it would seem that blazing fragments were carried into the air and taken some distance. Could the station itself be saved? A messenger had been dispatched to Kendal and eventually two fire appliances (horse drawn, of course) arrived. A further appliance was brought in on the railway ('as soon as steam could be got up'). Water was fetched by rail from Black Moss to replenish the barrels of the appliances. The efforts made by all concerned resulted in the station itself being saved, although there was some minor damage. How had the fire started? It was not clear but it was noted that the joiners shop was never secured and was occasionally visited by tramps who would spend the night there and, others, who would go there to have a smoke! The place was clearly full of highly combustible material and, something of a sign of the times as far as the local vigorous building programme was concerned, 'window frames, stairs and a vast quantity of other articles for the erection of houses'. Mr Harrison lost £500 of the total loss of £1,500 and he was no doubt grateful when 'a number of gentlemen in the railway carriage' the following morning, subscribed over £60 to help him. There were other donations made for tools and various implements. The moral seemed to be, for some, that a more local fire appliance was needed.

1854

The year started with a rather unnerving incident. On Tuesday 17th January one of the coaches forming the train which connected with the 6.01 pm and 5.57 pm trains at Oxenholme experienced brake failure. Following this, the train careered through Kendal station and eventually came to a halt at the bridge near Dockray Hall Mills. It so happened that the main running line was clear, although there had been something of a 'near miss' because only a few minutes previously the luggage train had passed through. The suggestion in the report is that there was only one carriage with a braking system and the view was expressed that the company should take the incident as a warning and fit all the carriages with brakes so that if one failed there would be others to brake the train. The point was further driven home by another incident the very next day, 18th January, when a not dissimilar event occurred. This time it involved the train from Oxenholme which was scheduled to reach Kendal at 7.00 pm. The line was described as 'greasy' and the person who had been responsible ('the boy' was the description used) was unable to apply the brake with the force needed. Once again the train sailed through Kendal station and on this occasion the main running line was not clear as there was a wagon standing on it. (The report describes it as a 'stray' wagon.) The impact caused when the train hit this wagon resulted in two of the three passengers being thrown out of their seats. Mr Backhouse, who was on his way to attend his mother's funeral the following day at Rydal received severe cuts about the face. The *Kendal Mercury* was keen in its criticism stating that,

> We regret to say that this line is becoming generally notorious in the very inefficient and reckless manner in which it is conducted and we have been given to understand that the company is liable to a heavy fine for running carriages on the line without an engine in front of them and we have reason to hope that if some change for the better does not soon take place, someone will be patriotic enough to look into the matter.

It goes on to berate the company for not taking heed and acting after the incident on the previous evening; further to make the point that there are numerous complaints about the inadequacy of the arrangements to meet trains at Oxenholme and describes incidents on the previous Saturday and previous Monday when all the passengers coming from the south on the 8.20 pm had been left behind.

Whether all this was the reflection of a certain apathy creeping in at this stage or just a feeling that things were moving along and needed less attention, there was a minor problem when members convened for the first half-yearly meeting; the lack of a quorum (which only needed five members!). There was a hasty drumming up of support and eventually the meeting could be held. The work on ballasting the track, called for the previous year, had been carried out and the iron seating of the chairs attended to as well. This had been at considerable expense and there had been others. There had been a considerable increase in operating costs because the Directors had tried to ensure that in order not to inconvenience the travelling public all trains run by the Lancaster & Carlisle had been met. This had resulted in an additional 8,000 miles being run compared to a similar period in 1852. Revenue from this action had not significantly increased, resulting in a drop in profits in this department. In addition, the Lancaster & Carlisle had decided to levy a rent on the Kendal & Windermere for the use of Oxenholme station. Although this had been paid, it had been done so grudgingly. Other costs had been incurred, not least ones relating to increases in the wages. The outcome was a dividend of 5*s.* 0*d.* per share. The meeting had lasted just a few minutes.

In early February there was a complaint made of a rather unusual nature. It seems that the Kendal town clock and the clock at Kendal station were at variance by some seven minutes and this to the disadvantage of travellers who were turning up for trains which had already left. (One is reminded of the comment by Will Hay in the film *Oh, Mister Porter!* when he was wont to announce 'Next train's gone!') Both clocks were monitored by the same person and there was considerable anger amongst some passengers for the inconvenience this situation was causing.

There continued to be cautious optimism at the second half-yearly meeting with profits having risen £469 5*s.* 8*d.* compared to the same period in the previous year. Once again there was concern about the amount of running involved to meet every train on the Lancaster & Carlisle and the fact that the latter company had decided to withdraw payments to the Kendal & Windermere for services performed at Oxenholme. During the past year the country had experienced a surge in the iron industry with an associated one in coal and this had been reflected in an increase in the amount of coal traffic on the Kendal & Windermere, which had resulted in an increase of the profit made. A dividend of 5*s.* 0*d.* was agreed again but then there was some questioning about payments made to the Directors. Dr Davy felt that given the duration of the meetings and the fact that last time there had not been a quorum, a figure of £100 seemed too high and that until the company was in a better financial state, the Directors should only be paid their travelling expenses. Dr Davy was to find himself in something of a dilemma about his proposal at the following half-yearly meeting.

Towards the end of the year there was more satirical criticism of the railway company. Some eight years previously, the coming of the railway had been heralded with jubilation but for many the golden age that had been eagerly anticipated had been somewhat tarnished, it would seem. 'Unfair criticism' some might have said, bearing in mind that this was a new enterprise which had brought improvements of sorts and those involved were still really on a steep learning curve; yet surely, after eight years, problems should have been ironed out. Punctuality was the main bone of contention, although there were other things as well. Certainly there had been complaints from passengers about time-keeping (or rather the lack of it!) and frustration as far the Lancaster & Carlisle company was concerned, telling its train crews not to wait if connecting services on the Kendal & Windermere were not on time. On 4th November the following appeared in the *Westmorland Gazette*:

A Railway Passenger's Timetable for the Kendal and Windermere Railway Co.

On and after Thursday 2nd November the Trains may run as under:

The Train previously advertised to leave Kendal at 12 at noon will on Thursday wait till the Friends meeting breaks up, in order to accommodate the Friends who live at Birthwaite.
The Train advertised to leave Kendal at 3.30 will wait till the Goods Waggons can be arranged and may not start till 4 or 4.15
The Train advertised to leave Kendal at 5.15, will, if the rails are slippery, not leave till 6 or 6.15 and in future will stop at Staveley and reach Windermere instead of 5.50 at 6.15.
As an additional comfort for passengers, LEAKY LAMPS will for the present be provided in the carriages by this Train and the Windows may not be able to be closed, especially as the Winter is coming on.
The Train leaving Windermere at 9.30 and advertised to reach Kendal by 9.54 may not arrive till 10.6 or 10.10.
The Public are respectfully informed of the above important changes, and in future may anticipate that they will not be varied from unless circumstance quite unlooked for arrive.

There is no indication who was the author; not even a pseudonym is given. There may have been humour in some quarters but almost certainly not in the railway company. Further, as if to rub salt into the wound, in the very same column there appears a report on a proposed line from Barnard Castle to Hackthorpe. In extolling the virtues of such a line, it points out that 'no fever of a speculative era has quickened the project' and goes on to comment that it is the deliberate forecast of men who have the sagacity to appreciate and provide for 'the growth of the wants of the country'. The moderate cost is noted because there is, according to the writer, 'cool prudence in the decision to make the line a single one'. The sting comes next with the comment 'Had the Kendal and Windermere been so inaugurated it might, even despite all its other disadvantages, have been a paying concern'.

1855

At the meeting which was held on Thursday 25th January, the Chairman John Gandy was ill and the Vice-Chairman J.J. Wilson had decided to retire and so it was John Whitwell who took the chair. Yet again the matter of meeting all the trains was seen as a factor in influencing the profit margin. After looking at the overall state of things, a dividend of 6*s*. 3*d*. was proposed and this was agreed. The matter of remuneration for the Directors was opened up again with a proposal that £100 should be made available. This put Dr Davy on the spot because following J.J. Wilson's retirement he had been appointed a Director to replace Wilson and so he now found himself about to vote on an issue about which, only at the last meeting, he had expressed strong views! Whilst reminding the meeting of his former proposal opposing such a payment he now wriggled out of the dilemma by informing those present that more recently he had come to have a better opportunity to understand the demands made on the members of the Board and felt it was justified, given that only those Directors who attended should receive payment.

John Gandy was still indisposed at the half-yearly meeting which took place on Thursday 26th July and by this time John Whitwell had become Vice-Chairman. There was some gloom in the air. Passenger receipts had fallen; especially relating to those travelling first and second classes. There was a marginal increase in those who travelled third class but only by some 413 people. There were other causes suggested, including the long hard winter and the inclement weather during the spring. Freight receipts had also fallen. There was some encouraging news. The house building project near Windermere station was now complete and tenants were in and paying rent. The person occupying the Windermere Hotel had asked for further accommodation and the Directors had approved an extension which was already in use. In commenting on the state of affairs, the Chairman made the observation that although there had been a marked increase in the population of the Lake District, it did not seem, in his view, to be having a beneficial impact on the company's returns. In addition, the slowing down of building work which had been taking place, had had an adverse effect on the carriage of associated freight. A discussion then ensued which was initiated by Mr Kennedy, who was clearly not happy with the present state of affairs. He could see that the falling number of passengers and the drop in goods traffic, together with the increased expenses of maintaining the permanent way and the locomotive power, seemed to have swallowed up the dividend. Changes were needed, he argued, and these could well begin with an overhaul of the season ticket allocation. It was not right, he felt, to be carrying passengers at a cost (to the company) greater than they were paying. Mr Kennedy maintained that season tickets should be issued at a fixed price and family tickets should be discontinued and he did not seem convinced by the Secretary's reassurance that they did result in an increase in revenue. He also pointed out that the company did not put on special trains to convey trippers at cheap rates, and by implication, without these cheap rates there would be less revenue on the trains. At the end of the debate a considerably reduced dividend of 2*s*. 6*d*. was agreed. No doubt, after making his views plain, Mr Kennedy was not happy about a move the Directors made later in the month. When the

Windermere College reopened under new management on Wednesday 1st August the Directors agreed to convey all the day-boys from Kendal free of charge!

Banking engines were in use at this time to help trains up the incline from Kendal to Oxenholme and an incident early in September reflected the possible hazards involved in the early days of this practice. The 8.00 am mail train left Kendal on Monday 3rd September, with a considerable number of people on board who were taking a cheap trip to Hest Bank, Lancaster and Preston. The train had only travelled a few hundred yards out of Kendal when a violent impact was felt in the carriages, resulting in several passengers being badly hurt and others greatly alarmed. It seems the whole prospect of a day out was completely ruined for some of those on board. Fortunately there were no fatalities. The impact had been caused by a banking engine, possibly in the charge of an over zealous driver, running hard up against the mail train in order to help it up the bank to Oxenholme. There was a great deal of indignation expressed about the practice and it was even suggested that such a procedure may not be legal!

On 30th October, George Jardine, an engine driver, was arrested and charged with stealing 12 sovereigns from the company's booking office at Windermere. The money had been in the drawer of the booking office just before the 4.00 pm mail train had left but shortly afterwards the clerk discovered the money had gone. The case would come up in January.

1856

From a description of what had happened on that October afternoon, when driver Jardine had been accused of stealing from the company, there seemed to be certain irregular practices taking place and not a little negligence. The booking clerk had not followed procedures as he should have done and it became clear that there was not a strong case to suggest that George Jardine had been the person who had taken the money. Witnesses were unconvincing in their evidence in the sense that what they said did not have any real bearing in indicating that the accused was guilty. The jury was not convinced and even while the witnesses were still being heard, signified a unanimous view that George Jardine was innocent. This decision appeared to be shared by the court. The lesson seemed to be that there was a need to tighten up on procedures.

When the first half-yearly meeting was held in January, there had been a significant change. Lawrence Heyworth MP had become the Chairman, replacing John Gandy (who was, nevertheless, present). In what might be described as a very pedestrian meeting with nobody rising with issues about the way the company was being run, it was pointed out that the gross income for the half was down on the same period in the previous year by some £220. This was attributed in the main to the manner in which 'a neighbouring company' (the Lancaster & Carlisle - who else?) had changed the system for forwarding goods traffic destined for Kendal. There had, however, been a considerable reduction in the running expenses although much of this had been absorbed by increases in rates and taxes.

In the meantime, Mr Hunt had advised the Directors that a new locomotive was needed to help deal with the traffic and this had been agreed. The company turned to Carrett-Marshall of Leeds. This was an interesting company to choose; some would say surprising, because Carrett-Marshall, at the Sun Foundry on Dewsbury Road in Leeds, was not noted for building railway locomotives but rather for steam driven road vehicles. (There is no mention of this locomotive or company by Ahrons in his very exacting survey.) The connection may have been that Carrett had originally been with E.B. Wilson & Co., leasing engines to the Kendal & Windermere. The locomotive purchased was originally named *Grasmere* but later became *Dwarf*. It was a 2-2-2 with a central large pair of driving wheels and two other sets of smaller wheels, one under the smokebox and the other, at the rear, under the coal bunker. It was, in effect, a tank engine.

The matter of the forwarding of goods would soon become a major bone of contention as far as the Kendal & Windermere was concerned. It related to a practice, which was being adopted by the Lancaster & Carlisle, of moving goods destined for Kendal by unloading them at Oxenholme and taking them to their destination by road rather than using the Kendal & Windermere for forwarding them.

In fact the matter was not raised at the second half-yearly meeting, held in July; rather there was satisfaction expressed that the decision to use their own locomotives had proved to be a wise one and had saved a considerable amount of expense. However, towards the end of the year the Lancaster & Carlisle made it clear that the policy of carting goods to Kendal from Oxenholme would be the norm from the beginning of the following year.

This is the only locomotive the Kendal & Windermere Co. ordered to be built. The builder was Carret-Marshall of Leeds. The locomotive was originally named *Grasmere* but when it was taken into LNWR stock it was renamed *Dwarf*, the change of name probably being necessitated by the fact that the LNWR stock already had a *Grasmere*.

Author's Collection

1857 – A remarkable meeting with an alarming episode

This was the year in which a chillier wind started to blow through the affairs of the company. The first half-yearly meeting was both lengthy and in some ways the cause of disquiet as the Directors faced challenges about some of the ways in which they were conducting the company's affairs. The Directors' report, which was read by the Secretary, began with a statement which was intended to reassure the shareholders that in spite of there being inappropriate actions reported in some other companies, a careful scrutiny of their company's affairs had shown that all was in order and no money had been improperly expended. However, there appeared to be certain areas where improvements could be made, including the way in which the capital account details might be stated and changes that could lead to greater clarity. A detailed description followed relating to how this might be achieved. It was conceded there had been an error but this was brushed aside and the assertion made that this had not had any impact on the overall position of the company's finances. By adjusting the presentation of the figures, it could be concluded that the line had cost £20,000 per mile to build and this amount included the infrastructure as well. When considering the company's financial standing, the Directors felt a dividend of 2*s.* 6*d.* would not be inappropriate. There was, however, a caveat. The decision by the Directors of the Lancaster & Carlisle for their company to make its own arrangements to move goods from Oxenholme to Kendal would be damaging as far as the Kendal & Windermere was concerned and although a number of trades people in Kendal had made representation about the practice, it was now effective and would, by implication, affect the financial position of the Kendal & Windermere.

After the report had been read, Dr Davy made certain observations about matters relating to the conveyance of goods between Oxenholme and Kendal by the Lancaster & Carlisle. He suggested they might be out of order by acting in the manner in which they were doing and even put forward the view that what was being done was tantamount to building another line and diverting goods along it and this without an Act of Parliament.

If all this was not trouble enough, worse was yet to follow. Present at the meeting was Mr Sharp. He was something of a mystery character. When he took the floor he appeared, in his opening remarks, to be, on the whole, in sympathy with the company's dilemma regarding the action the Lancaster & Carlisle had taken, although there was a hint of criticism in the way he couched his remarks. He pointed out that he was 'a small and recent proprietor' but, in spite of that, within no time at all he had launched into a critical analysis of the Directors' behaviour in certain aspects of their dealings. He expressed misgiving that the shareholders had not been given a copy of the report before the meeting in order to give them a chance to study it and he went on to say that when viewed with previous statements about the condition of the company, there seemed to be little evidence that they were dealing with the same one. He claimed to have scrutinized the previous reports and found inconsistencies and felt this was why the Directors had felt it necessary to make the comments in the current report. He went on to say that he had gone through the accounts and came up with what must have been a startling revelation to some of those present. Mr Sharp noted that the company had been authorized to borrow £56,000 but in reality £66,487 2*s*. 1*d*. had been borrowed. Even after a small amount had been paid off there was still more than £9,000 over the figure of £56,000. He was quick to point out that all loans in excess of their powers were 'utterly illegal'; the lender had no security and the company's property was in no way pledged as a security for the excess. As a shareholder, Mr Sharp said he wished to protest at what had happened and maintained that the company's seal had been illegally and improperly used. There was more.

Mr Sharp had noticed that £9,132 had been raised as a loan on the security of preference stock. This was also illegal. They (the Directors) had, claimed Mr Sharp, £18,739 of loans for which, in his view 'there was not a shadow of authority'. Interest had been paid on these unauthorized loans and this had adversely affected the dividend on the old shares. Mr Sharp was of the opinion that 'there had been some strange influence at work in the board' and he went on at length in his further analysis of the figures which, whilst he did concede did not indicate anything which would be to the detriment of the shareholders, 'imperilled the responsibility of the Directors'. He referred to the situation on the Board of the Caledonian Railway, where the Directors had to make good certain monies out of their own pockets.

The next issue to be tackled by Mr Sharp related to the Windermere Hotel, where he argued that certain items of expenditure were not sanctioned by the Act. Following this, Thomas Harrison, the treasurer, managed to get a word in and explained that this expenditure had been sanctioned by the shareholders. Mr Sharp was not going to be fobbed off by that and retorted that such approval did not make the expenditure legal. He reminded the meeting that a railway company was allowed to hold in its keeping a certain amount of land and no more. It was intended that that should be appropriated to the enlargement of their building premises, as occasion required, but they were forbidden to enter into building speculations generally, even if a general meeting gave a unanimous consent to such a proposal. There is no indication as to how the Directors were taking all this but they may well have been wondering by this time where (and when) it was all going to end!

In fact, at this juncture, Mr Sharp seemed ready to display a certain sort of magnanimity. He said he was not there to demand what the Directors should do in the circumstances but simply begged them to give serious consideration to the matters he had raised. They had rendered themselves, he told them, personally liable for these unauthorized expenditures. They must face up to the situation, together with the auditors. At this point a most remarkable thing happened. Whether Mr Sharp had been rather animated during his delivery is not made clear but the chair on which he was sitting collapsed! The attitude of the meeting may be judged by the fact that when this happened, there was laughter and the Chairman seemed relaxed enough to remark that the honourable gentleman had broken down. In spite of this minor interruption, Mr Sharp quickly gathered himself together and he continued to lecture the various officers about their responsibilities. There followed another tirade in which he reminded the Directors of the perilous state in which they found themselves.

Once Mr Sharp had had his say, it was the turn of Messrs Whitwell and Harrison to mount what, in effect, was a defence. This was done with great aplomb and there was a succinctness that possibly shook Mr Sharp somewhat. It was Mr Whitwell who really led the reply. He explained the situation as far as the role of the auditor was concerned; he put forward a response in connection with the objections raised regarding the Windermere Hotel, arguing that amongst other things it was an essential element of the company's business and that the traffic of the railway could not have been conducted properly without it; he accused Mr Sharp of wasting 'professional eloquence' on making these observations; he dealt with the financial matters and detailed the rationale relating to the loans and the preference shares and also the bonds which had been issued and in spite of Mr Sharp's earlier protestations, Mr Harrison was able to point out that all was legitimate. One assertion which was made a number of times was that all had been done openly; there had been no attempt to hide what was happening and the shareholders had always been made aware of the decisions the Board had made. There were inferences, at times, that there might be ulterior motives coming into play associated with the allegations which had been made but this was denied. At the end it was observed that Mr Sharp repudiated, with some warmth, the imputation of personal motives in the matter but he could well afford to sit down under the imputation in silence.

The meeting was then able to deal with other items. There was a keen debate about whether or not a dividend should be paid. The figure of 2*s*. 6*d*. had been mentioned but in the end, following a vote, it was resolved not to pay a dividend. Mr Steele raised the matter of the closure of Burneside station and why it was that Mr Cropper was still allowed to alight there. (Burneside station had been closed the previous year (1856) because there had been a number of complaints from passengers that very often the train stopped there but nobody got on or off.)

Further, there was a strain on the locomotive when setting off, caused by the incline it had to cope with and this was the case in both directions. He was told that Mr Cropper had contracted £5 for this facility and in response Mr Steele offered to pay £30 per year to have it open. He reckoned this would be worth £50 per year but at this stage the Directors were not prepared to avail him of the facility. Matters would change and there would be questions to answer at a later date. It was, however, the situation regarding the steps taken by the Lancaster & Carlisle that was a cause for considerable concern and after discussion it was agreed to set up a committee to look into the whole business and even, if necessary, seek some form of arbitration.

So the meeting ended. Yet who was this Mr Sharp who had tried with considerable vigour to put the cat amongst the pigeons as far as the Directors were concerned? He was a lawyer; that was obvious and he was a newcomer. Were his intentions honourable or did he really have, as has been implied, what might in later years have been described as a hidden agenda?

On 24th January a letter appeared in the *Kendal Mercury*. It was signed 'A Kendal Tradesman' and began as follows:

> Sir, It is rumoured in the town that the Lancaster and Carlisle Company employed a solicitor to attend the meeting of the Kendal and Windermere Company to endeavour to shake the confidence of the public by attacking the Directors …

The following week the same writer had a further letter included,

> Sir, As you inserted my letter last week, I wish to trouble you with some more observations, and first I would remark that it seems Mrs Rumour was quite right and that a lawyer from Lancaster, who, within a few days, had a few shares transferred to him, at least as I hear, came over with a reporter from a Lancaster paper; the former attacked the Kendal and Windermere Company and the latter put down all he said. Then there was an article in the Lancaster paper - for a friend of mine lent me one to read – and it says the Lancaster and Carlisle Company want to make one thousand pounds profit out of carrying the Kendal goods …

All was revealed. It seemed the Lancaster & Carlisle had, in effect, declared war of sorts on the Kendal & Windermere and not only that, it appeared it was prepared to employ dirty tricks.

In spite of this incident, certain things seem to change little. As had often happened in the past, the Lancaster & Carlisle rescheduled some of its train times in July and the Kendal & Windermere had to follow this in order to make connections possible.

Leasing by the Lancaster & Carlisle is mooted

However, schemes of a more significant nature were afoot. Following the first half-yearly meeting, the Directors of the Kendal & Windermere approached the Board of the Lancaster & Carlisle with a view to the two companies amalgamating. In fact such a step would have required a Parliamentary Act and a leasing arrangement was therefore more realistic. With a readiness to consider an arrangement to bring the two companies closer together, the Lancaster & Carlisle prepared a list of possible arbitrators and gave the Kendal & Windermere the choice of whom should act. The outcome was that Mr Rotherham was appointed to put forward proposals to determine the terms by which the two companies might combine. When the report was published, towards the end of July, the terms as set out were, as the *Kendal Mercury* pointed out, difficult for the uninitiated to follow, referring as it did, for example, to 'one thirtieth and thirty eight decimals of the net income available for division…'. The Directors of the Kendal & Windermere put it into language which it was felt would be better understood and, in a pamphlet issued to the shareholders, pointed out that taking the average of the last three years, the proposed division of the net proceeds would, after paying interest on bonds and dividend on preference shares, yield each original share of the Kendal & Windermere about four shillings. However, on further consideration, the Directors had misgivings about the language of the report, feeling that it contained certain ambiguities. These misgivings had been further reinforced when they sought informal legal advice and as a result of what they had been told, felt more time was needed for them to properly establish the real intentions of the report. The two interpretations led to very different outcomes in terms of the award. Did Mr Rotherham, it was speculated, mean one-thirtieth and something more or one-thirtieth less something? If Mr Rotherham, it was alleged, meant 30.38, it would give one sum; if he had said one thirtieth *and* 38 decimals of another thirtieth, it would give a very different sum.

At the meeting on 11th August, those present were informed about the situation and eventually an adjournment was agreed. In the meantime the Directors were asked to take [the very best] legal advice on the matter. Mr Sharp had suggested that one course of action would be to approach Mr Rotherham direct for clarification but it was pointed out that it was not in order to contact an arbitrator in this way. In fact, it transpired that someone had already done so! Mr Blenkinsop had asked Mr Rotherham for clarification and had been informed by Mr Rotherham that such an approach was not really in order but, nevertheless, had expressed surprise that the award was not clear. The Directors, on hearing what had been going on, were quick to distance themselves from any activity of this sort and point out this had been the action of shareholders. On another front, a leading London accountant had been approached. Feeling did begin to run high and one person present said he would rather *give* his shares to the Lancaster & Carlisle than 'sell them for a paltry dividend of 4*s*.'

The meeting over, the Directors of the Kendal & Windermere set about trying to clarify what the award was actually all about. They did not meet with a great deal of success. The accountants who had been consulted were of the view that the company would receive the larger sum but the barristers took the opposite view. At the adjourned meeting, which was held on 27th August, the Directors had to point out that it was with this uncertainty in mind that a decision about whether or not to accept the recommendations in Mr Rotherham's report needed to be taken. However, at this point, allegations began to surface which suggested there had been some chicanery behind the scenes. It was Mr Sharp who, once again, claimed he had discovered the Directors had been less than open with the facts as they knew them. He [Mr Sharp] alleged that although he had been informed at the previous meeting that contacting an arbitrator was out of order, there had, in fact, been correspondence with Mr Rotherham *before* that meeting and the Directors were aware *at that meeting* what Mr Rotherham had said in reply! Mr Sharp asked for an explanation, feeling that, yet again, the Directors had dealt unfairly with the shareholders. There was a certain amount of 'buck passing' but in the end the arguments lost strength and the matter was dropped. It was Mr Heelis who came up with a proposal, namely that,

> ... this meeting accept the award that on the understanding that it gives to this company one-thirtieth and thirty-eighth hundredth of another thirtieth of the nett revenue of the joint Companies, but refuses the award on any other interpretation.

Mr Heelis was keen to point out that he felt Mr Rotherham's award was not based on just principles and in this respect it would be wrong to accept it. The motion was seconded. Clearly there was both confusion and uneasiness among some of the members about this proposal and, indeed, about the whole situation which seemed to be getting more and more difficult to resolve. An amendment was proposed by Mr Wakefield that the award should be accepted and its true meaning be settled afterwards. Mr Sharp readily seconded this and it is reported that he went on at great length to argue the case for acceptance; further hostility, he insisted, would simply make the situation worse. He became quite vehement in his description of what the future would hold for the Kendal & Windermere if the award was not accepted.

> ... they [the Kendal and Windermere] would find themselves in the hands of a body of pirates who would do all they could to annoy them and destroy them.

Yet the meeting remained sharply divided and when the amendment was put to the vote it was defeated by five votes for and eight against. So it was back to the original motion; namely the proposal put by Mr Heelis. A vote was taken and it was accepted, there being seven votes for it and two against. Some further discussion ensued and the Chairman expressed the hope that the other side would not turn out to be a band of pirates!

So had the award been accepted? It could be argued 'Yes or No'. In principle 'Yes' but with the proviso 'Only if' and in that sense 'No'. The matter was not fully resolved in these respects.

There were still important issues involved. The leasing of the Kendal & Windermere by the Lancaster & Carlisle would mean a much more integrated system and this would benefit Kendal in particular. In addition, the Lancaster & Ulverston Railway would soon be opened and there was a danger that traffic for the Lakes might well be carried along that line if the Kendal & Windermere did not have strong support. And, of course, there still remained the whole business of the Oxenholme-Kendal goods traffic and the associated problems. There had even been the suggestion in some quarters that if the proposals were not ratified, the only course of action open for the Directors of the Kendal & Windermere would be to resign. Once again pens were put to paper and letters appeared in the local press. Reference was made to the fact that there had often been no dividend paid by the Kendal & Windermere; that it would soon be facing heavy financial commitments because many of its bridges and its stations were made of timber and would need replacing. 'Scrutator', in a long letter, did a very careful analysis and concluded that the shareholders should support Rotherham's proposals. 'Shareholder', although expressing certain reservations about the lack of detail in the way the conclusions of the proposals had been reached, was of a similar view.

The proposed leasing was raised at the half-yearly meeting of the Lancaster & Carlisle which was held on Friday 4th September. There was clearly some bemusement and not a little misgiving about the behaviour of the Kendal & Windermere Board and there was also frustration about the way in which it was dealing with the proposals. It was felt that recourse to the law would achieve little and the Directors of the Lancaster & Carlisle were adamant it was not a course they wished to follow. Considerable reservations were expressed about whether the proposed union should be pursued further and they had turned down a request from the Directors of the Kendal & Windermere for further negotiations.

Concern about accidents on the line

Accidents, not least those resulting from trespass, seemed to be a fairly common occurrence on the line and this became a matter of concern for the company. There was a particularly unpleasant mishap during the evening of Monday 20th April. Henry Dodd, of Kendal, had been to a sale at Ings Hall where, the evidence suggested, he had been drinking heavily. It was thought that he decided to walk back along the railway line, the distance being shorter that taking the road. It was concluded he had been run down by the mail train which left Windermere at 8.30 pm. His decapitated body, which was described as 'a frightful spectacle', was found the following morning by Henry Dent, a labourer on the railway. The driver and fireman of the mail train said they had been unaware that the train had hit anybody. A verdict of accidental death was recorded. The incident prompted the company to place a notice in bold print in the newspaper the following week:

> That the Railway Servants have peremptory Orders to report *all* Persons TRESPASSING ON THE LINE and after the late melancholy Accident, it is hoped that this Notice will be a sufficient warning, not only of the illegality but the great danger in crossing or trespassing on the Railway.

A Royal visit

Whilst all this dialogue continued, the line did have an important visitor who may well have been the first member of the royal family to use the line. In May, the Prince of Wales, Albert Edward, later to become Edward VII in 1901, following the death of Queen Victoria, embarked on a visit to the North and had visited the Craven District. He had been to Leeds and then to Bolton Abbey and following this, on Monday 11th May, caught the 2.40 pm train from Skipton in order to travel to Windermere. The report of this visit may have been something of a scoop for the *Westmorland Gazette* because it appears there had been a plan to keep it at a low key. However, information had 'oozed out' (according to the *Gazette*, using the sort of language typical of the period!). Those who turned out at Oxenholme and Kendal in the hope of catching a glimpse of the Prince were disappointed; he was taken on to the Kendal & Windermere line without a change of carriage. On arriving at Windermere, the Royal party alighted and walked down to Bowness where those in the group were accommodated at the Royal Hotel. The stay lasted for about a week and during his visit the Prince visited a number of places including Grasmere.

John Ramsbottom takes over at Crewe

Further afield there were changes in 1857 which would have an impact on the running of the Kendal & Windermere. At Crewe, Francis Trevithick was pensioned off by the LNWR and his place was taken by John Ramsbottom, who would remain in office as chief mechanical engineer until 1871. During this period there would be considerable changes in the types of motive power used on this line, as, indeed, it would be over the whole of the Northern Division of the LNWR. The class 'DX' 0-6-0 goods would appear, as would the 'Problem' 2-2-2s, the 'Samson' 2-4-0s and the 'Newton' 2-4-0s, as visitors to the line. Locomotive design and development would move on apace.

1858 - A period of intensive meetings

The next two years would see a complex situation develop which would result in a considerable number of special meetings together with numerous adjournments. The Kendal & Windermere along with the Lancaster & Carlisle and eventually, also, the LNWR railways, would engage in lengthy and almost painstaking dialogue and debate as the means to find the most satisfactory way forward for the companies was thrashed out.

At the beginning of 1858, no binding decision regarding the proposed leasing had been made and as the year progressed, the attitude of the Kendal & Windermere towards the Lancaster & Carlisle become increasingly hostile. Although returns in some areas had been holding up and in some cases improving, there was still one aspect in which quite the opposite still proved to be the case. Passenger receipts had shown healthy growth and the financial situation of the company had been strengthened by the fact that there had been a considerable reduction in expenditure with regard to locomotive operations.

The problem continued to be in the transport of goods, where returns had dropped markedly. The main reason for this, as before, was the practice which had been adopted by the Lancaster & Carlisle of offloading goods at Oxenholme, which were destined for Kendal and district, and forwarding them by road instead of transferring them to the Kendal & Windermere for transportation. Feelings in the Kendal & Windermere camp were running very high about this practice. It was described as 'a positive injustice to the company' not least because the Kendal & Windermere was an important feeder of traffic for the Lancaster & Carlisle. The ill feelings were exacerbated by the fact that at a time when the Kendal & Windermere was only able to pay a dividend of 1¼ per cent, the Lancaster & Carlisle was paying its shareholders between seven and eight per cent. So much, then, for all the expressions of goodwill which the Lancaster & Carlisle had been wont to make. There was also the matter of the facilities which the Kendal & Windermere had made available for the storage of coal which it had assumed the Lancaster & Carlisle would use. It seemed incomprehensible that given the co-operation the Kendal & Windermere felt it always afforded the Lancaster & Carlisle, the latter should choose to act in the way that it had. There seemed to be no justification for it. Dr Davy had decided to take up the matter with the Board of the Lancaster & Carlisle but had been unable to make any headway in bringing about a change of attitude. At the first half-yearly meeting, held on Tuesday 19th January, when all this came out, there was even a suggestion that legal action should be taken against the Lancaster & Carlisle, in view of the course it was pursuing but it was pointed out that the case was by no means a clear one and a costly and protracted lawsuit might well follow. Another matter, raised at this time, was the circumstances following the closing of Burneside station. As mentioned previously, following the closure of the station, Mr Steele, who lived a Burneside, had proposed and had subsequently negotiated a deal with the Kendal & Windermere Directors, whereby he [Mr Steele] had guaranteed £40 per year if certain trains could stop at Burneside. However, it was pointed out that within about eight months of a 12 month agreement, this target of £40 had been realised and the income for the rest of the year had (presumably) gone into Mr Steele's pocket. (What may have made this a particularly sore point at this stage was that Mr Steele was also a Director of the Lancaster & Carlisle!) Once again the matter of what some considered exorbitant fares between Kendal and Oxenholme, was raised and the Directors were urged to review the passenger rates in order to increase the number of those who travelled on the line.

In spite of comments, apparently to the contrary, the Lancaster & Carlisle was, in fact, ready to discuss further the possibility of an arrangement between the two companies. In the light of this, a survey was carried out on the Kendal & Windermere line by the Lancaster & Carlisle Engineer to establish the state it was in. The result was encouraging and it was reported that although there were one or two wooden bridges requiring some repairs, the line was well made with good rails and sleepers and that maintenance costs would be on a par with those of his own company. Some works would be needed but the cost of building a warehouse at Kendal, if cartage into the town from Oxenholme continued to be by road, would be saved. The Directors of the Kendal & Windermere were adamant that a better deal than that recommended by Rotherham would be necessary (as resolved at the meeting) if the discussions were to succeed.

Then, on 17th April, there was a statement in the editorial of the *Kendal Mercury* which indicated that at last there appeared to a breakthrough in the negotiations between the two companies. It was stated that,

> We understand that this line [The Kendal and Windermere] is shortly to pass into the hands of the Lancaster and Carlisle Railway all the preliminaries being arranged for the transference so soon as the formal sanction of the respective directorates shall have been given ...

There was a new offer of one-twenty-eighth share of the earnings of the two companies which it was estimated would give 11*s*. a share. This was almost three times what would have been received under Rotherham's proposals.

The new offer is accepted

On 3rd May there was a special meeting of the Kendal & Windermere. Mr L. Heyworth, now Chairman of the company, presided. The meeting was, as anticipated, informed of the new offer and the income being considered also included that of the Lancaster & Preston. The lease, if approved, would, according to the terms be retrospective, and commence on 1st May. In addition to the various financial arrangements, the Kendal & Windermere Board would have one of its number on the Lancaster & Carlisle Board and there was a proposal, if the circumstances were right, to seek Parliamentary powers in 1859 for an amalgamation. The Directors felt they could recommend this offer and put forward a resolution that would make it effective. This was seconded and after a period of discussion, mainly about financial implications, it was put to the vote. Acceptance was unanimous. One significant observation made was that acceptance of the resolution would result in a cessation of hostilities between the two companies. Once the main business had been concluded there were various thanks extended to those who had borne the responsibility of the company over the years.

The Lancaster & Carlisle also held a special meeting on the same day to consider the position. Fewer members than usual turned out for this but E.W. Hasell, the Chairman, in spite of having been the victim of influenza for the previous three weeks, felt it was important enough to make the effort to be there. In fact he was faced with explaining to those present why his company had turned its back on the proposal put forward by Rotherham and appeared to have acquiesced to the Kendal & Windermere demand for the one-twenty-eighth settlement. Hasell pointed out that he was still of the view that Rotherham's proposal had been a just one but he turned, by way of explanation, to the cartage of goods by their company from Oxenholme down to Kendal. The company had chosen to do this and had felt justified in doing so, because, he maintained, there had been problems arising from the stance of the Kendal & Windermere over the use of the terminals. However, Hasell had to concede that the exercise had been a very expensive one, costing about £1,000 each year. This, he maintained, was clearly to the detriment of both companies, depriving one or both of them of this amount. He then argued that by leasing the Kendal & Windermere on the terms its Directors had put forward, there would be a saving of £1,000 to set against the £600 per annum that would have to be paid to the Kendal & Windermere over and above the Rotherham award. He also pointed out the other advantages to be gained from leasing the Kendal & Windermere; with, in effect, one company there would be greater economies and therefore greater profits, there would be greater probability of improving the line and giving more attention to local requirements and, very important, there would be no loss to the Lancaster & Carlisle.

He then made some very telling comments about the relationship between the two companies. He frankly acknowledged there had been something of a contest between the two Boards which had resulted in poor relationships between the two companies and had even led to allegations that the Lancaster & Carlisle, as the more powerful, had attempted to crush its smaller neighbour. This, again, was a reference to the Lancaster & Carlisle carting goods down to Kendal from Oxenholme by road and Hasell justified the action of his company by insisting that the Kendal & Windermere had imposed unreasonable rates and therefore left the Lancaster & Carlisle with no alternative. (Some might have seen this as being in contradiction to what Hasell had said earlier.) Hasell was then disposed to a degree of magnanimity in saying that he and the other Directors had always hoped for an opportunity to enter into an arrangement with the proviso that their company was not damaged. Hasell concluded on a somewhat conciliatory note by saying that 'whilst they had a legal right to do what they did with the Kendal traffic, he was almost sorry that they were driven to such an extremity by their Kendal friends'. There followed some discussion but no serious opposition to the proposal that the Lancaster & Carlisle should agree to lease the Kendal & Windermere under the terms discussed. In fact, E.W. Hasell was a man held in high esteem by those who met him, not least because of his fairness and sound judgement. When the proposal was put to the meeting, it was agreed unanimously. This was indeed a milestone for the Kendal & Windermere. The future of the company would now be inextricably linked to that of the Lancaster & Carlisle.

The Lancaster & Carlisle held the second half-yearly meeting on Friday 3rd September. It was reported that the company had actually taken possession of the Kendal & Windermere on 3rd May, the Monday on which both companies had agreed the terms of the lease. It was also recorded that as well as transferring £18,000 from capital to the credit of the locomotive account, £2,000 had been transferred to that account 'in respect of the Engines on the Kendal and Windermere Railway'. The feeling was that the new arrangement was working well; the public seemed to be finding the arrangements that had been made more convenient and the two companies appeared at that point to be benefiting. Lieutenant-Colonel John Gandy become a Director of the Lancaster & Carlisle for the Kendal & Windermere Board. One of the first improvements that would be carried out was the extension of the electric telegraph from Kendal to Windermere.

The next meeting of the Kendal & Windermere did not take place until Tuesday 28th September. It was brief. Mr Whitwell, the Vice-Chairman, took the chair and the only persons present were Dr Davy, J.J. Wilson, E. Harrison, John Gandy, George Crewdson, Isaac Whitwell and John Hudson. The meeting simply dealt with the various procedures which were carried out after the lease came into effect at the beginning of May and details of the financial matters involved. Dr Davy and Mr Whitwell were reappointed as Directors and George Crewdson as auditor.

1859 – Misgivings in the Kendal & Windermere camp

At the next shareholders' meeting, on Tuesday 8th March, at the Longpool offices, the opening section of the report referred again to the terms of the union. More people were present than had been at the previous meeting. The gathering was reminded that their company would receive one-twenty-eighth of the net revenue of the united companies, which amounted to £3,795 13s. 11*d*. After the deduction of the interest on bonds, loans and bank commission and the preference dividend which had been paid, there remained £1,010 17*s*. 6*d*.; this figure to be at the disposal for the shareholders. The Directors were reticent in making any recommendations about this in view of certain demands which might be made on the company. It was also reported that the Lancaster & Carlisle had a Bill before Parliament which it was believed, if it became an Act, would mean the Kendal & Windermere would be open to become fully amalgamated with the Lancaster & Carlisle. The Directors of the Kendal & Windermere had not been consulted about the terms but having obtained a copy of the proposals, had made certain recommendations to the Lancaster & Carlisle about some of the clauses which might, if realized, affect the operating conditions of the Kendal & Windermere.

There was some uneasiness about this move and in spite of the feeling that the lease would see the end of hostilities between the two companies, there were clearly those who did not trust the Lancaster & Carlisle Board and questioned the fairness of the deal. Mr Thomson was one such and he raised the matter of the 'Birthwaite Hotel' [Windermere]. The Kendal & Windermere had spent some £10,000 on it and received a rental of £400 per annum and now they would get back a 'paltry' twenty-eighth part! However, he went further than this. Although he was assured that the one-twenty-eighth had already been agreed he felt strongly that they had been 'taken in' and was all for the company appealing to the Lords for some sort of redress. The two issues, one relating to the award and the other to the Lancaster & Carlisle Bill, which appeared to offer amalgamation, became rather mixed up in the discussion which ensued but it was clear that Mr Thomson had a great deal of support from some of his fellow shareholders. The Directors were accused of taking no action as far as the proposed Bill was concerned but this was denied; there had been communications between the two Boards (it was said). In relation to the award, the Chairman conceded that the Lancaster & Carlisle had taken advantage of their weakness but what could they do? Having fought hard to get what they did get, not accepting the terms would have led to ruin. To the end of the debate Mr Thomson was adamant that there was a cause to be pursued but having lost the battle to convince others present had to be content with making the observation that 'There might not be retribution now but it would assuredly come'. Quite what he implied by this ominous remark was not made clear! The report of the Directors was approved as was a dividend of 4*s*. 6*d*. to be paid on 2nd April.

On 9th July there was a special general meeting of the Lancaster & Carlisle to discuss 'A Bill for authorizing the Lancaster & Carlisle Railway Company to make New Works and to make arrangements with other Companies to raise further Funds and for other purposes'. At this point the Bill had already passed through the committee stage and approval of the shareholders was now sought. One of the main features of the Bill was to enable the company to build a branch to Morecambe to facilitate the movement of South Durham coal. There was also a scheme relating to the possibility of the company having a hotel adjacent to the station at Lancaster. There was reference to the Kendal & Windermere having representation by a Director of that company, together with those from the Lancaster & Preston and London & North Western railways, on the Lancaster & Carlisle Board. When a vote was taken, the proposal that the Bill should go forward was passed unanimously.

A special meeting to discuss the Lancaster & Carlisle Bill

Perhaps Mr Thomson was not prepared to let the issue of the Lancaster & Carlisle Bill rest there and he may well have done some badgering in the days which followed. Certainly, on Friday 15th July, a Special Meeting of the Kendal & Windermere was convened at the room of the Chamber of Commerce to consider, yet again, the consequences of the Bill becoming an Act. After Mr Harrison, the company solicitor, had read the heads of the clauses, the Chairman, Mr Whitwell, proposed that, in the light of what was involved, the meeting should give its assent to the Bill and this was seconded by Mr Harrison. Not surprisingly it was Mr Thomson who was first to open the discussion, making the point that none of the clauses had been submitted to their solicitor and he objected to the fact that the terms of the 'amalgamation' would not be settled until after the Bill was passed. He felt it was alarming that £70,000 was about to be paid out by the Lancaster & Carlisle from which there would be no benefit for the Kendal & Windermere, yet they would be paying their portion of one-twenty-eighth to the payment of the interest. This, he argued, would leave them, in effect, penniless, with nothing for a dividend for the old shareholders. In addition he felt the 6 per cent preference might also be jeopardized. He felt that would not be the end of it and he went on at length to argue that they had been coerced into an agreement that had already been made. He urged an adjournment for a week to provide the opportunity for an interview with the Lancaster & Carlisle Directors to discuss the terms of the amalgamation. Mr Harrison opposed this saying the outcome, given the lateness of the Session for the Bill to go forward, could well result, if the clauses relating to the amalgamation were struck out, of a possible backlash from the Lancaster & Carlisle at a future date. In a sense they were already committed and action might result in the loss of their Director on the Lancaster & Carlisle Board. A dilemma indeed! After further debate, the motion for assenting to the Bill was put and passed but Mr Thomson was not finished yet; he demanded a poll but because of a technicality involving the proxies, this could not the held. The decision stood.

The Lancaster & Carlisle met the following day, namely, Saturday 16th July. The purpose was to bring before the shareholders the proposals in the Bill and seek approval for it to go forward. There was reference at this meeting to there being representation on their Board from the Kendal & Windermere. The meeting resolved that the Bill should go forward.

Events now began to gain momentum and further changes were on the way. Whilst these two comparatively small fish had continued, in spite of the leasing agreement, to squabble, a much larger fish had no doubt been watching them both carefully. Now was the time to pounce!

A meeting of the Lancaster & Carlisle was planned for 2nd September. The venue would be the Windermere Hotel. Perhaps this was chosen, following the leasing of the Kendal & Windermere, to make a point; or perhaps it was seen as being a pleasanter place to convene. Certainly the Chairman, E.W. Hasell, would not have to travel quite so far from Dalemain, where he lived. The purpose of the Special Meeting was planned to be the authorization to convert fully paid up shares into stock from time to time. However, this proposed trip to Windermere was not to be. The meeting was cancelled and moved to 10th September and, what is more, it would be held in Lancaster, as usual. The reason why this step of cancelling the meeting had been taken becomes apparent in a further clause which was added and for consideration. This refers to a proposal to lease the Lancaster & Carlisle (and therefore the Kendal & Windermere as well as the Lancaster & Preston) to the LNWR.

The meeting was informed that the Bill before Parliament was now an Act and much of what the company had been applying for had been granted. The Lancaster & Carlisle would now be able, if the Lancaster & Preston agreed, to amalgamate the two companies (which was approved at a meeting, later that day). However, there had been certain problems relating to some of the terms of the lease with the Kendal & Windermere. These involved properties and this is possibly where Mr Thomson felt he had a point to make (regarding, for example, the hotel at 'Birthwaite') because the Act now clarified this and a new lease would be drawn up. When this had been completed, a Director from the Kendal & Windermere would be added to the Board of the Lancaster & Carlisle. Now came the Special Meeting and the subject of that was to consider a proposal that the Lancaster & Carlisle should be leased in perpetuity to the LNWR. The Directors able to pronounce on this (clearly LNWR Directors on the Board were excluded) felt strongly that with many small companies now going down that road, resulting in larger and more powerful groups being formed, this would be a sensible step to take and recommended it. When the proposal was put to the vote it was approved unanimously. (There are reports that the outcome was greeted with loud applause.)

On the same day, 10th September, a meeting was held at Euston Square station. The purpose was to discuss, amongst other things, the leasing of the Lancaster & Carlisle. It was noted that the proposed agreement was of considerable importance (to the LNWR!). It was made clear that the Lancaster & Carlisle had an essential role to play in assisting the LNWR in moving traffic north and south. (It was described as 'a bridge' between Staffordshire and the Scottish railways.) Even so, it was felt that it would be important for the Lancaster & Carlisle to retain its independence. Understandably, much stress was placed on the interests of the LNWR in what would be tantamount to gaining control over this vital section it was seeking to lease but, on the other hand, the rewards for the Lancaster & Carlisle would be significant. Before the proposal was made it was observed, with some surprise, that with such an important step to be considered, the attendance was small but it was then put to the meeting that the LNWR should 'lease The Lancaster and Carlisle Railway, including The Kendal and Windermere and The Lancaster and Preston Railways for a term of 900 years'. The solicitor outlined the terms. The share capital was not to exceed £2,420,000 and the loan capital £430,000. The dividend of the Lancaster & Carlisle would in no case fall below 8 per cent per annum; when the dividend of the LNWR was 4¼ per cent, the Lancaster & Carlisle would be at the rate of 8½ per cent; when 4½ per cent, 9 per cent; when 4¾ per cent, 9¼ per cent, when 5 per cent, 9½ per cent and when 6 per cent, 10 per cent.

The Kendal & Windermere (along with the Lancaster & Preston) would receive its due proportion of the dividend. The LNWR would pay the necessary expenses of Directors, the audit and other expenses, not exceeding £1,525 per annum. After some debate, during which some of the LNWR shareholders did have slight reservations (and one expressed the hope that the company would not attempt to go south of the Thames!) a vote was taken and 43 members were in favour with 19 against. Following this, a poll was carried out and there was a majority for the motion of 207 shareholders. The meeting was then adjourned until Friday 28th October.

The next Kendal & Windermere meeting was held on Tuesday 27th September. Lawrence Heyworth was in the chair. There was a summary of the recent past events; the company was now leased to the Lancaster & Carlisle. The Lancaster & Carlisle Bill had now become an Act and the latter opened the door to possible amalgamation. The other significant development was that involving the LNWR and there was some concern on the Board that, yet again, it seemed that although their company would be affected by the proposals, there had been no consultation. This had prompted the Board, at a meeting on 28th August when it was realised what was afoot, to send a communication to the Lancaster & Carlisle pointing out that the Kendal & Windermere did not consider itself to be bound by the decisions that might be made on 10th September. The solicitor for the Lancaster & Carlisle had also sent a draft setting out the terms and conditions of the new lease which was considered to be necessary. The Directors were not happy with this as they felt that it varied from the terms of the original in such a way that would disadvantage their company. However, they were prepared to accept the matters relating to the property and effects of the company on the understanding that the Lancaster & Carlisle would carry out its part of the agreement. Once again differences arose between the two companies. This time it was because the Lancaster & Carlisle decided to withhold the paying of any dividend until the lease had been signed. In consequence, the Directors of the Kendal & Windermere had seen fit to send a missive to the Lancaster & Carlisle setting out their assessment of the situation. It is a long and rambling statement. It touches on the complex nature not only of the arrangements between the Kendal & Windermere with the Lancaster & Carlisle but also the proposals involving the LNWR. The Kendal & Windermere Directors imply that they have no desire to stand in the way of possible arrangements but that they have misgivings about proposals regarding the draft lease, intended to replace the existing lease, and also with the ramifications of this with future plans. There had been no formal response to this statement from the Lancaster & Carlisle, merely acknowledgement that it had been received. The LNWR, on the other hand, had given an undertaking that it would be considered by its Board. Those at the meeting were in support of what the Directors had done and there were some fairly harsh words spoken against the Lancaster & Carlisle with an inference that it was 'the enemy'. The best way forward, it was generally agreed, would be to accept that no dividend would be possible for the time being but wait for the LNWR to play its hand. Amongst those present, for the first time for a long time, was Cornelius Nicholson and that could only mean one thing; a stirring speech. The meeting was not disappointed! There was an analysis of the situation in very clear terms and strong support for the Directors for doing what they had done. He felt strongly there must be no *villenage* (an old Westmorland term for 'slavery', it seems) where persons were transferred like chattels along with the manors which they served. Those times had gone for ever 'and helpless as the Windermere Line has hitherto been against the oppression of its big Brother, it must and will now defend itself against *villenage*'. (There hadn't been a meeting as lively and uplifting as this for ages!) The rhetoric continued and Nicholson had certainly lost none of his gift for enthusing a group and in winning them over to his point of view. At the end of his oration he put forward the following resolution:

> That it is the opinion of this Meeting that the Board should be supported in its refusal to accept any new Lease from the Lancaster and Carlisle Company, notwithstanding the

> Resolution of that Company to withhold the payment of the dividend and the proprietors present are perfectly satisfied to defer the reception of any dividend until a satisfaction of the present difficulties is arrived at or until the lessees of the Line have fulfilled their engagements by paying the rents justly due.

This was carried 'by acclamation'.

A further motion was proposed by Nicholson which gave the Directors authority to take whatever actions they felt appropriate in dealing with the Lancaster & Carlisle and this was also approved unanimously.

Harrison, the company solicitor, did urge some caution. He pointed out that matters were progressing favourably with the LNWR and he felt it would be wise to avoid what he referred to as 'extreme measures'. It was clear that there had to be more discussion if satisfactory progress was to be made.

Talks with the LNWR did result in such progress and in early November it was possible to announce that the Kendal & Windermere had reached an agreement with that company. The LNWR would guarantee a fixed dividend of 3 per cent per annum on the ordinary share capital. In addition to this, the Kendal & Windermere would be able to participate in any future stock. The LNWR undertook to pay any establishment charges and the agreement could come into effect retrospectively from 21st July. On the other hand, there was no satisfactory outcome in the further discussions between the Kendal & Windermere and the Lancaster & Carlisle about the terms of the lease and the Kendal & Windermere Board felt it had no choice but to have recourse to the LNWR. There it had found a sympathetic ear (and also one which was anxious, no doubt, to settle the whole matter in the interests of its own company).

On 19th December there was an Extraordinary Meeting of the Kendal & Windermere. The purpose was to put before the members a proposition made by the LNWR. This was that the lease to the Lancaster & Carlisle should be executed and the seal affixed but at the same time that this lease to the Lancaster & Carlisle was executed, the agreement with the LNWR was also signed. The future dividend to be paid with these arrangements would be 6 per cent on the new stock and 3 per cent on the original stock. The telling aspect was that all the Kendal & Windermere responsibilities would be adopted by the LNWR, thereby (although this was not stated but inferred) releasing the Kendal & Windermere from the oppressive behaviour of the Lancaster & Carlisle. What would happen was that the whole responsibility of the Kendal & Windermere would pass to the LNWR and short of what would need an Act of Parliament, the company would be 'abolished'. All dividends would come from Euston and there would have to be a Secretary to deal with these unless ('if or when') full amalgamation with the LNWR took place. After some deliberation the meeting unanimously accepted the proposals put forward.

The 22nd December was the big day when all the threads came together. At a meeting held at the Castle station in Lancaster the seal was affixed to the new lease from the Kendal & Windermere to the Lancaster & Carlisle, as it was to the lease from the Lancaster and Carlisle to the LNWR and to the Agreement between the LNWR, the Kendal & Windermere and the Lancaster & Carlisle railways. There was the inevitable 'small print' but the essential business had been transacted.

No doubt there were many who had a particularly happy and stress-free Christmas over the next few days but probably none more than Lord Chandos, the Chairman of the LNWR and Richard Moon, an influential Director of that company, who may well have been instrumental in the background at this stage and one who was destined to play a major role in its future progress. The simple fact was that the LNWR had taken one very significant step nearer to controlling what would become the West Coast main line to Scotland.

Fresh fish and great days out

Amidst all these meetings and discussions about the future shape of these various companies, it was also necessary to actually run a railway and, where possible, enhance or improve facilities. With such aims in view, it was proposed that after the end of June, the people of Windermere, Kendal and Lancaster would have supplies of fish and game from Glasgow, Edinburgh and Greenock sent by passenger train. Presumably this would mean that these commodities would arrive fresher than they had done previously.

A number of trips out were planned. On Monday 18th July and 1st, 15th and 29th August (all Mondays) there were high tides at Hest Bank and someone had the bright idea of attaching excursion carriages to the 9.55 am from Kendal in order give people the opportunity to take advantage of this situation and bathe in the sea. The return from Hest Bank was at 5.04 pm. Another treat in store was a visit to see the ship the *Great Eastern* when it visited Holyhead. Special trains were run on 12th, 14th and 17th October. The fare from Windermere and Kendal was £1 first class and 13*s.* 6*d.* in a 'covered carriage'. The price included the boat trip between the pier and the ship and the visit on board was free. However, those wishing to travel from Kendal and Windermere had to set off the day before in order to catch the special train which left Lancaster at 5.00 am. After changing at Preston, they reached Holyhead at 11.15 am where they boarded a boat at the pier and were taken out to go aboard the *Great Eastern*. The train back left Holyhead at 4.30 pm.

By October 1859 there had been a considerable number of changes in the timetable. These included a reference to the 'Express' leaving Windermere. This train, in future would leave five minutes later, at 1.35 pm and proceed to Lancaster where it would join the 'Scotch Express' for the south. A month later, in November, there had been still more alterations and the 'Express' departure time from Windermere became 1.50 pm and it would join the express for the south at Oxenholme.

So it was that with the end of the decade and following protracted discussions, a new phase in the history of the Kendal & Windermere Railway was about to begin. The 1860s and 1870s would see yet more changes as this group of lines consolidated even further to give a more viable system.

Chapter Seven

The London & North Western: The 'Premier Line'

Some reflections

The advent of the railway, especially during the mid-19th century, rapidly brought forth a plethora of schemes. Some of these were the result of high aspirations and were planned to link centres of great importance such as London and Birmingham or Liverpool and Manchester. In contrast there were many others which were small, local enterprises, planned by groups of people, often the worthies of a particular town, who had various motives in embarking on a particular project. There was no grand overall plan for a railway system and the result was the very piecemeal way in which development occurred. In many ways this was hardly surprising. Although the so-called industrial revolution had begun, England was still predominantly rural and the shape of society reflected that; there even remained a strong flavour of medievalism in the way that society was structured and there was some way to go before real change would occur. The railway schemes which were proposed in this new age, understandably, usually had a powerful element of what would be referred to today as 'commercialism'. This was either directly, in the sense that the railway itself would make a handsome profit, or indirectly in that it would enhance the trade in the area it was intended to serve and so lead to greater prosperity within that community.

Nevertheless there were those who saw the coming of a railway as a sign of prestige and something which would ensure the future standing of a particular town. There were, of course, those on a darker side who saw the opportunity to be fraudulent and make a profit out of others' financial greed. It was in this climate and background that the group in Kendal had decided to make their bid for a railway. There is no doubt that their intentions were honourable but like so many others, they were treading on ground which had not, to any great extent, been trodden before. They were, it is not too far removed to say, pioneers. Whatever their shortcomings, and there were, at times, critics who perceived them to be many, they were successful in putting Kendal on the railway map and, at the same time, opening up the Lake District to large numbers of visitors, who, without this mode of transport, would not have been able to enjoy its beauty and its facilities. The time came, however, when it was apparent that what was needed was the support and the backing (not least financial) of those with greater expertise, experience and resources. The LNWR was a company well able to do this. It was formed in 1846 from the London & Birmingham and Grand Junction and Liverpool & Manchester railways (which had already merged in 1845) along with a number of other companies associated with these. Its influence gradually spread northwards from Euston and it steadily annexed more and more companies which not only formed the main route from London to Scotland but also many of those associated with it. The LNWR became such a powerful and influential railway that it was soon referred to as the 'Premier Line'. It even had the audacity, as some saw it, to include the figure of Britannia, the symbol of Great Britain, in its coat of arms. In the latter part of the 1850s there was one individual on the Board of Directors who was playing a very influential role in driving the company forward; that man was Richard Moon, who was mentioned in the last chapter. It has been said that he was determined to the point of being ruthless; that he was highly respected (possibly feared) by those with whom he worked and certainly by those who worked under him. It was clearly much to do with his ambitions for the company that the LNWR was advancing northwards and taking control of the companies already operating the route to Scotland. Richard Moon, who later received a knighthood, eventually became the Chairman of the LNWR in 1861. So it was that in 1859, the LNWR made a bid to lease the Lancaster & Carlisle and, inevitably, therefore, the Kendal & Windermere.

As we have already seen, the Kendal & Windermere had initially been leased by the Lancaster & Carlisle but in that arrangement, it continued to exist as a company. The Lancaster & Carlisle was now leased, along with the Kendal & Windermere, by the powerful LNWR. Although, again, both would remain, in a sense, distinct companies for a few years more, this process would herald considerable change.

A significant aspect of this move would be that the Kendal & Windermere would, in effect, in many ways, lose its local identity. Unlike others, for example the Cockermouth, Keswick & Penrith Railway, which retained its identity until the great amalgamation of 1921-1923 and was, as mentioned earlier, simply *worked* by the LNWR (together with the North Eastern), the Kendal & Windermere was virtually absorbed into the LNWR and in the process it lost its essential 'localness'.

When this happens, the history of a railway line, especially a comparatively small one, can become rather colourless. The local personalities, certainly at an executive level, disappear and the control of the line is from afar; in this case it was from Euston. It becomes a small cog in a large wheel. There are no more eloquent and often colourful speeches at half-yearly meetings, no haggling about what should remain as capital and what should be made available for dividends and none of the spice of intercompany dispute and rivalry. Life could become very dull; just trains puffing up and down a section of line according to a rather simple timetable.

However, the LNWR would not be slow to realize the potential that a railway serving an important part of the Lake District would have, both from a business as well as a tourist point of view and this realization would certainly not condemn the Kendal & Windermere to backwater obscurity, as happened in the case of some other branch lines.

Relocation

During the 1840s and 1850s, there had continued to be an influx of people from the rural areas and into the towns where there was work to be had in the factories and mills. However, the squalor and depravity which had resulted when large numbers came together without adequate provision and proper facilities, became a characteristic of cities such as Manchester and Liverpool, making them undesirable places to live for those who could afford not to have to do so. Also, the new rich, who had made their fortunes; the factory owners for example, often felt a desire to emulate the aristocratic way of life of which they were aware, not least by building large and impressive mansions which would sit in impressive grounds.

What better place for this than the Lake District? The coming of the railway now made this possible, providing a means of escape for those who had become wealthy. Large houses were built with the profits being made and so, eventually, this wealth came into the area, much as Cornelius Nicholson had predicted. There was an obvious advantage to be in close proximity to, say, Windermere or stations along the line and this would govern, to some extent, where building would occur. A classic case is Brockholes, situated on the road between Windermere and Ambleside. An area of land was purchased in 1895 by William Henry Adolphus Gaddum who had become wealthy as a silk merchant in Manchester. In addition to a grand mansion, he had five acres of formal gardens laid out and there were a further 25 acres of land giving panoramic views of the surrounding hills and the lake. Brockholes is now a visitor centre.

Others included Blackhall. This house was designed and built for Edward Holt and his family. Holt, who had been educated at Christ Church Oxford, became very wealthy as the owner of a brewery in Manchester. Blackhall, the family retreat, was built just outside Windermere on the road to Newby Bridge and also has fine views over the lake. It remains to this day and is now open to the public. In some cases the wealth created was used to purchase existing grand piles, as was the case with Merewood which also overlooks Lake Windermere and is now a hotel. This was built in 1812 for use by the first Earl of Lonsdale but it was eventually sold in this period to Mr Thwaites, the well known brewer.

These are just three examples of which there were many others. There was also a peripheral spin-off to all this for which the coming of the railway could claim a part. Not only did these wealthy families seek desirable residences, they also endeavoured, in many cases, to furnish them lavishly and to include in those trappings works of art produced in the contemporary art and craft genre popular in the age. These items were not to be of the mass produced variety but specially made by local craftsmen for whom, therefore, a living was provided.

So it was, then, that now there was a fully integrated railway system, the LNWR could make life for the man who had his business in the city but who wanted his 'estate' to be in the Lakes, a practical reality.

1860

Meantime, under the new regime, the half-yearly meetings of both the Kendal & Windermere company and the Lancaster & Carlisle company now dealt with basic matters such as dividends. The LNWR had completely taken over the running of the lines and so there was no discussion about policy and little opportunity for debate.

The first half-yearly meeting of the Kendal & Windermere, which was planned for 31st January, was subsequently adjourned until Thursday 16th February and took place at the Chamber of Commerce in Stricklandgate. Even at this stage, when it might have been thought that from here on it would be plain sailing, there had been problems in the dealings with the Lancaster & Carlisle.

Once again, the problem had been of a financial nature. The LNWR had paid over to the Lancaster & Carlisle the money due to the Kendal & Windermere, with regard to the interest on the bonded debt and loans, together with the preference interest. All that was needed now was for the meeting to authorize payment of this to the appropriate people. However, the Lancaster & Carlisle had initially failed in its commitment to pay over to the Kendal & Windermere the proportion of the profits due and this had resulted in the Kendal & Windermere being unable to declare a dividend. Following considerable correspondence, the money had been offered but without interest, and this offer was received 'under protest'. It had been anticipated that the interest would be four per cent. Eventually, after a good deal of discussion, the Lancaster & Carlisle had offered to pay 1½ per cent interest. It was pointed out to the meeting that from the payment which should have been made by the Lancaster & Carlisle, it would first be necessary to pay off all the liabilities of the company on revenue account and these must be liquidated before there was money available for a dividend. In fact the Directors were able to say that they had met the whole of these liabilities and the £940 remaining would give, if agreed, 3*s.* per share for the year ending July 1859 but the meeting was asked to decide on the matter of the interest being offered. After some rather heated exchanges the meeting agreed to the offer of 1½ per cent. There was a dividend agreed of 7*s.* 6*d.* from the agreement between the LNWR and the Lancaster & Carlisle companies and the 3*s.* 0*d.* proposed by the Kendal & Windermere Directors. This left a sufficient amount to pay the Directors a sum of £200 for their work. When the Lancaster & Carlisle held its half-yearly meeting on Monday 20th August, it was pointed out that the meeting was for the transaction of purely formal business and there was a good deal of self-congratulation on the present position of the company, especially in connection with the lease. A dividend of 9¼ per cent was announced. It was made clear that the line was now under the control of the LNWR and attention must be turned to the progress of the Lune Valley line (the Ingleton branch, as it would become known).

On the same day as this meeting, an inquest was held at the Globe Inn, in Kendal. It involved Jonathan Creighton, 'a remarkably fine little boy' aged 10, the son of Thomas Creighton, a butcher. Among those giving evidence was a nine-year-old boy who verified how, the previous day (Sunday 19th August) he, together with Jonathan and a group of other boys, had been playing with the railway wagons in a siding near Saint George's school in the vicinity of Kendal station. They had succeeded in moving wagons in the game they were playing but in the process, Jonathan had been crushed between the buffers. He was taken out alive and moved to a stable belonging to the Railway Tavern. Although Mr Longmuir, a 'surgeon', had been sent for, the boy had died shortly afterwards. The coroner, Richard Wilson, recorded a verdict of 'accidental death'; a sad case, which served to emphasize the dangers of playing on the railway.

From here on, the half-yearly meetings of the Lancaster & Carlisle were very much engaged with the Lune Valley line, although a point was raised in the meeting on Tuesday 26th February, 1861 that in connection with the lease, it might be advisable for the company to have its own solicitor. However, this was seen as an unnecessary provision, the Directors being of the opinion that the LNWR, in spite of its rapid and continuing growth, would act in the interests of those companies it was leasing.

Whilst this was going on, the Kendal & Windermere Railway was enabling business opportunities to open up, not only in Kendal but also in Windermere and other places along the line. In May, Mr J. Livesey at the Railway Inn, in Kendal, was not only able to thank his friends and customers for their support but he also 'begged to announce' that he was able to supply them with 'very superior hay and straw by railway at reasonable prices'; clearly an early example of diversification, thanks to the railway.

A 'new' station is planned for Kendal

There had been a considerable amount of local dissatisfaction about the poor condition that Kendal station was in and so there was a sense of relief when, in May, the LNWR decided to put matters right. The local press no doubt reflected the feeling of a good many users of the station. The *Westmorland Gazette* was particularly scathing about the state of the building, saying it was 'the worst railway station in the kingdom' (and, as if for good measure, it felt that the town hall had been pretty much as bad until this had been rectified) with the 'wooden sheds having long done duty for the purpose'. It was conceded that the Lancaster & Carlisle company had intended to deal with the problem but the merging of the companies had intervened and so no progress had been achieved. The *Kendal Mercury* displayed rather less acerbity in reporting the proposal, although it pointed out that it was felt Kendal, as far as its station was concerned, was behind other towns of its size in the kingdom. On a positive side, it was clearly a matter of some satisfaction that the contracts awarded by the LNWR for the construction, to a design by Mr Worthington of Manchester, had gone to local people. These included walling and masonry to Richard and John Thompson, carpentry and joinery to John Fisher and Samuel Compston, slating to Miles Thompson, plumbing to Messrs Winder and Gibson, painting and glazing, William Thompson and plastering, Joseph Steel; all of Kendal. The contract for the iron work was awarded to the Phœnix Foundry Co. in Lancaster. It was anticipated that work would take about seven months from starting and cost between £7,000 and £8,000. The *Kendal Mercury* held out the hope that 'their several contracts may turn out to be remunerative' and expressed the view that 'though designed with an evident disregard of all useless or unnecessary ornament and without much pretentions as to style, will nevertheless be at once handsome and substantial and replete in every convenience'. In short it would be a station of which Kendal could be proud. This would be the case in the following year.

Also, in May, on Saturday 18th, special trains were run, by the 'London and North Western, Lancaster and Carlisle Division' for the 'Whitsuntide Hiring' in Kendal. The train from Lancaster consisted of first, second and third class carriages. It left at 7.30 am and called at Hest Bank, Bolton, Carnforth, Burton and Holme, Milnthorpe and Oxenholme and arrived at Kendal 'at about' 8.32 am. Return was by ordinary service at 3.55 pm and by special train at 6.00 pm. In addition there was a special train which left Tebay at 8.10 am (again it had first, second and third class carriages). It called at Lowgill, Grayrigg and Oxenholme and arrived at Kendal at 8.45 am. The return journey could be made at 10.55 am (ordinary train) 2.12 or 6.50 pm. There was also a special train from Windermere which left at 8.30 am and called at Staveley and Burneside. Return on all trains in this case, was by ordinary train at 11.15 am, 3.55 or 7.10 pm. Whitsuntide turned out to be something of a mixed bag as far as tourism was concerned. There were misgivings in Kendal that the numbers of people who turned out for the special events were smaller than anticipated and this was put down to the cheap trips which the railway companies had on offer and which drew people away from the town.

On the other hand, there were several trips to Windermere. On Whit Monday, 290 people travelled on a Christian and Literary Institute trip from Kendal and there was a school trip from Blackburn, on a train made up of 24 carriages. On Tuesday, the Working Men's Library and News Room outing, from Kendal, was joined by 304 participants and two trains came from Preston. One carried Church of England Sunday School children, which had 24 carriages, and the other of Wesleyan Sunday School children, which consisted of 25 carriages. A further train from Todmorden had a train of 12 carriages. The LNWR was certainly ready to facilitate the use of the Kendal & Windermere on these high days and holidays.

Another significant, though probably less auspicious, event during the year was the arrival in Kendal of the first train carrying Durham coal. This was possible following the opening of the South Durham & Lancashire Railway between the North-East and Tebay. The load was consigned to George Gaskell and arrived on Thursday 4th July. Perhaps it was inevitable that, once again, the price of coal would fall and within three weeks of this delivery notices appeared to that effect.

In August it was announced that the 'Windermere Express' would be rescheduled from the 5th of the month. Instead of leaving Preston at 2.40 pm it would be moved on to 3.40 pm. Arrival at Windermere would be at 5.25 pm and in spite of being styled an express, it stopped at Oxenholme, Kendal, Burneside and Staveley. Before moving onto the branch it stopped at Lancaster and Carnforth. At about the same time, the LNWR invited tenders to be submitted for the renting of the refreshment rooms at Kendal station. The deadline was 2nd September and the documents had to be sent to the Castle station at Lancaster. Another event which drew the attention of the railway was a Temperance demonstration at Kendal on Monday 26th August. Those attending from Windermere and Staveley were able to take advantage of a concession whereby if they applied to the appropriate station master half an hour before the train left, they could travel out and back for a single fare. These tickets were available on the 9.40 am from Windermere and the 9.50 am from Staveley, returning at 7.10 pm from Kendal.

In September 'Nut Monday' was considered an appropriate day to run a special excursion to Belle Vue in Manchester. The train travelled down from Carlisle and there was a connecting train from Windermere at 6.36 am calling at all stations to 'Kendal Junction' and leaving there at 7.10 am. Passengers were set down at Longsight station and the train would return at 10.15 pm 'after the fireworks'. This must have been a particularly exciting outing at the time. Belle Vue was less than 30 years old at this stage but there were many attractions, including the famous zoological gardens, giving the residents of Westmorland an opportunity to see types of animals they had never had a chance to see before. There would also be a band concert. For those who were inclined to visit the seaside, a special train was chartered on the same day by the Kendal Christian and Literary Institute to take passengers to Barnard Castle, Darlington, Stockton, Middlesbrough and Redcar. This train had an earlier start from Kendal of 6.20 am and the party had, what for some might have been a dubious privilege, the Castle Mills Brass Band 'to accompany the trip the whole distance'.

A free delivery service

As the 1860s and 1870s passed so the railway continued to serve the community in very much the way it had become used to doing. During this period the railway company provided a free delivery service to certain parts of Kendal. The area included Kendal Green, the top of Beast Banks ('as far as the house of J.J.Wilson Esq.') and up Peat Lane 'as far as the Mayor's house'. This facility was almost lost in 1872 because 'some people, when receiving goods were taking it for granted that the [railway] company's servants were bound to place goods at any place the owner may desire as, for instance, the end of a long lobby or up stairs'. Only after much effort by the Kendal Chamber of Commerce did the railway company agree to continue the facility of free delivery but on the strict understanding that goods need only to be delivered to the door.

Reference has already been made to the use of horses and carriages for the conveyance of passengers arriving by rail in order to take them to their various destinations. These carriages were privately owned. The deliveries made by the railway were made using horses which usually belonged to the railway company. In this period horses were used by the railways to carry out a number of tasks. Very often they were used during the actual construction of a line and some contemporary reports (about other lines) suggest that they were often cruelly treated by those who were in charge of them. Horses were also used for marshalling operations (shunting!) but one of the most important types of work for which they were employed involved the conveyance of goods. In connection with providing customers with this facility, there were stables at Kendal and Windermere stations.

Some accidents and mishaps

There were several accidents during the 1860s and 1870s. One characteristic of the line, which gave rise to some of the problems, was the steep gradient down the final mile into Windermere station. Over the years it would catch out a number of drivers and others; misjudgement which would result in accidents on this section.

On 14th September, 1868 an incident occurred on this part of the line. The accident report, which was written by Colonel Hutchinson, after he investigated the circumstances, throws some light on certain operational procedures which took place. (It is of note that in reports of this period, the word 'break' is frequently used for what would more usually be expected as 'brake'. At no time has the process of arresting a vehicle been understood or written in this way and it can only be assumed this was a spelling error or misunderstanding on the part of the authors or those who actually printed the reports.) In practice, trains approaching Windermere station were usually stopped 100 to 150 yards from the foot of the incline.

The engine then left the train and ran through the facing points and into the shed. As soon as the locomotive had cleared the points, the brakes of the passenger train were eased off and the train was allowed to acquire enough velocity on the remaining part of the incline to carry it over the level part of the line and into the platform. It was usual to have two brake vans, one at the front and the other at the rear. If there was only one guard on the train, it was the duty of the foreman porter in the yard to take charge of the front brake from the point at which the engine had been dispatched but the rear guard was still considered to be responsible for the safe working of the train. On this particular day, the train due in at 4.35 pm consisted of the engine and tender, a brake third (in which the foreman porter at Windermere travelled from the junction at Oxenholme) a second, a third, a first, a composite, a third brake, four composites, a first, a second and a brake van with the guard; 13 vehicles in all. It appears that all was going well until it was realised that the speed of the train was too great. The result was that the brake power was unable to check it and it collided with the buffers. There was, in fact, no damage to the stock or, for that matter, the buffers. However, four passengers and 'some children' were slightly injured. It was concluded that the brake power was insufficient for 13 vehicles and Colonel Hutchinson noted that a train of the size involved would usually be provided with two heavy brake vans, with one at the front and one at the rear. However (he writes),

> ... by some carelessness of the foreman porter at Oxenholme a light break carriage had been put on the front on this occasion.

It was also stated that since the accident, orders had been issued that the engine should not be detached from the train until about 50 yards from the foot of the incline. However, it was felt that it would be far better to allow the engine to take the train right into the station for which (it is noted) there are the necessary facilities. He concludes,

> If, however, the Directors see fit to continue the present practice, it seems most desirable that the guard in the *front* van should be responsible for the safety of the train after the engine has left it.

Barely a year later, on the 2nd September, 1869, there was another accident at Windermere, this time involving an excursion train from Liverpool and Manchester. It was H.W. Tyler who carried out the investigation on this occasion. He also looked carefully at the procedures in use. He notes the falling gradient of 'about 1 in 80 for a mile' down to Windermere and that there was a fixed signal always at danger which was 236 yards east of the platform and trains are brought to a halt at this position. Thereafter the engine was usually detached from the train and was allowed to run down the line and then turned off into the turntable siding on the south side of the main line.

The carriages, as had been described by Colonel Hutchinson, were then allowed to descend by the force of gravity through a crossover road and to the north line platform. It was pointed out that if the north line platform was occupied by an 'ordinary' train, any excursion train was allowed to run into the south platform. In some cases, when the brake power was 'wanting', the engine was allowed to run down in front of an excursion train and into the platform.

Tyler observes that there was a public road level crossing 490 yards to the east of the fixed signal and from this level crossing a distant signal was worked 334 yards further east. The 'pointsman' went from the station to meet every train at the fixed signal. There was no distant signal from that signal or from the station but a woman, who acted as the gatekeeper for the level crossing, was expected to keep her distant signal at danger as long as any train was standing at the fixed signal. This woman was in sight of the fixed signal in clear weather and she could see vehicles standing to the east of it, even though the line was curved. She had, however, no means of communication with the 'pointsman' at the fixed signal other than by hand signals or whistles.

Tyler goes on to describe how between the fixed signal and the west end of the station there were five pairs of facing points over which a passenger train had to pass on each line of rails. Further, the levers of these points were in all places *at* (Tyler's italics) the points, which were weighted to stand right, on the north side, for the passenger trains entering the station and on the south side, for the turntable line, south of the down line, after passing the crossover road at the fixed signal. The points opposite the fixed signal required to be held over for a passenger train proceeding to the north platform and the points leading to the turntable for a train proceeding to the south platform.

On 2nd September locomotive No. 1408, a six-wheeled-coupled goods (weight 27 tons and 10 cwts) set off from Liverpool with an excursion to Windermere. The train was described as 'lengthy' but the make up was unspecified. The crew consisting of a driver and fireman was augmented by two other drivers who were riding in the cab, in order to gain experience when travelling the line to Windermere. It was on the descent into Windermere that problems started. It is reported that after reaching the summit and preparing for the descent, the driver, who had little experience of the line, noticed that the steam was low and also the level of water in the boiler and so he opened up the regulator to lift the water in the top of the firebox to save the lead plug and prevent damage to the top of the firebox.

The result of this action was to increase the speed of the train to 15 mph. At this speed the train was unable to stop at the fixed signal, travelling at speeds reckoned by different observers to be anything between five and 13 mph when passing it. One of the drivers jumped out. The 'pointsman', when he heard the whistle from the engine, went to the second set of points from the fixed signal, which lead to the turntable, intending to turn the train into the south platform line. When he saw the speed, however, he feared it would not be able to pull up at the station. He then decided to leave the points standing for the turntable siding and the train passed on to it and over the turntable. The engine then destroyed a mound of timber and stone and knocked down a portion of a wall. The engine was partially turned on its side, becoming embedded in soft ground. Fortunately only the leading wheels of the first vehicle went over the end of the rails. The locomotive was not badly damaged and was able to return to Liverpool without assistance. Twenty passengers complained that they had been injured.

Tyler suggested that an extra arm should be put in place on the post of the distant signal, worked from the level crossing, and worked from the fixed signal, so making the 'pointsman' independent of the gatekeeper. He also felt that the various point levers should be connected and interlocked. There is a note at the end of the report, possibly by way of a mild caveat, that the permanent way at the approach to the station is in need of improvement and a recommendation that 'various point levers should be connected together and be interlocked in a simple manner with signals for the admission of trains into the station'.

By the time the report was being prepared, the driver and fireman of the locomotive involved had been dismissed from their jobs. It is not clear, however, whether the dismissal resulted from this incident or whether there was another reason.

During this period, a significant quantity of gunpowder, manufactured in the area, was moved from Windermere and one aspect which the report did not raise but was described elsewhere as 'a rather worrying one', was that there had been a considerable quantity of gunpowder in one of the adjacent sidings. Fortunately, this had not been affected by the incident. These events involving runaway vehicles at Windermere were by no means the end of such occurrences.

Apart from runaway trains there were other accidents. On 21st February, 1870 there was an incident involving a group of platelayers returning from Windermere. They were travelling on what was described in the parlance of the day as a 'lurry', which was a small trolley used for moving the workforce about. When they were in the vicinity of Staveley one of the wheels came off the trolley which then careered off the rails. One or two of the men suffered severe injuries, especially one named James Carruthers. The trolley ran over one of his legs but fortunately Dr Dobson of Bowness came to his rescue and the leg did not have to be amputated.

In 1871 there were further changes at Crewe. Following (it has been said) a disagreement between John Ramsbottom and Richard Moon, Ramsbottom left the company and Francis Webb now took hold of the reins. His period of office, from 1871 to 1903, saw many new classes of locomotives introduced, some of which would continue in service well after the demise of the LNWR. Certain of these classes would be seen on the Windermere line; the 0-6-0 '17' 'Coal Engine' class (introduced in the late 1870s and until the early 1890s) with passenger trains being hauled by the 'Precusor '2-4-0 and 'Precedent' 2-4-0 classes (introduced in the late 1870s and early 1880s). Local services were soon in the hands of Webb's 2-4-2 tanks.

On 17th August, 1872 there was a collision in Kendal which, except for the swift action of the station staff, might have been far more disastrous than it turned out to be. Once again, it involved an excursion train and was probably caused by a driver who was not acquainted with the steep incline from Oxenholme down to Kendal. The station only had a single platform, on the down side of the line. The incident would seem almost to rival the sort of sequence that might be seen (though at a later date!) in a film drama. The driver of the excursion train, which was from St Helens and consisted of 28 'heavily laden carriages', appeared to have lost control and although the signals were set against the train, it came 'speeding' (at nine miles an hour!) down the line towards the 9.05 local which was about to leave for Oxenholme. Mr Collier, the station master, together with other members of staff, when they saw the train approaching, managed to get all but four of the passengers out of the local. When this had been achieved, the driver of the local stayed on the footplate and started to reverse the train in order to lessen the impact when the excursion train ran into it. There was little more than shock sustained by the passengers in the St Helens train although a man and a boy who jumped out suffered cuts and bruises. Once the 9.05 was out of the way, the other train continued to Windermere. It was observed that

> ... it is the general opinion that the general arrangements at Kendal Station are dangerously defective, especially at this season, when heavy excursion trains are daily passing through to Windermere in charge of strange drivers at all hours of the day. Unless a change is made it is far from improbable that we may hear of another heavily laden train repeating the mishap of Saturday with more terrible results. To remove this risk, the company ought at once to construct another platform on the north side of the station with egress into Longpool, so that the 'down' line may be always clear.'

It would be some years before this advice was heeded.

On 23rd December, 1876 there was a collision near Burneside. This time it was a local train, the 1.50 pm from Kendal, which ran into a luggage train. The latter had 'through some mistake' not been cleared from the down line. The passengers 'were thrown against each other with considerable violence' and they sustained cuts and bruises, some of them severe. It was reported that following the accident one gentleman was seen making off across the fields after commenting 'they will never again have the chance of killing me on the railway'!

Richard Moon visits Windermere

On 19th September, 1878 there was something of an auspicious meeting at Kendal station. The situation at the station was, by now, once again, causing a considerable amount of concern, this time through its inadequacy to deal with the amount of traffic it was handling and possibly the implications in the report following the accident six years before. It was clear that measures were needed to effect improvements. A group of Kendal worthies, including Alderman Whitwell MP, together with five others, met a group of representatives from the LNWR. It was led by no less a person than Richard Moon and one could not ask for better than that if wanting to make a case. The Honourable W. Lowther was also in the party. Richard Moon pointed out that the Directors of his company would do all they could to help the situation at Kendal. They had, he informed them, been aware for some time that action was needed and, in fact, plans had been prepared 12 months before to effect considerable changes to the station. The intention had been to increase the platform accommodation by over 100 yards, to improve the offices and alter the track layout. It was estimated this would cost in excess of £5,000. The past tense here was not without significance because Moon went on to say that such extensive plans would not be implemented 'at the present time' but rather something less ambitious which could be put in place immediately. Forty yards would be added to the platform accommodation, there would be some modification to the offices with provision for first class and second class tickets to be sold from separate windows. Perhaps any improvement was better than no improvement at all and the Kendal deputation accepted the offer graciously.

There was, in fact, another matter. The engine shed which stood near to Peat Lane bridge would be moved to Oxenholme and it was felt this move would please the residents of Castle Street. Although the railway Directors were not drawn to comment on the possible implications of a proposal to build a new bridge at Sandes Close, with a road which would give even better access to the station, the general feeling by the Kendal party was that the meeting had been a satisfactory one.

The LNWR gains complete control

The significant event of 1879 was that by Local Act 42 and 43 Victoria I, c.cxlii, the control of the Kendal & Windermere Railway, in conjunction with the Lancaster & Carlisle Railway, passed into the complete control of the LNWR. 'The Kendal and Windermere', strictly speaking, was no more; it became, quite simply, the line from Kendal (or perhaps more realistically Oxenholme) to Windermere and just a very small part, albeit an important one, of the powerful LNWR.

The 28th February, 1879 saw an unpleasant accident at Kendal station when Mr Nelson was saying his farewells to his father who had been visiting him in the town. The son had the misfortune, when standing on the carriage step and chatting to his father, to fail to realise the train was about to set off. As it did so he slipped. He clearly thought the best action was to throw himself under the train but in trying to do so was dragged along by it and several of the wheels passed over his leg. The train was halted and Mr Nelson was rushed off to hospital where he had to have the leg amputated.

On 20th May, 1879 the Royal Train stopped at 'Kendal Junction' to take water whilst on its way north to Balmoral. On board were Queen Victoria, Princess Beatrice and Prince Leopold. However, those who might have hoped to catch a glimpse of the Royal party were disappointed because, it is reported, the station was 'strictly private' and during the stop 'the blinds of the Royal carriages were down'.

The original station at Oxenholme was quite a modest affair. In 1881 the decision to rebuild the station resulted in some radical changes. The main one was to reroute what became the B6452, Kendal to Kirkby Lonsdale road, in order to create much more space for the station facilities. The old road became, in effect, what is now the subway of the present station and the new section of road was taken in the large U-shape to the south; a development which, obviously, did not have the car in mind. The rebuilding was extensive as can be seen on the OS map (*page 220*) with, for examples, large capacity cattle pens being erected, a goods shed and more lines being added to a larger engine shed.

In 1884 Kendal station was further enlarged and improved. Some might have said that it was not before time. It was six years since Richard Moon's visit. However, the plea made some 12 years earlier, following the collision involving the excursion train and a local service train, was, seemingly, at last taken into account and an up platform was provided.

Plans for the Kendal, Windermere & Ambleside Railway

There had always been, albeit, somewhere in the background, from the earliest days, a notion that the logical development of a railway built to Windermere (or Low Wood, as originally intended) would be an extension to Ambleside (and possibly beyond). This hope, in the initial project, had been ruled out, in effect, by strong objections by certain landowners beyond Birthwaite who influenced the scheme in a way which resulted in the line terminating there. Aspirations to carry the line on had never been completely extinguished and when mutterings and grumblings (for such there were) from the Ambleside community began to resurface again in the early 1880s, it seemed the time was right for action.

The disquiet centred on a number of issues but they were based on a general premise that the inhabitants of Ambleside were being disadvantaged by their neighbours in Windermere and the key reason for this was that the latter had railway facilities. At 8.00 pm, on Tuesday 17th March, a meeting was held in the Mechanics Institute in Ambleside. The purpose of this meeting was 'to promote the movement for the extension of railway communication to Ambleside'. It was very well attended. (It was said that there were even a few ladies present!) In the company there were some influential persons. W.H. Heelis, and Mr Taylor (who owned 'Queens Hotel' and leased the 'Salutation Hotel'), were on the platform and 'on the front row' were Stanley Hughes la Fleming, George la Fleming (both of whom lived at Rydal Hall) and several clergymen, together with other worthies.

The meeting was addressed by the Revd George Alton, a Wesleyan Minister, who held the floor for a quite a period as he expounded the arguments for extending the line from Windermere to Ambleside. He spoke with clarity and conviction which made his case very convincing and he was often backed with shouts of 'Hear, hear' and cheers. The main thrusts of his argument were, firstly, that the people of Ambleside were victims of a monopoly when it came to the transport of passengers (although he did not say so in as many words, this he believed to be so because 'Riggs' coaches had an agreement with the LNWR) and, secondly, that the price for the carriage of goods made the cost of these at market uncompetitive when compared with the price of similar goods from Windermere. In a nut shell what he wanted was cheaper and better means of transit between Ambleside and Windermere and this meant promoting a railway between the two.

When it came to which railway company would best serve their purpose, he had no clear view. The three which would attract consideration would be the LNWR, the Midland and the Furness. In that sense it could be assumed the field was wide open! However, he already had thoughts which might indicate the direction in which to move. Then again, he was of the opinion that a five mile stretch of line as they had under consideration would not be seen as a worthy candidate for investment by the 'North Western' but if that company became aware that another one was ready to push ahead that might encourage it to undertake the project. (There seemed to be something of Cornelius Nicholson in the Revd George Alton.) The arguments for cheaper coal and other commodities which would be made possible by a railway were then rehearsed. He did concede that there was not a great deal produced in Ambleside that might benefit from railway facilities although he was aware that bobbins made in Staveley were cheaper than those made in their locality and this difference was down to the cost of transportation. And then, of course, there was that key issue, namely, summer visitors, and, coupled with this, the business of attracting the wealthy to set up houses there (just, he affirmed, as they had done in Windermere). When Alton suggested a railway would bring 'crowds of trippers', there were loud cheers.

When it came to dealing with the critics of the scheme there is a certain amount of *déjà-vu* when looking back over the issues which arose in connection with building the line to Windermere; the despoiling of the scenery, the disturbing of those who sought solitude in the district and the arrival of vulgar hordes who would not appreciate the beauty as the more discerning did and so ruin it. He became particularly eloquent at this point (shades of Cornelius Nicholson again) defending these maligned hordes whom he demonstrated did have an eye for beauty as he himself had witnessed. He countered the suggestion that writers and artists would no longer find a place of tranquillity in the area and would therefore desert it, as being unfounded in the light of experience. There were many comparisons drawn with Windermere and its resulting prosperity following the arrival of the railway. This he argued could be the lot of Ambleside if they had a railway. When Alton sat down, after a long and erudite presentation, there was a great deal of support which was expressed in loud cheering, with one gentleman proposing, albeit with tongue in cheek, that Mr Alton should be given 50 shares immediately. Other speeches followed, much in the same vein as Alton's. If rhetoric could carry the day, the railway was as good as built! A proposal was made, seconded and resolved (but notably, perhaps, with one dissentient),

> … that the resources of Ambleside and the neighbourhood for the maintenance of their progress and general prosperity are at present unsatisfactory and demand the serious attention of all who are interested in the welfare of the place.

Strangely there was no mention of a railway here but that was soon rectified by a second proposal. Somewhat along the lines of the first, it contained the vital element,

> Its progress is much retarded by want of railway facilities; that the extension of a railway or railways from one or more of the termini to Ambleside would be a great boon to the neighbourhood

It went even further,

> … and would give occupation to the working classes by encouraging wealthy families to reside in the district and by the general development of suitable industries and would also be a greater advantage to visitors and tourists in providing quicker and cheaper means of ingress and egress.

There was more waxing eloquent about the advantages a railway would bring and when this proposal was eventually put to the vote it was agreed - but again with one dissenter. A third motion was then put to the meeting. This simply reaffirmed the view that a railway would in no way detract from the natural beauty of the landscape. This was passed - yet again with one dissenter.

Now was the time to form a committee and 19 people agreed to serve. Their job, initially, would be to show to the companies which might be involved, that the scheme would pay. At this point Mr Walker commented that 'the opposition chap hasn't spoken yet'. Did they know who he was? In the event the membership of a committee was approved unanimously.

At this point what had clearly been a very lively meeting ended. There had been much cheering and support shown with frequent cries of 'Hear, hear'. The whole business was looking very promising. No company needed to be formed and therefore no subscriptions were called for at this stage but it would appear to leave any group or committee ready to pursue possibilities to fund its own expenses.

Inevitably, perhaps, the letters then began to appear. The first writer (Q.R.) supported the scheme but felt the Furness should do the building, leaving the present line to Windermere as it stood and bringing in a line from Grange to Lakeside, through Sawrey and Hawkshead and so to Ambleside. Another letter, which is simply signed 'A Windermere Resident' and appears to have been written by someone with considerable knowledge and insight, opens up the proverbial can of worms, namely matters relating to 'Riggs' coaches.

Although the writer commends the group for taking the initiative to put Ambleside on the railway, he takes issue with George Alton's assertion that there is a monopoly at work as far as the movement of passengers is concerned. Regulation, he points out, takes place at the station, which is normal practice in such situations, but there are alternative means for passengers to use. He goes on to suggest that the promoters do themselves no favours by saying at the outset that the line will not pay. What company, he argues, in its right mind, would agree to build a line which will operate at a loss? Certainly not the LNWR while Richard Moon was in charge.

Another point raised is that the promoters should consider the use of a tramway. This letter brought an immediate response from 'XIT'. He is quick to clarify the position over the use of 'Riggs' coaches and 'Windermere Resident' found himself having to concede that he had made an error. The fact of the matter was that the railway company, working in conjunction with 'Riggs', would, in many instances, include the cost of the journey from Windermere to Ambleside in the total price and so although a traveller could opt or inadvertently decide to make the journey on another coach, this would be charged, resulting in paying twice for the ride. There were other letters, often with suggestions about the development; for example that a branch line should be built from Windermere to Bowness and there were various notions about the route a line to Ambleside should take.

Certainly the inhabitants of Ambleside had a point, not least as far as building work was concerned. A report in the same year as they mustered their arguments indicated that in Windermere a great deal of building had taken place and more was to follow. In the report it is noted that although for some time there had been a scarcity of building land available, large amounts had recently come on to the market. The Old Field Estate almost filled the gap between Bowness and Windermere and lodging houses, residences, two churches and a school had been built. Then there was the Ellerthwaite Estate and a portion of Rayrigg. However, this glut had resulted in a slump as far as prices were concerned and bids of 2*s*. 6*d*. a yard for certain sections were well under expectation. Nevertheless the population was growing and this could well mean business for the railway as well as a boost for the local economy. Ambleside wanted to share in this.

At the end of October 1884, it was possible to report that the Ambleside committee had been in contact with a number of railway companies about getting railway communication for the town. The two companies which appeared as favourites were the LNWR and the Furness. However, it was felt options were still open, although Mr Cropper reported that the LNWR was 'carefully watching what was being done by other bodies'.

The question of whether or not there should be a rail link for Ambleside was one which created interest within a number of groups in the locality and on Friday 6th November the Ambleside Literary & Scientific Society decided to give it an airing. The proposal before the group was couched in a rather negative form, being 'That it does not appear that the advantages of the proposed railway to Ambleside will outweigh the disadvantages'. Once again it was the clergy who came to the fore, the Revd E.M. Reynolds, normally the chairman but standing down on this occasion in order to take an active role, gave a spirited speech in defence of the motion. Much of what he had to say had been said by others before and elsewhere; the detrimental effect on the beautiful countryside ('steam and scenery would never harmonise') the value of property would fall if more people moved into Ambleside and, that, by now, old chestnut, namely the unwelcome effect a deluge of trippers would have on the town.

It was the vicar of Ambleside, the Revd C.H. Chase who spoke next. He expressed uncertainty about whether or not railway facilities for his parish would be a good or bad thing. He drew a comparison with his previous parish in Weston-super-Mare, expressing reservations about the impact of 'trippers' in that place; something he would not like to see occur in Ambleside. This particular experience, therefore, lead him to think a railway would not be good for the town. He went on to rehearse the argument for retaining tranquillity for those who sought it in the area.

Yet another cleric spoke next; this time the curate of Ambleside. He spoke quite strongly against the motion, maintaining that there should be an opportunity for more people to experience the beauty of the area. He opposed the view that a railway would deface the countryside and felt visitors who were not well off would find the 2*d*. or 4*d*. to travel from Windermere by train much more attractive than having to pay 2*s*. to travel on the top of a coach. One further observation he made was that there were many men 'hanging about' in the district for want of work and the building of a railway would give them employment.

Other speakers were keen to point out ways in which a railway would be an advantage. It was suggested that a line from Greenod would mean Ulverston was directly accessible from Ambleside and the former would be the foreign port for Ambleside. This would result in a wide variety of merchandise coming, in effect, directly to Ambleside thereby reducing by considerable amounts the cost of carriage and in addition to this, the time involved in the transporting of foreign goods such as wine, which presently had to come via Liverpool. This argument, on the other hand, might move the LNWR to decide to extend the railway from Windermere and this would involve some 4½ miles of line. In addition it was felt the worthies of Kendal would not be happy with a line to Ambleside which by-passed their town and so would try to put pressure on the LNWR for an extension. There was clearly little support for the motion with one speaker suggesting that the proposers, if they felt so strongly about preserving the tranquillity of the area, should petition the LNWR to remove the link from Oxenholme. 'Look at Windermere,' exhorted another contributor,' from whatever point you look at the railway there is nothing to be seen in it but a boon.'

Another clergyman, the Revd H.S. Callender added his voice to the debate. He was confident that a railway for Ambleside was inevitable and strongly favoured the Windermere extension. The debate continued without showing any signs of flagging and by 10.00 pm the acting Chairman decided it was time to bring the proceedings to a close. He summed up the pros and cons and then asked those present to vote 'without selfish or personal feeling' bearing in mind what would best for the district. Only two or three hands were raised in support of the motion which was soundly defeated. Of course, this was simply a formal debate which carried no clout as far as decisions were concerned. Nevertheless it was a clear indication of how a good many people felt about railway provision for Ambleside.

In the midst of all this activity, the LNWR announced that it was proposing to put a Bill before Parliament to give the Midland Railway a joint interest in the lease of the Lancaster & Carlisle and the Kendal & Windermere railways together with the Lancaster & Preston Railway.

1885 – The Ambleside quest continues

In the days ahead there would be more moves made to secure the link to Ambleside but the year opened with a bit of a broadside from 'Commercial Traveller' writing in the *Kendal Mercury* on 2nd April. Once again it was the matter of fares which was at issue, in particular the price of travel from Kendal to Oxenholme and vice-versa. In the 21st century there are often complaints about what appears to be unfair price structuring on the modern railway system but on the face of it this is nothing new. The writer points out that to travel from Preston to Kendal costs 3*s*. 9*d*. but from Preston to Oxenholme the cost is 3*s*. 4*d*.; making the fare from Oxenholme to Kendal a disproportionate 5*d*. This is not an isolated case; Carlisle to Kendal 4*s*. 7*d*., to Oxenholme 4*s*. 2*d*. and this 5*d*. difference applies to all bookings between Preston and Carlisle. Booking separately from Oxenholme to Kendal and vice-versa costs 2½*d*. and so by rebooking at Oxenholme, 2½*d*. could be saved. This may not sound a great deal by present day standards but not a paltry sum then and certainly not in relation to the rest of the fare. 'Commercial Traveller' is keen to make others aware of this situation, especially 'the poor working man'. The writer does express his appreciation of the improved Kendal station which he feels is very befitting the status of the town.

On Wednesday 16th April, the Ambleside Extension Committee met again, this time at the Queen's Hotel in Ambleside. The level of interest was once more evident in that there were representatives from Ambleside, Hawkshead, Grasmere, Langdale, Troutbeck, Satterthwaite and Sawrey. By this time, people were being invited to subscribe to the fund and there was a call to seek more who would support the project in this way. There was a feeling that the Manchester Waterworks Co. would soon be starting work in the area and this might provide a further incentive for the LNWR, whose Directors would be urged 'to take early action'.

No doubt the events of Whitsun simply added grist to the mill of the Ambleside Group when they realised what the area might be missing. On the Monday of Whit week, 'there was the usual influx of cheap trippers' at Windermere as heavily laden trains came in from Leeds, Bradford, Liverpool (two trains) Blackburn and Wakefield. These were met by a large number of three-horse omnibuses and 'well appointed' four-in-hand district coaches. They went off to Keswick, Ullswater and Coniston. (Ambleside is not mentioned!) Later in the week there were excursions from Manchester, Miles Platting, Crumpsall, Oldham, Longsight and Stretford with an estimated 3,000 passengers. On the Friday there were even more, bringing more excursionists from places in the Manchester area. Apparently, when the time came to leave, the 'trippers' behaved in a 'most staid and respectable fashion' and there was no unseemly behaviour or disturbance in the vicinity of the railway station (as, it seems, there had been in the past). Mr Becket, the station master, together with his staff, sent off the various 'specials' on time. The smoothness of the operation was attributed, in part, to the extensions made to the Windermere platforms in the previous year. O that Ambleside could have had a slice of this lucrative cake!

By June, the Furness Railway had decided it could not help with the Ambleside project but on Thursday 26th June, 40 Midland Railway representatives who had turned up in Ambleside the day before and had stayed at the Salutation and Queen's Hotels, went for a tour in four-horse conveyances to visit Keswick and Ullswater. There seemed to be some uncertainty about the real purpose of this visit but the idea that the Midland would provide Ambleside with its railway link seemed rather unlikely, unless the Committee was clutching at straws. Certainly there was still a strong prevailing notion that with the advent of Manchester Waterworks it would not be long before the LNWR would make the link to Ambleside.

1886

As 1886 progressed there seemed to be little or no activity from the Ambleside Group and it begins to look as though the project is a lost cause. The Windermere branch on the other hand remained very active with a variety of special trains being run. These included, as well as the usual excursions, a train for those returning to Burneside, Staveley and Windermere following the Spring Concert of the Kendal Choral Society (100 voices) on Thursday 1st April and what was described as 'a fast excursion train' for the 'Liverpool Grand National Steeple-chase' on 26th March. Although this 'fast' train actually started at Lancaster it was possible to book cheap tickets from stations on the Windermere line, with the journey from stations on the line being on scheduled services. In July there was a special excursion which brought in the Wine and Beer Retailers Association of Leeds. A large number of people were in the group but in the afternoon, the outing was spoilt by a very violent thunderstorm which drenched them all; perhaps to the satisfaction of the Temperance Society! A development during this period, which it was noted would have something of an impact on the railway, was the proposed opening of Sandes Avenue. This, it was suggested would give better access to Kendal station from Stricklandgate. In connection with this project, £3,000 was loaned to the Corporation in 1886 for the purpose of building a new road bridge over the River Kent.

On 23rd May what was described as a 'violent' collision occurred at Kendal station. In the early morning, a locomotive was shunting near the goods warehouse when the coupling on the engine gave way with the result that 24 trucks careered down the incline into the goods yard. Although three men were able to jump onto the moving wagons and apply the brakes, the vehicles failed to stop because rain

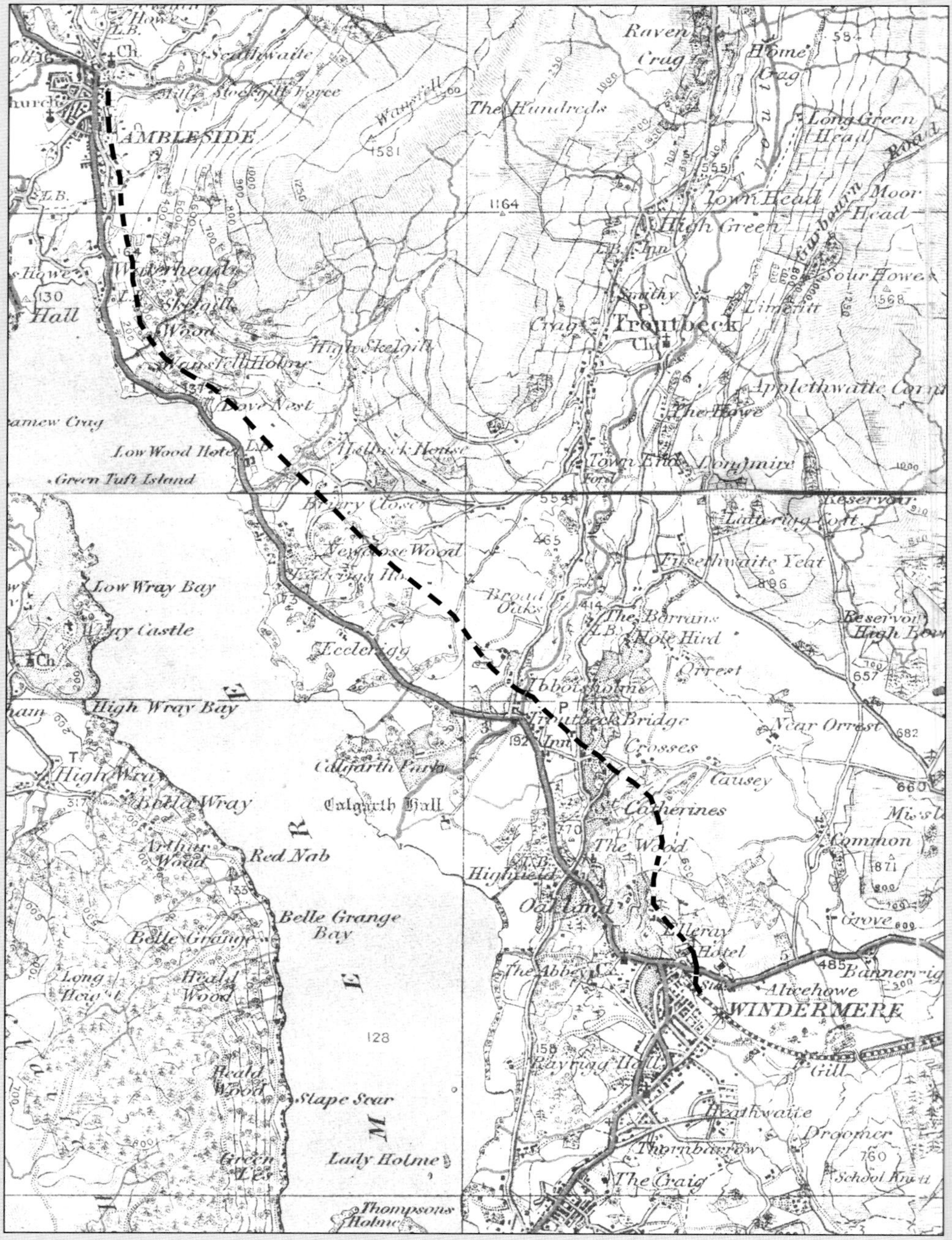

Map showing an outline sketch of the proposed route of the railway from Windermere to Ambleside. This is superimposed on a 1904 map. The extension would not have been made as an 'end on' connection to the existing line but would leave it just before the station. This would prove inconvenient for through trains to Ambleside if they were scheduled to stop at Windermere as a reversal would have been necessary.

had made the rails greasy. There was a collision with a stationary group of trucks and a considerable amount of damage was caused with some trucks being smashed to pieces. One of the vehicles involved was a gunpowder van belonging to the Elterwater Gunpowder Co., but fortunately it was empty.

The Ambleside scheme gains momentum

Any notion that the apparent silence of the Ambleside Project Group meant there would be no further pursuit of getting a rail link to Ambleside, was completely dispelled at the end of October. The scheme had clearly been smouldering away and suddenly burst into flames again with fairly dramatic consequences. On Friday 22nd October, a meeting was held at the Queen's Hotel in Ambleside with a view to carrying forward plans to acquire rail facilities for the town. The meeting had been called by Mr Taylor, the hotelier mentioned earlier, a fact that was soon to draw comments from the opposition. Also among those present were Mr Leane, an engineer and Mr Baker, a solicitor. Colonel Rhodes, who described himself as 'a resident ratepayer of Ambleside' but gave his address as 'Westhaugh, Pontefract, Yorkshire', was appointed the chairman. Although originally a member of the committee, Colonel Rhodes eventually decided to stand down to avoid the allegation that he was not really a local resident. In spite of this, he often attended the meetings and not infrequently took the chair. The colonel asked Mr Baker to provide the meeting with some information. What followed, both at this meeting and others, that were held later, and also the reactions in various quarters, once again had a remarkable sense of *déjà vu* going back 50 years to when the line for Kendal was being mooted. Mr Baker told those present that he had some 25 years' experience dealing with railway matters and that he had been very surprised to discover that Ambleside had no railway. He felt the line to Windermere should be extended to Ambleside but as to any further extension beyond that he did not feel it appropriate to speculate at that time.

Two possible routes for the line were put before the meeting. The first would actually leave the existing line before Windermere and go round Orrest, passing near to Troutbeck and thence to Ambleside. This was described as the 'higher line' and would be the cheaper, even though it would be about a mile longer. The second line would be a continuation of the line which terminated at Windermere station. The first of these proposals, although cheaper, had considerable drawbacks; there would be severe gradients which would be difficult to work and there would be the great disadvantage that trains travelling to Ambleside but calling at Windermere would have to reverse out of Windermere before continuing on their journeys. There was a suggestion that the number of visitors envisaged could well give a return of 5 per cent. The cost of getting a Bill to Parliament would be £1,500 and Mr Baker advocated that as many people as possible should buy £10 shares, paying £1 on each to raise the funding needed. The hope was expressed that between £25,000 and £30,000 might be raised locally with other revenue coming from further afield. The engineer, Mr Leane, stated that he favoured the second scheme which had been

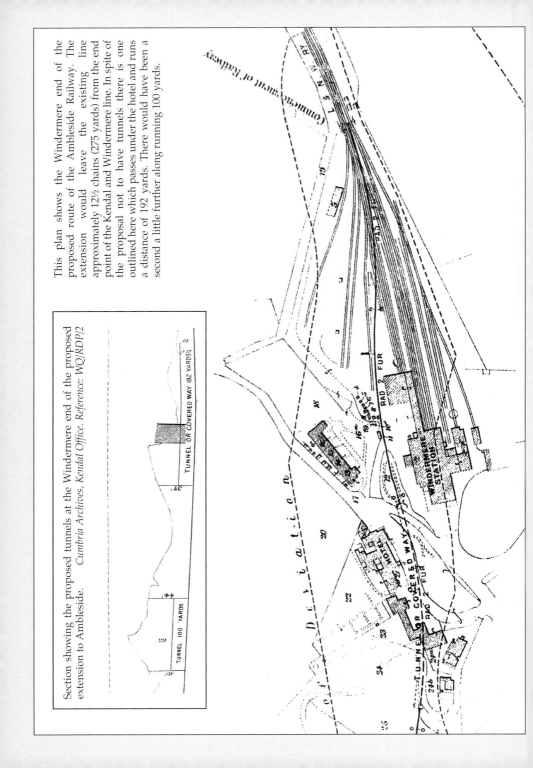

Section showing the proposed tunnels at the Windermere end of the proposed extension to Ambleside. *Cumbria Archives, Kendal Office. Reference: WQ/RDP/2*

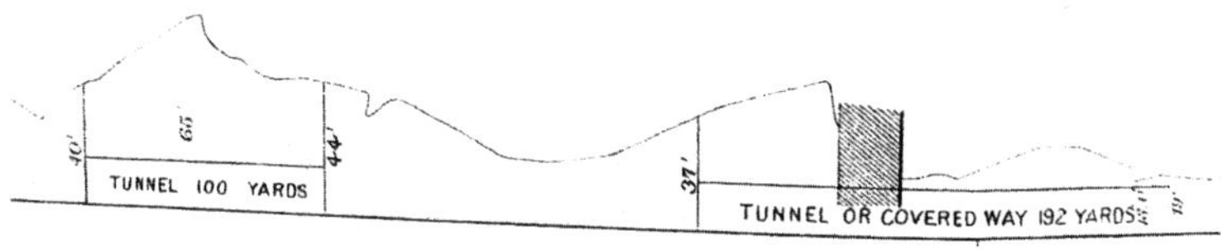

This plan shows the Windermere end of the proposed route of the Ambleside Railway. The extension would leave the existing line approximately 12½ chains (275 yards) from the end point of the Kendal and Windermere line. In spite of the proposal not to have tunnels there is one outlined here which passes under the hotel and runs a distance of 192 yards. There would have been a second a little further along running 100 yards.

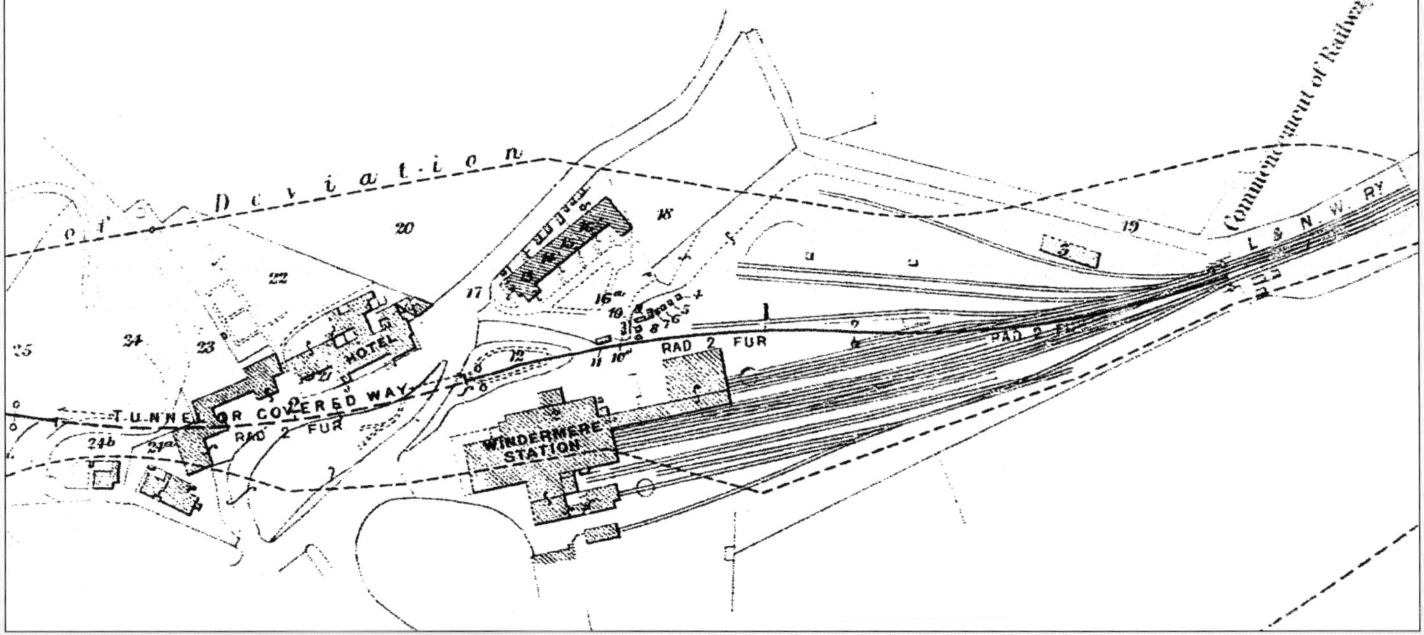

discussed; the viaduct over Troutbeck on this scheme would be 170 yds long, compared to 433 yards on the 'higher' one. He disagreed with the original assessment on cost, saying that he felt the 'lower' scheme would prove to be cheaper. Without further prompting, Mr Taylor said he would take 100 shares.

Three resolutions were passed unanimously:

(1) That it is most desirable in the public interest that a line of railway should be constructed from the London and North Western Railway at Windermere to the town of Ambleside.
(2) That such a railway should be laid out as far as possible to form a continuation of and suit the convenience of the London and North Western Railway due regard being had to avoid unnecessary interference with the properties of the landowners and the scenery.
(3) That this meeting calls upon the owners of property, inhabitants and other persons interested in the welfare of Ambleside and district to take the necessary steps for introducing a bill into the next session of Parliament for power to construct such a railway and to subscribe for share capital.

No doubt there were those who, originally, had seen any idea of a railway for Ambleside as 'pie in the sky' but now things were clearly getting serious and anyone who was considering mounting opposition to the project would have to move quickly. Initially the opposition was rather sporadic and there was no group or body of persons who met formally to form an opposition party. However, this would change. In the meantime there was by no means universal acceptance of the project. In November, an article appeared in the *Pall Mall Gazette* and a copy of this was published in the *Kendal Mercury* on 26th of that month. The writer started by describing the scheme as hanging like the Sword of Damocles over the much worried lovers of the Lakes and so it was obvious which side the author would be taking. There is a detailed account of the points being put forward in the argument for the promotion of the 'Ambleside Railway' and these are summed up as being commercial and industrial; quarries, mines and gunpowder works would appear in the vicinity and there would be an easier way for tourists to reach the lake (Windermere) rather than by having to catch a coach after alighting from the train at Windermere station.

There is a verbal swipe at Mr Taylor (although he is not mentioned by name) when it is stated that 'the most active supporter of the scheme, a local innkeeper at Ambleside, offers to take a large number of shares in the hope that it will bring him the business which he now has to divide with his brethren at Bowness and Windermere'. There is also an attack on Colonel Rhodes, whom it is maintained would benefit from the sale of land he holds and, in addition, to further his own ends has offered to give the company land on which to build a station.

This is followed by that well worn argument that the things which visitors come to the Lakes to enjoy would be diminished if the railway is built. The writer envisages 'a soot blackened atmosphere, decaying trees, defiled streams and all the litter, dirt, poverty and squalor which are the common characteristics of our mining and manufacturing districts'. Remarkable, perhaps, that five miles of railway and only just an extension of an already existing line, could do all this!

With that salvo over, the action now passed to the local boards. The first to meet was the Ambleside Local Board. This meeting, on Monday 13th December, was specially convened to consider a notice which had been received from the promoters of the railway regarding the property of the board through which the proposed line would pass and to establish whether or not the board would assent or dissent to the plan. One of the members, Mr Russell, proposed that the board should assent with the proviso that the station was at Blue Hill. However, Mr Jones, the Chairman, pointed out that the scheme would seem to be too advanced to allow this. Whilst it may have been thought this board would have been the keenest of all to see the project advanced, this was by no means the case. There was a proposal to assent, which was seconded but then an amendment was proposed that the board should remain neutral. When voting took place, two of the six voted for the original proposal, one voted for the amendment and the rest abstained. Hardly an enthusiastic response! On a more encouraging note, the Grasmere Local Board voted to support the plan.

1887

Next up was the Kendal Town Council, which met on Tuesday 11th January. It was a lengthy meeting and at one point, during the course of it, what may be seen as a rather surprising suggestion was made. The meeting had been called following representation from the Ambleside Group. The tenor of the whole meeting was extremely positive with no voice being raised in opposition to the scheme. Councillor Wilson informed those present that this was not the first time over the intervening years, following the opening of the Kendal & Windermere, that the council had been approached by those wanting to progress such a scheme and he had been one of a committee of three which had considered the question. However, now there was real action in making the plan a reality. There was criticism of 'people of old antiquated notions like Mr Ruskin and others' who could not or would not see the great benefits railways brought to residents of a particular neighbourhood. It was acknowledged that commerce must be allowed to thrive and that there was benefit in creating the facility for tourists to have access to the area. When the resolution was put that the board should do all it could to support those who were trying to ensure that Ambleside would have a railway, it received unanimous support.

The decision was made to hold a public meeting to discuss the proposal. And the surprise? It was the suggestion that 'they should find if their good old friend Cornelius Nicholson would give them a lift, seeing that he lent his assistance in the formation of the Kendal & Windermere Railway and that he might give them a lift in making a Jubilee branch from Windermere to Ambleside'. (The term 'Jubilee' might well have had two edges to it because not only was it 50 years since the scheme to build the Kendal & Windermere had been formulated but 1887 was the Jubilee year for Queen Victoria and a period when various schemes to celebrate the event would be up for consideration.) Cornelius Nicholson, who was now elderly, was living in Ventnor on the Isle of Wight. After moving from the Kendal district he had been very involved with railway projects and eventually held the post of Superintendent Director of The Great Indian Peninsula Railway.

The last of the local boards to consider the Ambleside Group's proposal was the Windermere Local Board, which met on Wednesday 12th January. There would be no prizes for guessing correctly how they would view the scheme! The initial feeling at the meeting was that it seemed unlikely that the project would succeed and therefore there was little to fear. However, when it was discussed further and it was made clear it was necessary for the board either to assent or dissent, the issue went to a vote and there was a unanimous decision to dissent!

The hope that Cornelius Nicholson might show his arm in the endeavour to bring the railway to Ambleside was not entirely in vain because on 21st January the *Kendal Mercury* published a letter he had written. The content indicates very clearly that in spite of his advancing years, he had changed little in his views about his own achievements. He starts by referring to 'the friendly illusion' Kendal Town Council had made at its meeting to his 'exertions' 50 years previously in bringing the railway to Kendal but then goes off at a tangent to explain why he has not succumbed to the pressure to write a history of the local railways. He acknowledges that he is 'not distinguished by great humility' and recognises such a history would be full of 'egotisms'. He goes on to recall the events leading up to the opening of the Kendal Railway and the word 'I' appears a great number of times. Eventually he gets down to the business in hand,

> My opinion, as an absentee, is of little value, one way or the other, but I am astonished at the want of foresight of the London and North Western Railway Company as owners of the line to Windermere. I came home, in the past summer, taking the Midland Railway at Lakeside and was much struck with the facile approach to Ambleside by the Western shore of the Lake. [And then there is a caveat] Depend on it, as sure as tomorrow's sun succeeds the darkness of this night, the Midland Company will push that line forward before the London and North Western Company are roused from their torpor. That Kendalians is your rival. Beware of it! Who stands still, falls into the rear and loses the goal. I can only prate now at a distance.

In true Nicholson style there follows a quotation,

> I can say with Southey, as fervently as he said it, 'Every valley vale and stream are clear to my memory' ... [and he finishes] ... Still, I cannot be insensible to the material interests of dear old Kendal and my native Ambleside.

Would the magic work again after all those years?

Other letters were published, both in the local and national press, during this period, supporting or opposing the scheme. The whole issue became much more than just a local one. The Ambleside Group were soon alleging that outsiders were interfering to stop the coming of the railway and that such parties should let the local people decide what facilities they felt were in their best interests.

The Bill drawn up for consideration by Parliament, proposed,

> A railway four miles, six furlongs and six chains in length, commencing in the parish of Applethwaite by a junction with the Kendal and Windermere branch of the Lancaster

> and Carlisle Railway of the London and North Western Company at or near the centre of the bridge carrying the said branch railway over Orrest Lane, and terminating in the parish of Ambleside at a point in the field belonging to Colonel Godfrey Rhodes,16 yards or thereabouts south of the fence dividing the said field from the road leading from Ambleside to Stock Ghyll and 43 yards or thereabouts measured in a south westerly direction from the south west corner of the Stock Ghyll bobbin mill.

There were sections which dealt with other aspects, including the proposal to build a roadway and footpath linked with the viaduct over Troutbeck. There was also a proposal for a working agreement with the LNWR. Even so, from the outset the enterprise was seen as what might be described as a private one, promoted by a group of individuals without the co-operation of, or in conjunction with, the LNWR. It might have been thought this company was strangely quiet through the proceedings; not, it was to transpire, without good reason. The capital was put at £155,000 in £10 shares. The Bill was placed before the private examiner for Bills on 21st January. As this stage was a formality, it did not invite any opposition; this, if it was to be made, would come later.

The 21st January was quite a day for the project. Not only did the Bill go before the examiner and the *Kendal Mercury* publish Cornelius Nicholson's letter but the Mayor of Kendal, prompted by the wishes of the town council, when it had met to discuss the issue of extending the Kendal & Windermere Railway to Ambleside, called a public meeting.

Rather like the meeting of the Kendal Town Council, the public meeting was long and lively. Sir Douglas Fox, who would draw up the schemes for the line, spoke warmly in favour of it. Speaker after speaker rose to add support to the proposal for the extension of the Kendal & Windermere to Ambleside and it was seen as a way to bring added benefits to Kendal. There were one or two voices heard which expressed a lack of conviction in the wisdom of such a development. One such person was Mr Whitwell, who said he had four questions to put to those who were promoting the line but he seemed unable to get an opportunity for answers. Perhaps the most telling question was why the LNWR, itself, had not taken the step of building the extension. 'Why, if it was to bring an "El Dorado" had the London and North Western not pursued it more vigorously?' asked Mr Wilson. However, such voices were few and far between and when they were raised the speakers tended to be virtually ridiculed. The mention of Cornelius Nicholson's name and his views, as expressed in his letter, brought shouts of 'Hear, hear'. In spite of what had gone before, there still seemed to be a spectre hanging over the situation that the Furness might build a line to Ambleside and this would be detrimental to the interests of Kendal. When, after a lengthy debate, a proposal was put to the meeting that the extension would be a benefit to Kendal, it was carried with only two dissenting. The Council must have felt that in spite of the vilification it had received from some quarters after supporting the scheme, the public meeting had vindicated its position.

The next move caused quite a stir. On Tuesday 1st February, in Manchester town hall, no less, there was a meeting of a substantial number of influential businessmen. The purpose of this meeting was to consider ways in which the Bill for the rail link to Ambleside could be defeated. One of the people responsible for calling the meeting was William Bell who was one of the honorary secretaries of the Manchester Committee of the Lake District Defence Society. W.H. Hills was also present. Indignation was expressed about the contemplated damage to 'the playground of England'. ('But whose playground?' was the question that would inevitably follow by those who viewed the group as having a certain interest in keeping it for themselves.) Although there was a feeling that the Bill would not become an Act, there was unanimous agreement that the scheme should be opposed and a special committee was set up with the brief 'to take such steps as they thought desirable to oppose the suggested railway'.

By the time the Bill came up for consideration at a meeting of a select committee, the LNWR had shown its hand. It opposed the Bill and was ready to make representation to that effect. The company did not want to build the line or operate it, even if it was built. Nevertheless, at this stage, it may not have had the option, as far as running the line was concerned, if the Bill, incorporating such a clause, became an Act. For all sides, therefore, there was still everything to play for.

The hearing

The Select Committee convened on Tuesday 15th March. The hearing would last for five days, ending on Monday 21st March and there would be detailed questioning over this lengthy period. Sir Henry Selwyn Ibbotson MP presided.

For the purpose of the hearing the business was summed up as considering,

> ... the Ambleside Railway Bill the object of which is to incorporate a company for working a railway from the Kendal and Windermere Railway from Windermere to Ambleside with a roadway and boatway in connection with the railway viaduct over Troutbeck, to charge tolls for the road traffic, to use a portion of the Kendal and Windermere Station, to make working arrangements with the London and North Western Railway and to pay interest during construction.

The proposers were represented by Mr Pember QC who was assisted by Mr Rigg and Mr Faber. On the other side, there were Mr Littler QC, Mr Pope QC and Mr Moon representing the LNWR. Also in opposition were Mr Jeune, for the Earl of Bradford, and, in addition, Captain Dunlop and Mr Cripps for a group of local landowners. Some minor formalities were dealt with and then battle commenced in earnest.

Mr Pember was first up and went through the proposals in some detail. He spent a considerable length of time putting forward the arguments, by now rehearsed many times, which, in the view of the promoters, justified their case. After this protracted presentation he called forward those who would give evidence. The first person to be called was Colonel Rhodes. Whilst the colonel was speaking, there were, at times, outbursts of laughter. It is not clear whether these were of a derisive nature or simply because, for some reason, some of those present found his comments amusing. Certainly, the chairman did not call for silence or chide those who behaved in this manner. For example, when Rhodes said he took a great interest in local [Ambleside] affairs and more so than most, there was laughter. Was this derisory? On the other hand when he stated that there had been opposition 'by aesthetic people who were in the moon' or when he referred to the [Lake District] Defence Society as the 'Offence Society' the laughter was easy to explain. In that first session, evidence was also given for the submission by Mr John Fleming and Mr William Barton, who was agent for the Bank of Westmorland. Littler challenged Barton on the sort of figures that would give rise to a viable scheme and these were considerably higher than it had been thought. At this point the day's deliberations came to a close and resumed again the following day. There was further questioning of William Barton, again, on matters of finance and his evidence, or possibly the lack of it may have played an important role in the outcome of the hearing. Following William Barton came Mr Taylor who, not surprisingly, laid great emphasis on the tourism element in promoting the line. In so doing he was at pains to point out that if the line was to spoil the scenery then it would be defeating the objective which he felt was of great importance. Taylor did point out that the opposition by the 'North Western' was 'a new thing'. Mr Moses Bownass was then called to give evidence and, as a farmer, drew the committee's attention to how he would benefit in this capacity if there were railway facilities. When asked by Littler if he felt that the refusal of the LNWR to work the line would be 'a fatal blot on the scheme', Bownass had to concede that it would. When Mr Horrax, of the bobbin mill, gave evidence, he pointed out the advantage of being able to move goods out without having to transport them to the railhead at Windermere. Mr Jackson, a builder, also felt his and other trades would benefit from the close proximity of a railway. When it was pointed out that there were other witnesses who could be called, if the committee so wished, the chairman made a very pertinent request. He commented 'we would like to be strengthened on one point - that of finance.' The witnesses who followed conveyed little further evidence and were questioned more about their ability and intention to invest in the scheme. Finance was becoming a key issue, it seemed.

During the remaining days there was more searching questioning. Naylor's firm had been provisionally appointed as the contractor for the line and there had been much questioning of those giving evidence for the promoters about how much they were aware of the conditions this company had set out in connection with carrying out the work and how the costs would be met. There were several who seemed to show little knowledge about this aspect and there had been one or two surprises as far as these people were concerned when certain points had been made by those representing those opposing the Bill. In view of this apparent confusion it was agreed, on the advice of Mr Faber, for the promoters, that on day three (Thursday) Naylor should be called to give evidence. Before this happened there was another long stream of witnesses called in support of the Bill and included was the Mayor of Kendal. There is a suggestion that the committee chairman was beginning to feel that whilst it was clear there was a large number of people supporting the Bill there was a certain adequacy achieved already. The one significant question that came up time and time again was 'Would you buy shares in the scheme?' and this was answered in a variety of ways. Some would, some might and some admitted that they could not afford to do so. In the event Mr Naylor was not called on Thursday but Mr Leane who, together with Sir Douglas Fox, had designed the line was called to give evidence. He explained how, of the two projected routes, the one which was less obtrusive on the scenery had been chosen; that the cost would be £32,000 per mile, there would be no tunnels (a strange remark, given the plans) and, further, although he had experienced a hostile reception from the LNWR, he was surprised the company had come out in opposition to the scheme which was, after all, simply an extension of the its line from Windermere.

Friday was another long and taxing day for the promoters. Sir Douglas Fox was questioned and once again cost was very much on the agenda. There was even a suggestion that if the LNWR declined to operate the line, the Ambleside Railway would build its own station at Windermere. When it was disclosed it had been suggested it would be on LNWR property (presumably by some form of compulsory purchase) there were eyebrows raised in the London & North Western camp! At the end of the day Mr Holme, a surveyor, stated that the compensation necessary for those who lost land would be of the order of £24,000.

After the weekend the final day involved very close questioning about financial aspects. Mr Holme, the architect and surveyor, was recalled and asked about the cost that would have to be met by the company to pay those whose land was needed. Again, he put the figure at £24,000, considerably less than the £80,000 that had been suggested elsewhere. However, this figure was challenged and it was thought the figure for the Earl of Bradford's land would be of the order of £20,000. The possibility of easements rather than purchase was discussed as a means of bringing costs down but how such easements would work also presented a problem. Then Mr Naylor was called. When closely quizzed, he said his firm was prepared to make the deposit of £8,000 permanent if the railway was sanctioned. He also felt that if his company took shares in the project, the capital required would be raised locally. He was adamant that his company could build the line for £165,000 and therefore there would be no question that the cost would exceed the capital being asked. It became clearer which way the process was moving when he was asked whether he would start, even though the full capital had not been raised at that stage and what he would do if the balance was not forthcoming. Here he hesitated and said the company would go on with the building but he was not sure what sort of amount his company would be prepared to put in to realize the completion.

The hearing was closed and the Committee retired to consider the Bill. When it reconvened it was announced that the Bill had been thrown out. The reason, on the face of it, had nothing to do with spoiling scenery or unduly taking land but rather a financial factor. The Chairman stated,

> While the Committee sympathised with the inhabitants of the district in their desire to have the line they had come to the conclusion to throw out the bill on the preamble on the ground that they were not satisfied with the financial aspects of the scheme.

So, the hopes for a railway to Ambleside were dashed. There would be those who would lay the blame for this decision squarely on the LNWR, for although the outcome had rested on financial issues it would be felt that the support of the 'North Western' would have carried the day. Instead, the company had chosen to oppose the Bill and what rubbed salt into the wound, was that it had been the prime opponent. Yet the outcome was merely a reflection of the sign of changing circumstances. The time had passed when a small group of individuals in a district such as that around Ambleside could float a scheme to build a railway, even one of just four or five miles long. It was now the great railway empires such as the one based at Euston that would be the planners and the decisions as to what should or should not be built would be taken at central executive levels, not in local village halls.

Cornelius Nicholson summed it up and poured some oil on the wounds in a letter published in the *Kendal Mercury* on 25th March. He wrote:

> I took so prominent a part in originating and carrying a railway through Westmorland, your readers will, I feel sure, excuse my ringing the true knell of the Ambleside project. The noticeable thing about the formal decision of the Select Committee is the declaration of their '*sympathy* with the desires of the inhabitants of the district to have *improved railway facilities*'. This amounts to a moral triumph for the promoters; and is uncalled for by the decision, and unusual in such cases. The routine practice of a Select Committee on a private bill would be to say simply in these words 'Preamble not proved'. So as between the Utilitarians and the Sentimentalists, the latter go to the wall by the judgement of the committee. But the project broke down by the provisions of the contract for the construction of the line, and I am bound to say that any projector with railway experience, looking at these provisions, could have no confidence in the success of the bill. It could not, as the proverb says, possibly hold water.

There is a sort of dramatic irony in this letter. It was probably the last Cornelius Nicholson was to write on any railway matter. He died just over two years later on 5th July, 1889. His last observations, like his first, some 50 years before, had been about a railway in his 'beloved home district'. He died at Ventnor on the Isle of Wight and by then carried the letters FGS, FSA, JP, DL. In the *Illustrated London News* he was described as 'one of the chief pioneers of railway work in England'.

A period of consolidation

With this episode over, things settled down and the line from Oxenholme to Windermere provided services during a period when railways were usually the first choice for the conveyance of passengers and freight. This would be the case for at least the next 16 years. Then the tide would turn with the beginning of World War I and following which, there would be the commencement of radical social and economic change.

The LNWR clearly had an eye to the welfare of its employees (borne out, not least, in the manner in which it provided for those who lived and worked at Crewe) and so it could be reported in January 1888 that the annual supper for those working at Kendal station was held at the Temperance Hotel in Stramongate. The meal was described as 'excellent' being prepared by Mr Taylforth and the men who had to be on duty were not forgotten as 'a good meal was sent to each'. They did, however, miss the entertainment which followed, with the musical section being accompanied by a piano lent by Mr Taylforth and an American organ provided by Wilkinson & Sons. There were comic songs, some solos and readings. At the end Mr Kirkby proposed a toast to the tradesmen of the town and commented that it was pleasing to see a revival in trade which he hoped would be felt in Kendal. After the singing of *Auld Lang Syne* the party ended.

> **Windermere Branch**—The last Train or Engine which will run on the Windermere Branch from Kendal to Windermere, and vice versa, each night (*i.e.*, between the last ordinary Train of one day and the first ordinary Train of the following day), will be targetted between Oxenholme and Windermere with an additional Tail Lamp, which will be painted white and show a white light. When there is no Special, Relief Train, or Engine to run between these hours, the last ordinary Train in each direction must carry the special target. Messrs. PRESTON, Oxenholme, and RHODES, Windermere, to make arrangements for this being strictly carried out. Gatekeepers at Level Crossings must keep a sharp look-out and not close for the night until the last Train or Engine, carrying the special target has passed, unless otherwise advised.

Extract from the LNWR Rule Book 1899.

An idea of the timetabling in this period can be seen in the one given on pages 160 and 161. And so the 19th century drew to a close. There was no real reason to expect things would change very dramatically as the 20th dawned and certainly for a period this proved to be the case.

The 20th century - Years of plenty

Although as early as 1861, George Measom in his *Official Illustrated Guide to The London and North Western Railway* had described Kendal as 'the Halifax of Westmorland', with a walk along the river bringing into view 'more dyed and tanned hides than green fields or trees or flowers', the town never really became the industrial centre which some had envisaged and hoped for 50 years or so before and, indeed, others had feared. Nevertheless, the town and surrounding area did diversify and develop its manufacturing base with the result that rail freight would become increasingly significant during this period. Coupled with this was the increasing demand for commodities such as coal and other consumer items and these would keep the freight element on the Oxenholme to Windermere line high on the agenda for the LNWR.

One of the long standing industries of Kendal, or to be more precise, of Burneside, which still remains today and which used the railway to good effect, was Cropper's Paper Mill. Cornelius Nicholson was associated with this enterprise in the early days of its existence but it was James Cropper who built up an extremely successful business venture. Although not part of the railway, it had strong links with it through men such as James Cropper, who was influential in the promotion of the Kendal & Windermere Railway and, also, the Lancaster & Carlisle Railway. In 1907 he became a Director of the latter. The mill was extensive enough to have its own railway system which originally was narrow gauge. This was eventually converted to standard gauge in order to be compatible with the main railway by which raw materials came in and the finished products were taken out.

In 1903 Webb retired and Whale took over at Crewe. His tenure was a comparatively short one but during his time larger engines made their debut and the 'Precursor' 4-4-0s and 'Experiment' 4-6-0s would visit the line. There would also be the 4-4-2 'Precursor' tanks and the 4-6-0 '19 in. Goods' which were tender engines.

L. & N. W. Ry.

KENDAL and WINDERMERE BRANCH.

With Connections North and South.

	WEEK DAYS.																						SUN	
	ngt	ngt	mrn	mrn	mrn	mrn	mrn		aft	mrn	aft	mrn		mrn	mrn	aft	aft	aft	aft	aft	aft	aft	aft	mrn
LONDON (E'tn) dp	10 0	12 0	..	..	..	..	5 15	..	Mon. & Sats.	7 15	..	..	..	1030	..	..	..	..	..	2 10	..	4 10	†10 0	10 0
Rugby .... „	1155	2 8	..	..	..	..	7 12	..		9 5	..	..	..	1220	..	..	..	..	..	3 58	..	6 2	†1155	1218
Birmingham .. „	1115	3 10	..	..	..	..	7 20	..		9 0	..	..	..	1140	..	..	..	..	..	3 40	..	5 50	†1115	1215
Crewe .... „	2 1	4 42	..	6 0	..	6 40	9 20	..		11 5	..	..	..	..	2 5	..	2 35	..	..	5 40	..	8 5	2 1	2 40
L'pool { L. & N. W.	1245	..	..	7 35	6 10	8 30	9 40	..	1110	1110	..	1210	..	..	2 20	..	3 55	..	..	5 30	..	7 35	1245	2 10
L'pool { L. & Y.	2 40	mrn	..	..	6 10	8 53	10 5	..	11 7	1133	..	1210	..	..	2 47	..	4 10	..	..	5 15	..	6 45	..	1 22
Manc'r { L. & N. W.	1 0	..	..	8 0	6 0	8 15	10 0	..	11 5	11 5	1145	1240	..	..	2 45	..	4 15	..	..	5 40	..	7 30	1 0	3 0
Manc'r { L. & Y....	..	..	..	..	7 5	8‡45	9 50	..	1025	1125	..	..	..	..	2 40	..	4 10	..	..	5§55	..	7 0	1 10	1 30
Wigan	3 1	5 29	..	8 30	7 15	9 35	1043	..	1156	12 7	..	1 10	..	..	3 8	..	4 51	..	..	6 35	..	9 8	3 1	4 10
Preston	3 28	6 10	..	8 58	8 10	1010	1112	..	1225	1237	1245	1 48	..	3 7	3 50	..	5 16	..	..	7 5	..	9 35	3 28	4 50
Lancaster	..	6 38	..	9 26	9 0	1058	1138	..	1249	1 5	1 33	2 10	..	3 33	4 16	..	5 42	..	..	7 31	..	10 6	..	5 46
20 Barrow .. dep.	..	..	..	..	7*0	10 0	10 0	..	..	..	1 5	1 15	..	1 50	1 50	..	4 25	..	..	5 40	..	9 0	..	4 45
20 Ulverston	..	..	..	..	7 31	1029	1029	..	..	..	1 25	..	..	2 21	2 21	..	4 45	..	..	6 11	..	9 22	..	5 16
Carnforth .....dep.	..	6 52	..	9 49	9 25	1116	1155	..	1 5	1 21	1 58	2 26	..	3 49	4 33	..	5 58	..	..	7 48	..	1021	..	6 10
OXENHOLME arr. S.	4 17	7 17	..	10 3	9 55	1134	1212	..	1 23	1 40	2 26	..	..	4 7	4 52	..	6 15	..	..	8 12	..	1040	4 17	6 37
KENDAL....... arr.	4 27	7 30	..	10 9	1015	1155	1225	..	1 31	1 54	2 35	2 48	..	4 20	5 0	..	6 22	..	..	8 20	..	1046	4 27	6 50
Glasgow .....dep.	9 5	..	..	Mons. & Sats. only	..	..	..	..	..	..	..	SATURDAYS ONLY.	1010	..	..	..	..	2 1	..	..	..	6 55	mrn	aft
Edinbro' ..... „	9 10	..	..		..	..	..	..	..	..	..		1020	..	..	2 0	..	2 5	..	..	..	6 0	..	..
Carlisle ....dep.	1210	..	6 50		8 40	9 30	..	..	..	..	..		1 40	1 50	..	4 12	..	5 38	..	..	7 40	8 41	12 5	4 30
Tebay .... „	M	..	7 54		9 38	1051	..	1122	..	..	..		2 37	3 14	..	5 17	..	..	6 55	..	..	A	..	D
14 K'by Lonsdale	..	..	..		8 50	1043	..	..	..	..	..		1 50	..	..	..	..	..	6 8	..	..	..	..	..
14 Sedbergh.. „	..	..	..		9 12	11 2	..	..	..	..	..		2 12	..	..	..	..	..	6 27	..	..	..	..	..
Lowgill .... „	..	..	8 8		..	1123	..	..	..	..	..		..	3 25	..	..	..	..	7 9	..	..	..	..	..
Oxenholme arr. N.	1 29	..	8 20		9 59	1124	..	1239	..	..	..		2 56	3 44	..	5 35	..	6 51	7 26	..	9 15	..	D	6 18
OXENHOLME...dep.	4 23	7 25	8 30	10 4	1010	1150	1220	1246	1 26	1 50	2 30	..	3 5	4 15	4 55	5 45	6 18	7 0	7 35	8 15	9 30	1042	4 23	6 45
KENDAL .....arr.	4 27	7 30	8 35	10 9	1015	1155	1225	1250	1 31	1 54	2 35	2 48	3 10	4 20	5 0	5 50	6 22	7 5	7 40	8 20	9 35	1046	4 27	6 50
Burneside	..	7 38	..	..	1023	..	1233	..	..	2 3	..	Sat ony	3 19	4 29	..	..	6 31	7 13	..	8 28	..	..	..	6 58
Staveley	..	7 45	..	..	1030	..	1238	..	..	2 10	..		3 24	4 31	..	..	6 36	7 18	..	8 33	..	..	..	7 5
WINDERMERE..	4 47	7 55	..	1028	1040	..	1250	..	1 50	2 20	..	3 5	3 35	4 45	5 20	..	6 48	7 30	..	8 45	..	..	4 47	7 15

☞ **FOR COACHES, WINDERMERE TO KESWICK,** see page 41.

D—Stops when required to set down on notice being given.

M—Monday Mornings only from Edinburgh, Glasgow, and Carlisle.

*—Mondays only leave Barrow 7-50, Ulverston 8-10.

§—Saturdays excepted.

†—These times refer to Sat'dy ngt.

‡—Mondays & Sats. excepted.

A—Passengers from Carlisle travel via Carnforth.

Kendal & Windermere line, summer 1897, down trains.

L. & N. W. Ry.

KENDAL and WINDERMERE BRANCH.

With Connections North and South.

WEEK DAYS. / SUN

	mrn	mrn	mrn	mrn	mrn	mrn		mrn	aft	aft	aft	aft	aft	aft	aft	aft	aft	aft	aft	aft		Sun aft
WINDERMERE dep.	7 45	..	8 10	..	9 20	1056	..	1115	1 5	1 35	2 20	..	3 15	..	4 25	5 50	..	6 45	6 50	9 0	..	5 45
Staveley	..	..	8 17	..	9 29	11 4	..	..	1 13	..	2 29	..	3 23	..	4 33	5 59	..	..	7 0	9 8	..	5 58
Burneside	..	..	..	..	9 35	1110	..	..	1 19	..	2 35	..	3 28	..	4 38	6 5	..	..	7 6	9 13	..	6 2
KENDAL	7 59	7 10	8 25	8 50	9 41	1115	..	1129	1 24	1 52	2 40	3 15	3 32	4 0	4 42	6 11	6 45	7 3	7 12	9 18	..	6 7
Oxenholme arr.	..	7 14	8 30	8 55	9 50	1128	..	1138	1 32	2 0	2 48	3 20	3 40	4 5	4 50	6 20	6 50	7 11	7 20	9 24	..	6 14
OXENHOLME dp. North	MONDAYS ONLY.	7 21	..	..	10 0	1137	..	1216	1 43	..	..	3 30	..	4 10	..	6 22	..	MONDAYS and SATURDAYS.	..	..	..	6 40
NORTH. Lowgill arr.		7 40	..	..	1019	..	..	..	..	..	..	3 49	..	..	..	6 44	..		..	..	..	..
14 Sedbergh arr.		7 52	..	..	1031	..	..	..	..	..	..	..	..	5 2	..	7 21	..		..	..	..	..
14 K'by Lonsdale "		8 17	..	..	1056	..	..	..	..	..	..	..	..	5 25	..	7 45	..		..	..	..	..
Tebay arr.		7 48	..	..	1027	1155‡	..	1233	3 5	..	..	3 57	..	4 32	..	6 52	..		..	..	..	C
Penrith "		8 23	..	..	11 5	1 8	..	1 3	2 38	..	..	4 34	..	5 5	..	7 29	..		..	..	..	7 37
Carlisle "		8 50	..	..	1146	1258	..	2 45	3 5	..	..	5 10	..	5 42	..	8 5	..		..	..	..	8 18
Edinburgh (via Cal) "		1232	..	..	..	3 45	..	..	5 50	..	..	8 18	..	8 18	..	1045	..		..	..	..	..
Glasgow .. (via Cal) "		1237	..	..	..	3 40	..	..	6 0	..	..	8 18	..	8 18	..	1035	..		..	..	..	..
OXENHOLME dp. South	..	7 17	8 32	8 58	10 4	1128	..	1146	..	2 10	2 59	..	3 43	..	4 52	6 30	6 55	7 12	7 30	9 27	..	6 22
SOUTH. Carnforth arr.	8 20	7 41	8 48	9 24	1020	1154	..	12 4	..	2 27	3 15	..	4 17	..	5 10	6 48	7 10	7 31	7 56	9 45	..	6 50
17 Ulverston arr.	..	9 4	1019	1019	1228	1228	..	D	..	..	4 21	..	5 31	..	6 54	..	D	..	9 4	..	..	8 29
17 Barrow (Central) "	..	9 35	1050	1050	1255	1253	..	2 0	..	..	4 42	..	5 57	..	7 25	..	8 5	..	9 35	..	..	9 0
Lancaster arr.	8 35	7 56	9 0	9 45	1035	..	..	1216	..	..	3 27	..	4 38	..	5 27	..	7 21	7 42	8 18	10 4	..	7 18
Preston "	9 9	8 48	9 32	1040	1110	..	..	1250	..	3 5	4 0	..	5 38	..	5 58	..	7 55	8 15	9 17	1035	..	8 15
Wigan "	..	9 27	10 1	..	1155	..	..	1 23	..	3 34	4 50	..	..	..	..	..	8 21	8 53	10 5	1122	..	1110
Manc'r L.N.W. (Exc)	10 6	..	1030	..	1234	..	..	2 58	..	5 8	5 17	..	7 6	..	7 6	..	8 59	9 28	11 6	..	..	†1230
Manc'r L. & Y.	1033	10 3	1052	..	1230	..	..	..	..	4 18	5 8	..	7 20	..	6 58	..	9 0	..	1037	1210	..	10 0
L'pool L.N.W. (L.St.)	..	..	1050	..	1240	..	..	3 15	..	4 45	5 40	..	7 15	..	7 15	..	9 10	9 40	11 5	12 0	..	12 0
L'pool L. & Y.	..	1013	1030	..	1225	..	..	..	..	4 37	5 34	..	7 10	..	7 10	..	8 52	..	1117	..	..	1012
Crewe arr.	..	1027	1135	..	1232	..	..	2 34	..	4 30	6 0	..	..	..	7 23	..	..	..	..	12 8	..	12 7
Birmingham "	..	1230	2 6	..	2 45	..	..	4 35	..	6 40	7 55	..	..	..	9 30	..	..	..	..	2 32	..	2 32
Rugby "	..	1228	1 40	..	2 18	..	..	4 20	..	6 30	8 7	..	..	..	..	..	..	..	..	1 58	..	1 56
LONDON (Euston) "	..	2 20	3 30	..	4 15	..	..	6 15	..	8 25	1015	..	..	..	1045	..	..	..	..	3 50	..	3 50

FOR COACHES, KESWICK TO WINDERMERE, see pages 40 & 41.

C—Calls to set down on notice being given. D—A Carriage slipped.

‡—Departs Tebay at 12.9. † Passengers for Manchester change at Warrington, and arrive London Road Station.

Kendal & Windermere line, summer 1897, up trains.

WINDERMERE BRANCH.

DOWN TRAINS. — WEEK DAYS.

Dist'nce	STATIONS.	1 Pas	2 Goods	3 Goods	4 Pas	5 Pas	6 Fur. Pas	7 Pas	8 Pas	9	10 Furn. Pas	11 Pas	12 Pas	13 Pas	14 Pas
	Leave	a.m.	a.m.	a.m.	a.m.	a.m.	a.m.	a.m.	a.m.		a.m.	a.m.	a.m.	p.m.	p m
...	Oxenholme	4 25	6 35	6 50	7 25	8 20	8 55	9 37	10 10	...	10 20	11 30	11 55	12 25	1248
2⅛	Kendal arr.	4 29	6 45	7 0	7 30	8 25	9 0	9 42	10 15	...	10 25	11 35	12 0	12 30	1253
	Kendal dep.	4 32		7 40	7 32				10 17	...				12 32	
4	Burneside	...	See	8 0	7 38	...	...	N.E. Train	10 23	...	...	...	...	12 38	...
6⅝	Staveley arr.	...	note.	8 10	7 43	...	...		10 28	...	...	...	...	12 43	
	Staveley dep.	...	...	8 25	7 45	...	...		10 30	...	...	...	...	12 45	...
10¼	Windermere arr.	4 47	...	8 40	7 55	...	...		10 40	...	...	...	...	12 55	...

STATIONS.	15	16 Road Van Goods	17 Pas	18	19 Pas	20 Pas	21 Pas	22 Fur. Pas	23 Pas	24	25 Pas	26 Pas	27 Exp. Pas
Leave		p.m.	p.m.		p.m.	p.m.	p.m.	p.m.	p.m		p.m.	p.m.	p.m.
Oxenholme	...	1 10	1 50	...	2 34	2 40	3 5	3 20	3 50	...	4 35	5 50	6 4
Kendal arr.	...	1 20	1 54	...	2 39	2 48	3 10	3 25	3 55	...	4 40	5 55	6 8
Kendal dep.	...	2 5	1 57	...		2 50	3 13			...	4 43		6 10
Burneside	...	2 25	2 3	...	...	...	3 19	...	...	...	4 49	...	Frids.
Staveley arr.	...	2 35	2 8	...	...	S O	3 24	...	...	...	4 54	See	only.
Staveley dep.	...	2 50	2 10	...	.	...	3 26	...	...	...	4 56	Note	...
Windermere arr.	...	3 5	2 20	...	...	3 5	3 35	...	...	...	5 5	...	6 25

DOWN TRAINS. — WEEK DAYS—continued. / SUNDAYS.

Distance.	STATIONS.	28 Pas	29 Fur. Pas	30	31 Pas	32 Pas	33 Goods	34 Pas	35	36 Pas	Sun. 1 Pas	Sun. 2 Pas	Sun. 3
	Leave	p.m.	p.m.		p.m.	p.m.	p.m.	p.m.		p.m.	a.m.	p.m.	
...	Oxenholme	6 28	7 10	...	7 30	7 45	8 0	8 35	...	11 0	4 25	6 45	...
2⅛	Kendal arr.	6 32	7 15	...	7 35	7 50	8 10	8 40	...	11 5	4 29	6 50	...
	Kendal dep.	6 34		...				8 43	...		4 32	6 52	...
4	Burneside	6 40	...	...	...	...	...	8 49	..	...	...	6 58	...
6⅝	Staveley arr.	6 45	...	...	...	...	...	8 54	...	...	...	7 3	...
	Staveley dep.	6 47	...	..	...	...	...	8 56	...	...	...	7 5	...
10¼	Windermere arr.	6 57	...	...	...	...	...	9 5	...	...	4 47	7 15	...

UP TRAINS. — WEEK DAYS.

Distance.	STATIONS.	1	2 Pas	3 Pas	4 [illegible]	5 Pas	6 [illegible]	7	8 Pas
	Leave		a.m.	a.m.	a.m.	a.m.	a.m.		a.m
...	Windermere	...	...	8 0	8 30	...	...	...	9 15
3⅝	Staveley	...	...	8 7	M O	...	...	...	9 24
6¼	Burneside	...	...	...	...	...	...	...	9 30
8⅛	Kendal arr.	...	...	8 15	8 45	...	...	...	9 36
	Kendal dep.	...	7 10	8 16	8 46	8 55	9 15	...	9 40
10¼	Oxenholme arr.	...	7 14	8 20	8 50	9 0	9 20	...	9 45

UP TRAINS. — WEEK DAYS—continued.

Dist'nce	STATIONS.	9 Pas	10 Goods	11 Pas	12 Pas	13	14 Goods	15 Furn. Pas	16 Pas	17 Pas	18 C. Empt. W'gns	19 Pas	20 Pas
	Leave	a.m.	a.m.	a.m.	a.m.		a.m.	p.m	p.m.	p.m.	p m.	p.m	p.m.
...	Windermere	N.E. Train	9 40	10 45	11 45	...	...	...	1 0	...	1 10	2 15	...
3⅝	Staveley		10 0	10 54	11 54	...	...	...	1 9	...	1 25	2 24	...
6¼	Burneside		10 25	11 0	12 0	...	...	...	1 15	...	1 40	2 30	...
8⅛	Kendal arr.		10 35	11 6	12 6	...	...	...	1 21	...	1 47	2 36	...
	Kendal dep.	10 30	10 50	11 10	12 10	...	11 55	12 55	1 25	1 45	1 55	2 40	3 30
10¼	Oxenholme arr.	10 35	11 0	11 15	12 14	...	12 3	1 0	1 30	1 50	2 5	2 45	3 35

STATIONS.	21 Pas	22 Pas	23 Furn. Pas	24 Goods	25 Pas	26	27 Pas	28 Pas	29 Furn. Pas	30 Pas	31 Exp. Goods	Sun. 1 Pas	Sun. 2	Sun. 3
Leave	p.m.	p.m.	p.m.	p.m.	p.m.		p.m.	p.m.	p.m.	p.m.	p.m	p.m.		
Windermere	...	4 20	...	4 35	5 50	...	6 40	...	...	9 0	...	5 45	...	...
Staveley	...	4 28	...	4 50	5 59	...	6 49	...	...	9 8	...	5 56	...	...
Burneside	...	4 33	...	5 10	6 5	...	6 55	...	...	9 13	...	6 2	..	...
Kendal arr.	...	4 37	...	5 17	6 11	...	7 1	...	...	9 18	...	6 7	..	...
Kendal dep.	4 5	4 40	5 30	5 50	6 15	...	7 5	7 30	7 50	9 20	9 35	6 9	...	...
Oxenholme arr.	4 10	4 45	5 35	6 0	6 20	...	7 10	7 35	7 55	9 24	9 45	6 14	...	...

No. 2 Down—Will when required run forward to Windermere, departing Kendal 7.55 a.m. On Mondays leaves Oxenholme at 6.10 a.m.

No. 16 Down—On Mondays runs Engine and Break only, Oxenholme to Kendal; on Saturdays does not call at Burneside, and arrives Windermere at 2.45 p.m.

No. 26 Down—When required the Engine of this Train goes forward to Burneside to work a Special to Kendal. Mr. Hafford to provide Breaksman and Break Van.

LNWR timetable for 1899. Note the Furness Railway trains indicated in the appropriate column headings (*see comment about the 'Kendal Tommy' on page 181*).

1904 – Buffalo Bill in Kendal

In 1904 Kendal experienced what could only be described as a remarkable visit. On the morning of Thursday 22nd September Colonel Cody, popularly known as Buffalo Bill, came to town with his Wild West Show. The previous day it had been in Barrow-in-Furness, so there was only a comparatively short distance to travel. The 800 performers and 500 horses were conveyed in waggons, specially designed for the purpose. They made up three trains which were hauled by locomotives belonging to the railway company. The unloading of these trains was apparently done with careful precision, much to the fascination of those who turned out to watch and the whole retinue was taken to the field at Longlands, just opposite the place where the agricultural show was held in that period. It was set up surprisingly quickly and ready for a 2.00 pm performance. About 9,000 people attended this performance and 8,000, the evening performance. Many visited the various side-shows during the day. The whole event was seen as a great spectacle which would not have been possible without the facility of the railway!

Plans for an improved station at Windermere

Also in this period (1906-08) the LNWR rolled out a very impressive plan for upgrading Windermere station (National Archive RAIL 10/1180). The scheme included a new booking hall with a new façade at the western end, a new house for the station master, storage for luggage brought in advance, extra toilets and a parcels office. In addition there was an improved cab and omnibus stand to the north of the station. The estimated cost of the work was £4,500. The result was a station 'more befitting the importance of the terminus'.

A further boost to facilities was agreed at a meeting of the Directors of the LNWR on 15th November, 1907. It was resolved to provide improved accommodation at the refreshment room at Windermere station. The cost of the refurbishment would be £500 and as a consequence of doing the work it was decided that in future the company would take over the management of this area.

At the outset of 1908 things did not change significantly; in fact there was a measure of growth. An incident with a certain sense of *déjà vu* occurred at the beginning of July when the end carriage in a set of empty carriages which was being moved down to the end of platform three at Windermere, jumped the buffers ('stop block' in the parlance of the day) and crashed into the end wall. There was some alarm but no injuries. And there was some good news for Mr H. Johnson, when he was informed, in July, that his lease of the area for accommodating cattle at Kendal would be renewed for a further 10 years at a cost of £10.

It was in this era, early in the 20th century, that the 'Club Carriage' was introduced. Businessmen with their splendid residences, some of which have already been mentioned, travelled regularly, if not each day, to Manchester or Liverpool and the district around, in order to run their various enterprises. In many cases, these men had grown used to a level of opulence which they no doubt felt fitted their position. Motivated by this desire to have the best

This photograph shows the track layout to the north of Oxenholme station. The express is on the up main line. The branch to Kendal sweeps away to the top left of the picture with the tracks on the left linking the branch to platform 3. The tracks crossing the centre of the photograph are the connections from the branch to platform 1 and to the branch from platform 2.

Margaret Duff Collection

An unidentified LNWR 2-2-2-2 locomotive is seen at Oxenholme with a southbound passenger train around the turn of the 20th century. *John Alsop Collection*

available, they wished to embody this in their journey to business by rail and so they arranged for a specially adapted carriage to be placed at their disposal. It became known as the 'Club Coach' and was used on a morning train out from Windermere and on an evening train back. It boasted sumptuous Edwardian elegance with all the facilities, within the constraints of a railway carriage, which a gentleman's club should have. There was, as befitted such an environment, a well defined protocol of practice and behaviour. London gentlemen would repair to their clubs after a day's work; these northern gentlemen were able to do the same but their club was on wheels, conveying them home after the labours of the day!

Tourism booms

Tourism, as well as industry, was on the ascendant in this period and this was true for both incoming tourists making their way to the railhead at Windermere and, further, at certain times of year, especially holiday periods, significant numbers of local people going out to visit and, possibly, holiday in other places which were increasingly further afield. The LNWR, keen to promote the line as serving a tourist destination, introduced sets of postcards in order to publicize this. These cards did not show pictures of locomotives with their trains, as some companies had done, but rather beauty spots were depicted, albeit, in rather artistically glowing tones.

A reflection of the growth is shown by figures for 1908. In this year, for example, the Easter excursions advertised by the LNWR included trips, on Maundy Thursday from Windermere and Kendal for three, five or six days to London and for five, eight or 15 days to Brighton, Hastings, Portsmouth, Bournemouth, Guernsey and Jersey. There were also trips to Bath, Bristol, Exeter and Plymouth from Kendal for five, eight, 10 or 15 days. For those wanting to go north, there were trips to Carlisle, Glasgow, Edinburgh and Aberdeen from Windermere and from Kendal, for four, nine or 17 days. Merthyr, Cardiff, Carmarthen and Swansea were also possible destinations from Windermere and Kendal and these trips were repeated on the following Saturday. Those who were possibly less adventurous or had a more limited purse could take a trip to Manchester or Liverpool from Windermere and Kendal for four or five days.

On Good Friday there were less ambitious offers; to Windermere from Kendal and Carnforth and also Morecambe from Windermere and Kendal. This was also the case on Easter Monday when there were trips to Carlisle and Morecambe.

All this illustrates what was possible, by this time, when getting away for a holiday, for those who had the means to do so. In effect, nowhere was really out of reach. The people of Windermere, Kendal and district were able to travel the country with ease.

In commenting on the heavy traffic experienced over the Easter period, it was reported that on Good Friday some 400 people went to Windermere with 263 doing so on Monday. On Monday 470 went to Morecambe and it was noted that only 'a few' went to Blackpool on either day!

This crowd of people standing outside Kendal station in LNWR days would, judging by the large (but sadly illegible) banner, be on some form of rally. Rallies were very popular in this period and the railway enabled large numbers of people to gather together. Note the children's clothing and the little girl standing on her own in the centre. *Margaret Duff Collection*

Kendal station with bookstall on the right *circa* 1905. There are numerous direction signs to be seen. *John Alsop Collection*

Kendal station looking towards Windermere *circa* 1900. *John Alsop Collection*

Kendal *circa* 1905 looking towards Oxenholme. *John Alsop Collection*

A general view of Windermere station in 1900. *John Alsop Collection*

Windermere *circa* 1905, note the well stocked bookstall and associated advertising.
John Alsop Collection

However, by 1908 there had been significant growth in the motor industry, resulting in more and more cars appearing on England's roads. This was as much the case in the Lake District as anywhere else. The impact of this was manifest in a number of ways. There was the startling increase, in the district, of incidents involving motor cars which led to prosecutions. Then again, whilst the wrath of those who wanted to secure the sanctity of the Lake District had once been vented, initially, on those who planned the Kendal & Windermere Railway, it now turned on those who promoted what was seen as the intrusion of a far more damaging invader. One writer, for example, laments the fact that once winding roads have been straightened out (they were even tarring some of them!), hedges and walls have been replaced by iron railings and everywhere there seems to be noise, dust, smell and the sound of hooting. In short, it was argued, the Lake District was being ruined by this onslaught. Yet this onslaught was destined to continue and, indeed, to grow. It would pose a threat to the railways; a threat the like of which had never been experienced before. What is more, its real effects would have been felt much sooner had the advance not been stemmed, at least for a time, by the outbreak of war. In these most unfortunate circumstances local railways gained something of a reprieve.

Whale retires and Bowen-Cooke takes over at Crewe

There was an important change at Crewe in 1908. Whale retired. Bowen-Cooke took over and in the next 11 years some of his locomotives would be seen on the Oxenholme to Windermere line. These would include the 4-4-0 'George the Fifth' and 4-6-0 'Prince of Wales' classes. Towards the end of Bowen-Cooke's time, his 0-8-0 'G1' goods and the 4-6-0 'Claughtons' appeared, the latter hauling the through passenger services. Many of Bowen-Cooke's engines would still be running after the LNWR had passed into history.

1911

Various track modifications were carried out from time to time, particularly at Windermere. Reports occasionally drew attention to anomalies, as in late July 1911, when it was stated that a new siding connection with the down running line at the Oxenholme end of the station was ready for inspection. (Some notes made at the time point out that the signal box has 33 levers in use, six spaces and one spare lever.) An observation was made that the arrangements were inconsistent. There was a disc signal for entering the siding but no signal for coming out of the siding. This was in contrast, according to the report, to a siding alongside the new one, which had a signal for leaving the siding but no signal for entering it! Colonel Yorke, who carried out the inspection wanted to know why the two sidings had been treated differently. There seems to be no reply to this query but by October it was pointed out that a disc signal had been installed to control the exit from the new siding. Scribbled across the memo folder, in what might be perceived to be a rather grudging manner, are the words 'I suppose we should now sanction the use of the works'. This was done on 3rd November.

N.D.—No. 45 8 <>

L. & N. W. R.

THE BUSINESS AND PLEASURE LINE

Every Wednesday & Saturday to

KENDAL & WINDERMERE,

(L. & N. W. or LAKE SIDE)

and Each Week-Day to

LANCASTER & MORECAMBE

During JANUARY, 1914, and until further notice,

CHEAP DAY EXCURSION TICKETS

WILL BE ISSUED AS UNDER :—

FROM	Times of Starting. To Kendal & Windermere. Wednesdays and Saturdays.		To Lancaster and Morecambe. Each Week-day	To Lancaster and Morecambe. Sats. only.	RETURN FARES. To Kendal and Windermere. Wednesday & Saturday. First Class.	Third Class.	To Lancaster and Morecambe. Each Week-day. First Class.	Third Class.
	a.m.	a.m.	a.m.	a.m.				
LIVERPOOL (Lime St)	6 5	9 50	8 20	11 35				
,, (Edge Hill)	6 10	9 55	8 25	11 40				
Broad Green	...	...	8 30	11 45				
Huyton	6 22	9 27	8 37	11 52				
Garston	...	8 23	7 25	...				
Prescot	6 28	9 33	8 43	11 57				
Eccleston Park	...	9 36	8 46	noon 12 0				
Thatto Heath	6 35	9 40	8 49	12 4				
Widnes	7 14	9 45	7 14 9 34 10 39	... ...				
Appleton	...	...	...	...				
ST. HELENS B	6 42	10 14	8 57	12 10				
St. Helens Junction	6 59	9 46	8 15	12 0	8/-	4/-	6/6	3/3
Carr Mill	...	...	...	12 14				
Garswood	6 51	9 6	9 6	12 19				
Bryn	6 55	9 10	9 10	12 23				
WARRINGTON B	7 11	9 58	8 35 9 58	a.m 11 55				
Earlestown	7 22	...	8 45	12 4				
Pennington	8 10	...	7 29 9 9	... ...				
Newton-le-Willows	7 38	...	9 6	12 8				
Lowton	7 41	...	9 10	12 11				
Golborne	7 47	...	9 14	12 15				
Bamfurlong	7 52	...	9 19	12 24				
Howe Bridge	6 36	...	9 4	11 40				
Hindley Green	6 40	...	9 8	11 44	7/6	3/9	6/-	3/-
Platt Bridge	6 46	...	9 15	11 50				
WIGAN	8 5	10 34	7 15 8 5 9 30	p.m. 12 40	7/6	3/9	5/6	2/9

B—Tickets from these stations to Kendal and Windermere are issued on Thursdays and Saturdays.

SEE OVER.

Excursion fares to Kendal and Windermere etc. LNWR, January 1914.

The Great War

On Monday 3rd August, 1914, Mr Prudholme, a postal worker, stood on Kendal station waiting to catch a train. He found himself amongst a considerable throng as holiday makers jostled on the platform around him. However, Mr Prudholme stood out in the crowd because he was in the uniform of a naval reservist. He was one of the first, possibly *the* first, from the locality to go off to the war. When he boarded the train for a journey which would eventually take him to Chatham, a cheer went up from a group of friends and relatives who had come to say goodbye. Two days later, about 70 men of H Company of the Territorials assembled at 8.00 am at the Drill Hall in Windermere. They then marched through the village to the railway station and, being in good spirits, whistled as they marched. At the station the men were met by a large group of people, including wives and relatives, who had come to say their farewells. The 9.25 am left with fog detonators exploding and hats and handkerchiefs being waved. There were other men to follow on the trains at 10.50 am and 11.30 am. The stations on the line were experiencing a new phenomenon; that of men going off to war. Many would never return but would be buried near the battlefield where they had fallen. At midnight on 4th August, under 'The Regulation of Forces Act (1871)' the railways of Britain were put under Government control. On 14th August, it was announced that the summer services on the line would be suspended. These would be replaced by the winter timetable.

This war, terrible though it was, had little impact on the line from Oxenholme to Windermere. It was during this period that Windermere engine shed was closed, never to reopen.

1919-1923

The aftermath of World War I, the 'Great War', as it became known, was to have a profound effect on the way the railways would be organized. When the war was over there appeared to be reluctance on the part of the Government to hand back the railways to their appropriate groups of Directors. Some play was made on the fact that during the war the Government had invested considerable sums of money into the railway system and it was anxious to claw back some of this. A good deal of rumbling started to take place in certain Boardrooms with a lot of anxiety as far as some of the smaller companies were concerned. Over the next few years, the Government would reveal its real intention behind the reticence shown; a move to rationalize the railway system and replace the numerous companies with just four large ones.

The result of this decision would be that the LNWR, as a company, would also be consigned to history; it would become part of the London Midland & Scottish Railway: the LMS.

So what difference would this make to the line between Oxenholme and Windermere? The answer was that in most respects it would make very little;

The approach to Windermere station in LNWR days as depicted on a contemporary postcard
John Alsop Collection

A photograph taken outside Kendal station. The date is unknown but the vehicle would seem to be a charabanc waiting for passengers. *Margaret Duff Collection*

until, that is, another war began. In fact, initially, after the end of the war, perhaps partly because of the uncertainty, there seemed to be some reticence on the part of the LNWR to revitalize tourism in the Lake District by way of excursions. There is little evidence in the press of advertisements for outings, in a way there had been in the past. In contrast, the local operators of tours by (motor) coaches were much quicker off the mark. Three years after the end of the war (1921) there seemed to be little in the way of railway excursions and yet companies such as Rutter's Tours and the Winder Motor Co. were offering day trips from Kendal, during the summer months, to a wide variety of local destinations, with some further afield, for example to Blackpool and, for a three day tour, Edinburgh. The prices were not unreasonable ranging from 5*s*. 6*d*. to Grange and Newby Bridge to 10*s*. 0*d*. for Blackpool.

In 1922 there was what might have been seen as a greater threat to the line to Windermere. The Kendal Motor Bus Co. Ltd announced that from Good Friday, 14th April, it would be operating a daily service (except on Sundays) between Kendal and Bowness. The list of places at which the bus would call was given as Burneside, Staveley and Windermere. Yes! They were exactly the same as those served by the railway. However, the bus would go on to Bowness. A 'Workman's' bus would leave All Hallows at 7.15 am with further departures at 10.00 am, 1.30 and 4.15 pm. There would be additional services on Good Friday and Easter Monday and there would also be special services on Thursdays and Saturdays. The price of a single fare ranged from 3*d*. for the journey from Kendal to Burneside to 1*s*. 3*d*. from Kendal to Bowness. In addition, on the 'workman's bus', a return fare could be had for the usual price of a single journey. There would be connections in some cases to travel to Ambleside, with coaches owned by Feirns Ltd. The 'sting in the tail' was in the statement 'The bus will pick up and set down passengers where desired'. This was something the railway could not do! Perhaps the LNWR was losing heart or perhaps there was too much to be done in readiness for what was about to happen to Britain's railway system. Although it was reported that large numbers of people came to the area by train (and, incidentally, by 'motor vehicles of the small private type and motorbikes with side-cars by their hundreds') at Easter, there were still no signs of special excursions from Kendal and district for the holiday season. Times were certainly changing as was evident by the large numbers of advertisements in the local press for motor vehicles, both for goods and passengers. A new era was dawning and the railways would need to look to their laurels.

A review of motive power up to the demise of the LNWR

The first locomotives for use on the Kendal & Windermere Railway came from what had been the Grand Junction Railway but which by 1846 had been absorbed into the LNWR. These engines came from Crewe. There were four at the outset (although on occasions additional ones were borrowed) and they were of the Crewe-Allen (or Trevithick-Allen) type. There were 2-2-2 types used for goods and 2-4-0 types for passenger work. One of the 2-4-0 engines was

Ramsbottom 'Newton' class 2-4-0 No. 1532 *Hampden* and its crew and other staff at Windermere in LNWR days. *(Both) Margaret Duff Collection*

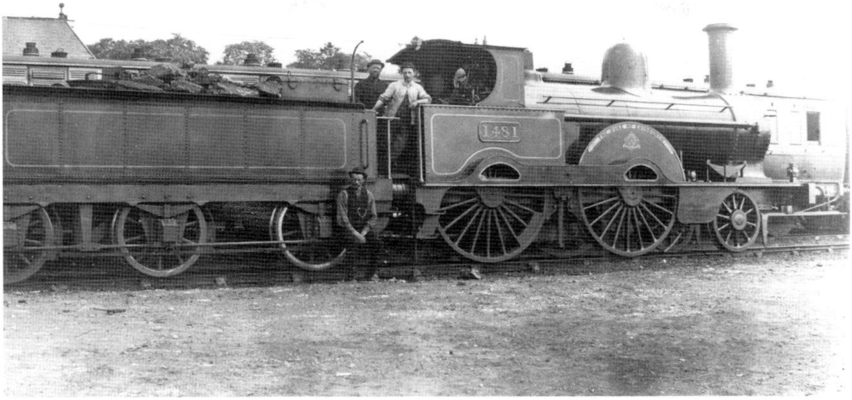

'Newton' class 2-4-0 No. 1481 *The Duke of Edinburgh* at Windermere in LNWR days.
Margaret Duff Collection

named *The Lady of the Lake*, a name which was to be carried over to other locomotives when the original had been scrapped. Later, under the E.B. Wilson regime, which lasted from 1850 for two years, that company, which was also building 2-2-2 tank engines and 2-4-0 types with inside cylinders for hauling passenger trains, supplied the motive power.

In 1856, the Kendal & Windermere asked Carrett-Marshall of Leeds to supply it with a locomotive. It has already been noted that this was, in some ways, an interesting company to choose because Carrett-Marshall, at the Sun Foundry on Dewsbury Road in Leeds, was not noted for building railway locomotives. The locomotive purchased was a 2-2-2 with a central large pair of driving wheels and two other sets of smaller wheels, one under the smokebox and the other, at the rear, under the coal bunker. It was, in effect, a tank engine. It was originally named *Grasmere* but later became *Dwarf*. There were changes at Crewe in 1857 which later became apparent on the Kendal & Windermere Railway. John Ramsbottom became the chief mechanical engineer (CME), holding the post until 1871. During this period, after the leasing in 1860, there were considerable changes in the types of motive power used on the line, as, indeed, there would be over the whole of the Northern Division of the LNWR. The class 'DX' 0-6-0 Goods appeared, as did the 'Problem' 2-2-2, the 'Samson' 2-4-0 and the 'Newton' 2-4-0 classes, as visitors to the line. (And there may be a clue here about why, and approximately when, the Kendal & Windermere locomotive originally named *Grasmere* was renamed *Dwarf*. It was during his first three years in office that Ramsbottom started production of the 'DX' 0-6-0 class and No. 532 was named *Grasmere*. When the LNWR leased the Kendal &

An LNWR 'Whitworth' class 2-4-0 on a Windermere express at Kendal *circa* 1905.
John Alsop Collection

Windermere in 1860, using two locomotives named *Grasmere* was probably not seen as being appropriate. Could it be that this is why the original *Grasmere* became *Dwarf*?)

In 1871 Francis Webb followed John Ramsbottom at Crewe and his time there, which lasted until 1903, witnessed the introduction of further new classes of locomotives with many seeing service after the LNWR had passed into history. The Windermere line saw his 0-6-0 '17 in. Coal Engine' class, the 'Precursor' 2-4-0 and 'Precedent' 2-4-0 classes. Webb's 2-4-2 tanks worked the local services. It was under Webb's successor, George Whale, when larger engines made their debut and his 'Precursor' 4-4-0s and 'Experiment' 4-6-0s visited the line. There were also the 4-4-2 'Precursor' tanks, used on local services, and the 4-6-0 '19 in. Goods' which were tender engines. Under Bowen-Cooke, who came after Whale in 1908, the LNWR reached its zenith in locomotive building. The Oxenholme to Windermere line would see Bowen-Cooke's 4-4-0 'George the Fifth' and 4-6-0 'Prince of Wales' classes and, later, his 0-8-0 'G1' goods and the mighty 4-6-0 'Claughtons' hauling the through passenger services. These locomotives had a working life of many years left in them after the passing of the LNWR.

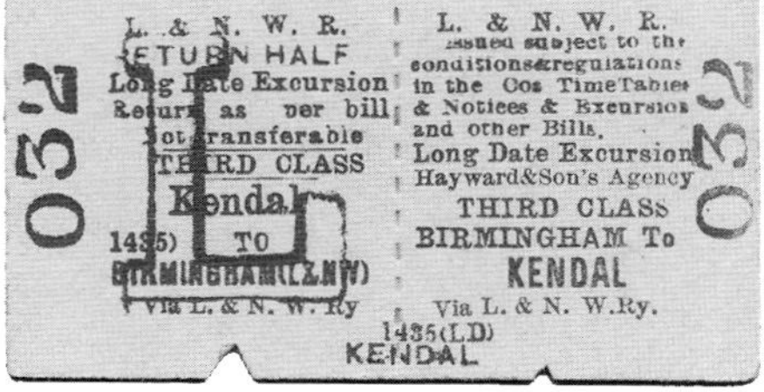

Chapter Eight

Grouping, Nationalization and Privatization

Under the Act of 14th August, 1921, which was not to be fully implemented until 1st January, 1923, in order to give the railway companies time to carry out the necessary administration, the railways of Britain were to be grouped into four companies. The Government had stopped short of nationalization, so avoiding the huge financial commitment that it would have to meet, following the financial ravages that the war had inflicted on the railway system. In this scheme, the LNWR became part of the London Midland & Scottish Railway, so finding itself side by side with what had been, on many previous occasions, an old rival, namely the Midland Railway. There has been much debate about which of these two companies had the greater influence in shaping this new group. In some ways, the Midland can be seen as the stronger contender in this respect, in spite of the fact that Euston became the operational headquarters and the new CME was George Hughes. Hughes had taken up the role of CME in the LNWR after its amalgamation with the Lancashire & Yorkshire Railway during 1921. He was considered to be senior to H.P.M. Beames who had become CME, following Bowen-Cooke, in 1920.

The impact on the line between Oxenholme and Windermere was not particularly dramatic. The LMS in annexing the Furness Railway, did acquire the boats on Windermere which the latter had previously owned and there was a more integrated approach to services because of this.

However, the LMS soon set to work revitalizing the excursion trade that the Oxenholme to Windermere line could offer to those who lived within the vicinity. Advertising under the heading 'LM&SR', on 23rd March a special train was run from Windermere to Aintree for the Grand National. It left Windermere at 8.10 am with provision for both first class passengers (15*s*. 7*d*.) and third class (9*s*. 4*d*.). It called at Staveley, Burneside, Kendal and Oxenholme and thereafter Milnthorpe, Burton and Holme. The return from Aintree was at 6.10 pm.

Easter saw a large range of excursions. These were to London, Birmingham and the Midlands; also to the South Coast, to Lancashire towns and coastal resorts and the West of England. On Thursday 29th March, these could be for five, six, eight, 10 and 15 days and on Saturday 31st March for three, four, six, eight and 15 days. And these were not the half of what was on offer! Also on 29th March there were excursions for five, six, eight, 10 and 15 days to North Wales; to Oswestry, Welshpool, Aberystwyth, Barmouth and the Cambrian District. In addition there were destinations including Skipton, Ilkley, Harrogate, Keighley, Shipley, Bradford, Leeds, Sheffield, York and Scarborough, Newcastle, Tynemouth, South Shields &c [*sic*]. These were all from Windermere, Kendal and Oxenholme. There were further excursions on Easter Monday. The simple fact was that if the tourist wanted to travel any distance in reasonable comfort and time, there was no alternative to the railway. The coach operators may have started to make inroads into the trade but at this stage, realistically, they were only able to offer destinations that were relatively close at hand; places such as Keswick, Grange-over-Sands, Morecambe and Blackpool.

Working Timetable for the Windermere Branch 1923 (LMS)

Weekdays - Down Trains

				MO		MO		MX								†	#	SO
		1.40am Pass. from Crewe	Work Goods train	C Goods men's Edge Hill	1.40am Pass. Goods Lancaster	7.30am Pass. Goods Grange	8.08am Pass. from Preston	7.55am Pass Grange	10.05am Pass from Lancaster	11.50am Pass. from Lancaster	11.50am Pass. from §	Pass. from	Pass. from	Pass. from	Pass.			
			am	am	am	am	am	am	am	am	am	am	am	am	am	am	pm	pm	pm
Oxenholme	dep.		4.57	5.55	6.10	6.20	6.55	7.30	7.50	8.19	8.30	8.38	9.55	10.20	10.35	11.40	12.32	12.32	
Kendal	arr.		5.02	6.03	6.16	6.30	7.05	7.40	7.55	8.24	8.35	8.43	10.00	10.25	10.40	11.45	12.37	12.37	
	dep.		5.15		6.19	6.55	8.45		8.05		8.38			10.30		12.05	12.45	12.45	1.00
Burneside					6.24	7.15	9.05		8.10					10.35		12.10		12.50	1.08
Staveley	arr.				6.30	7.25	9.15		8.16					10.41		12.16		12.56	1.15
	dep.				6.33	7.35	9.25		8.19					10.44		12.19		1.00	1.18
Windermere	arr.		5.30		6.42	7.50	9.40	*	8.28		8.53			10.53		12.28	1.00	1.10	1.27

		SO	SO	SX	MO	ThO														
		6.45am Goods ¶ Euston Branch	1.20pm Pass from Lanc Manchester	2.55pm Pass from Grange	11.10am Pass. from Springs ≠	5.05pm Pass from Arnside	4.15pm Pass. from M'chester	5.05 Goods from M'chester	6.35 Pass from Grange	Live- Pass. from	7.10pm Pass. train Carnforth	5.15pm Pass. from Liverpool/	Seasonal Pass. Crewe Preston	10.12pm stock from	Pass. from	Pass.	from	excursion	Pass.	
			pm	pm	pm	pm	pm	pm	pm	pm	pm	pm	pm	pm	pm	pm	pm	pm	pm	pm
Oxenholme	dep.		1.30	1.47	2.10	3.17	3.27	4.46	5.10	5.24	6.10	6.34	6.56	7.05	7.10	7.20	7.40	9.00	9.10	11.23
Kendal	arr.		1.40	1.52	2.15	3.22	3.32	4.51	5.20	5.29	6.15	6.39	7.01	7.10	7.15	7.25	7.45	9.05	9.15	11.28
	dep.		2.30	1.58		3.25		4.55				6.42	7.04		7.55	7.28		9.10	9.30	
Burneside			2.50	2.03		3.30		5.00				6.47				7.33		9.15	9.35	
Staveley	arr.		3.00	2.09		3.36		5.05				6.53			C	7.39		9.21	9.41	
	dep.		3.15	2.12		3.39		5.09				6.56				7.41		9.26	9.46	
Windermere	arr.		3.30	2.21		3.48		5.18				7.05	7.19		8.25	7.50		9.35	9.55	

Notes

*	When required, runs to Windermere.
†	Except Saturdays until 1st June, then daily.
#	Saturdays only. Will not run after 26th May
§	Commences 2nd June
¶	Runs to Kendal only on Saturdays. On Mondays leaves Oxenholme at 1.15 pm, arrives Kendal 1.25. Forward unaltered.
≠	On Saturdays leaves Oxenholme at 11.31 pm, arrives Kendal 11.36 pm
C	Conditional (runs only when required)
MO	Mondays Only
MX	Mondays excepted
SO	Saturdays only
SX	Saturdays excepted
ThO	Thursdays only

Working Timetable for the Windermere Branch 1923 (LMS)

Weekdays - Up Trains

		ThO Pass. for Lancaster	C Pass. for Lancaster	Pass. for Pass.	Pass. for M'chester	Pass. for Preston	Excursion Grange	Empty goods Pass.	Pass. for Pass.	Pass. for †	Goods Pass.	Goods Crewe	Grange	Pass.	Pass.			
			am	am	am	am	am	am	am	am	am	am	am	am	pm	pm	am/pm	pm
Windermere	dep.			7.00		8.30			8.40		9.10	9.25	10.25	11.25			11.40	1.00
Staveley	dep.			7.10					8.50		9.20	9.45	10.35	11.35			12.20	1.10
Burneside	dep.			7.16		*			8.56		9.26	10.05	10.41	11.41			12.45	1.16
Kendal	arr.			7.21		8.42			9.01		9.31	10.12	10.46	11.46			12.55	1.21
	dep.		7.00	7.25	8.15	8.44	8.50	8.56		9.04	9.35	10.35	10.50	11.49	12.50	1.00	1.10	
Oxenholme	arr.		7.06	7.31	8.21	8.49	8.56	9.02		9.10	9.41	10.45	10.56	11.55	12.56	1.06	1.20	

		for Pass. Branch	for Lancaster SO	Pass. for Springs SX	Goods for Arnside	Pass. for Pass.	Pass. for Preston	Pass. for Ingleton	Goods for Grange	Pass. for Pass.	Goods Preston	Goods Grange	Pass. Preston	Pass.	Pass.		
			pm	pm	pm	pm	pm	pm	pm	pm	pm	pm	pm	pm	pm	pm	pm
Windermere	dep.		2.15				4.00	4.35					4.45	5.30	6.30		8.35
Staveley	dep.		2.25		#		4.10							5.39	6.40		8.45
Burneside	dep.		2.31		2.37		4.16						5.25	5.44	6.46		8.51
Kendal	arr.		2.36		2.45		4.21	4.50					5.35	5.49	6.51		8.56
	dep.		2.40	3.25	3.40	4.00	4.25	4.55	5.05	5.15	5.40	6.40	7.30	5.51	7.00	7.55	9.02
Oxenholme	arr.		2.46	3.31	3.50	4.06	4.31	5.01	5.11	5.25	5.46	6.50	7.40	5.56	7.06	8.01	9.08

Sundays
Down trains

		Pass. from Crewe	1.40am Excursion §	10.00pm Excursion Pass. Morecambe	from §	Excursion to Excursion Pass.
			am	pm	pm	pm
Oxenholme	dep.		4.57	2.36	7.10	10.45
Kendal	arr.		5.02	2.41	7.15	10.50
	dep.		5.15	2.42	7.19	
Burneside	dep.			2.47	7.24	20th May
Staveley	arr.			2.53	7.30	to
	dep.			2.56	7.33	23rd Sep.
Windermere	arr.		5.30	3.05	7.42	

Up trains

		§	Lancaster	
		pm	pm	pm
Windermere	dep.		5.10	8.00
Staveley	dep.		5.20	8.10
Burneside	dep.		5.26	8.16
Kendal	arr.		5.31	8.21
	dep.	12.50	5.34	8.22
Oxenholme	arr.	12.56	5.40	8.28

Additional notes

* Calls at Burneside at 8.38am on Tuesdays to pick up, arrive Kendal at 8.43; depart 8.44 am. † Runs on Tuesdays, Thursdays and Saturdays only. # Conditional Burneside to Kendal. § Runs 20th May to 23rd September.

In 1924 the thrust to promote tourism continued. In February it was announced that the LMS had agreed to pay an equal share with the combined contributions of the Windermere Advertising & Development Committee, following the decision for it to join the Federated Lake District Advertising Association, and this would result in the printing of 10,000 posters promoting the Lake District. These would be displayed on 2,000 stations which would not be confined only to LMS stations but would include some stations on the Southern Railway as well. This seemed to be effective because large numbers of tourists visited over the Easter period, although they were no doubt also encouraged by a particularly welcome spell of very good weather.

Once again, as the summer season approached, there appeared advertisements for a wide range of tours from Kendal to many places throughout England. Other types of excursions began to be available, not least day outings to football fixtures; Preston North End and Everton being high on the list. In 1930 it was possible to leave Windermere at 11.15 am and for 4*s*. 6*d*. return, travel to Liverpool, watch Everton play and leave Liverpool at 10.25 pm to travel home. For four shillings, fans of Preston North End could travel on the same train and get off at Preston. The stipulation was that seats had to be booked in advance. Tourism continued to thrive with visitors coming in at holiday times such as Easter, in their thousands, brought by special trains from Manchester, Liverpool and the industrial towns and cities in the North of England. Fares for those coming in on excursions to visit Windermere often had included in the price of a ticket, a trip up to Ambleside on one of the boats.

Traffic reaches a peak

So it was that for 21 years, following World War I, the line would continue to provide a service for the local community and bring in the visitors from a wide variety of destinations. For many, this was an era with a sense of euphoria, following the horrors of the years of war. The period actually became known as 'the roaring twenties' and in spite of the economic depression which followed, in the 1930s, for many in this country holidaying in places such as the Lakes became fashionable and popular. The railways were able to capitalize on this trend and the line from Oxenholme to Windermere would enjoy a level of considerable prosperity as a result. For Kendal, in particular, this period would also be one which would see a marked increase in the considerable activity associated with the handling of goods traffic. This would reach a peak which would continue through until the outbreak of another war. Coal remained a substantial part of this trade as an incoming commodity. It would be used by industrial consumers including, for example, Kendal Gas Works. The domestic supplies would be handled by the coal merchants, of which there was a considerable number, based in the station yard. The railway also brought in other types of fuel; oil and petrol among them. Fish came in and was readily available. Timber arrived in large quantities for both those whose products depended on joinery and those who acted as timber merchants. The list of outgoing commodities was very impressive. This included the machinery made by the engineering works of Ibis and Gilks and there was Kendal snuff, renowned for its quality; carpets and other soft furnishings made in the locality were also taken out by rail. Cropper's Paper Mill, as it grew and flourished, required very large quantities of coal and raw materials. These were brought in by rail and the finished products taken out in the same way. K Shoes was an extremely important and thriving local industry which used the railway for bringing in tons of raw materials and sending out a vast amount of its finished products. All this coal, wood pulp, timber, oil, petrol, fish, paper products, shoes, snuff, carpets and furniture required transportation and the simple fact of the matter was that at the time there was only one possible way of moving such large amounts and that was by rail. Without the railway, the movement of goods on this enormous scale just would not have been possible. The consequence, needless to say, was a considerable string of freight trains which started bringing in the materials early in the day, continuing throughout much of the morning and then taking the produce out as the day progressed. And this produce was distributed widely. One of the most notable departures was the 'evening goods' from Kendal to Euston (later re-routed to Marylebone) which took out a whole range of items including a large consignment from K Shoes. Some of these products were dropped-off en route.

On another front, it was still possible, in the 1930s, to see the station master at Windermere turn out in his regalia each morning to welcome those who, having collected their copies of *The Times* newspaper, came to board the Club Coach.

Throughout the country, this period was something of a heyday for local rail services. A multitude of small (and some not so small) tank engines were hurrying and bustling about, each pulling a few coaches (often of mixed origin and some decidedly past their best). They would be taking people off to work in offices and factories; they would be taking folk to the shops or for a day out and they would be taking children to school. The area around the Lakes was no exception. As far as Kendal was concerned, this activity included trains carrying in passengers who lived in the Cartmel Peninsula and Barrow. The 'Kendal Tommy', first run in the 1870s, continued to run from Grange and travelled via Arnside, Sandside, Milnthorpe, Heversham and Oxenholme into Kendal. Originally this service had been operated by the Furness Railway and was hauled by an engine shedded at Grange. It is not clear when it was given the title the 'Kendal Tommy'. Ron Thompson, now in his nineties, and living in Cartmel, recalls travelling on this train in the 1930s, from Grange; together with other office workers going to Kendal. After the day's work was over, the train would take them home. Some say the morning train was the 'Tommy'; others that the title applied, as well, to the train returning in the evening but not, it is insisted, to the service during the day! It ceased running during the war years, in May 1942. Another train was named unofficially the 'Kendal Whip'. This was the last train of the day to Kendal and arrived late on Thursdays and Saturdays from Morecambe, although it has to be said that there is some debate about this and whether or not the name was given to a Preston train. What seems to be the general consensus is that it was well-known for the fact that amongst the passengers there would be late night revellers returning home! It is possible people used the term loosely and applied it differently over the years. The

The Ingleton to Kendal 'market day' train en route for Kendal in 1927. Motive power is a 'Precursor' 4-4-2 tank. *J. McGowan*

Oxenholme station looking south. A Fowler 'Royal Scot' class 4-6-0 on a main line train is waiting at platform 2 on the left with a Stanier 4-6-0 on a Windermere train at platform 3 on the right. *Margaret Duff Collection*

origins of the names 'Kendal Tommy' and 'Kendal Whip' are uncertain and seem to be lost in the mists of time, although there are plenty who feel that they have the explanation (but not always the same one) and will readily provide a rationale for these unusual titles.

A further service operating between the wars gave the people of Ingleton, Sedbergh and district the opportunity to go to Kendal market. In each direction two reversals were needed, one at Lowgill and the other at Oxenholme. The return service, which left Kendal at 5.05 pm, included horse boxes and cattle wagons for the benefit of those needing to get livestock back after a day at the market. The service was operated by an Oxenholme engine which, in this period, was usually a 'Precursor' tank. It seems Yorkshiremen did not feel the need to come up with a name for this particular train! It was also in this period that the 'Lakes Express' became very much a feature of the services provided for Windermere. The train, running between Euston and Windermere, was operating as a through fast service when the LMS took over and acquired the title in the late 1920s. Windermere was not the only destination as it had a section for Keswick as well. The train left Euston at mid-day and the Windermere section arrived at 5.25 pm. The up train left Windermere at 11.15 am and was joined by the section from Keswick at Oxenholme. Arrival in London was at 4.50 pm. The passengers in the Windermere section might have thought themselves to be somewhat privileged because it was their section which initially included the restaurant facilities! This service lasted well into the period when the railways were nationalized.

All in all, then, these were busy years on the Oxenholme to Windermere stretch of line. In this period it seems that for many, life was well measured and had a clearly defined sense of order to it. Yet all this was soon to end. In 1939, Britain found itself at war with Germany once more.

England declared war on Germany in September and, as on the previous occasion when this happened, there would be Government control of the nation's railway system; this came into effect in the same month. Later in that month, the LMS issued what was described as an 'Emergency Timetable'. The line from Oxenholme to Kendal still enjoyed a good service. The timetable for the local service is as follows:

Weekdays

Down	*am*	*am*	*am*	*am*	*noon*	*pm*	*pm*	*pm*	*pm*	*pm*
Oxenholme *dep.*	5.54		8.33	10.15	12.00	2.17	5.20	6.30	7.13*	9.40
Kendal	5.59	6.13	8.41	10.24	12.06	2.24	5.27	6.36	7.20	9.47
Burneside			8.45	10.28	12.10	2.28	5.31	6.40	7.24	9.51
Staveley			8.52	10.37	12.18	2.37	5.40	6.49	7.32	10.00
Windermere *arr.*		6.28	9.02	10.46	12.28	2.47	5.50	6.59	7.42	10.10

Up	*am*	*am*	*am*	*am*	*am*	*pm*	*pm*	*pm*	*pm*	*pm*
Windermere *dep.*	7.00	8.00	9.25	11.15	11.55†	1.53	3.35	5.40		8.35
Staveley	7.07		9.33	11.24	12.02	2.00	3.42	5.47		8.44
Burneside	7.12	8.07#	9.37	11.30	12.07	2.05	3.47	5.52		8.49
Kendal	7.18	8.12	9.45	11.39	12.15	2.12	3.54	5.57	6.07	8.58
Oxenholme *arr.*	7.74	8.20	9.51	11.45	12.22	2.18	3.59		6.13	9.04

* – Except Saturdays, † – Saturdays only, # – Stops on Tuesdays and Fridays to take up.

Timetable from 27th September, 1948

Weekdays§

Down trains	*am*	*am*	*am*	*am*	*am*	*pm*	*pm*	*pm*	*pm*	*pm*	*pm*	*pm*	*pm*	*pm*	*pm*
								S	E			E	E		
Oxenholme *dep.*	4.49	8.12	8.52	9.35	10.15	12.20	2.12	3.30	4.10	4.42	5.15	6.42	6.59	9.25	11.40
Kendal	5.01	8.21†	9.03	9.41	10.24†	12.28	2.20	3.36	4.16	4.49	5.21	6.48	7.06	9.33#	11.45
Burneside		8.25	9.07	9.45	10.28	12.32	2.24	3.40	4.20	4.53	5.25	6.52	7.10	9.37	
Staveley		8.32	9.14	9.54	10.37	12.40	2.33	3.48	4.28	5.02	5.34	7.00	7.17	9.46	
Windermere *arr.*	5.16	8.42	9.24	10.03	10.46	12.50	2.48	3.58	4.38	5.12	5.44	7.11	7.24	9.56	

Up trains	*am*	*am*	*am*	*am*	*noon*	*pm*	*pm*	*pm*	*pm*
					S				
Windermere *dep.*	6.30	8.10	9.20	11.00	12.00	2.00	3.25	5.45	8.30
Staveley	6.37	8.17	9.27	11.07	12.07	2.07	3.32	5.52	8.39
Burneside	6.42	8.22	9.32	11.13	12.12	2.12	3.37	5.57	8.44
Kendal	6.49	8.29	9.40	11.21	12.19	2.19	3.44	6.05	8.54†
Oxenholme *arr.*	6.55	8.35	9.46	11.27	12.25	2.25	3.50	6.11	9.00

Sundays

Down Trains	*am*	*pm*	*pm*	*pm*
Oxenholme *dep.*	5.48	12.08	2.50	6.15
Kendal	6.07*	12.15	2.55	6.21
Burneside		12.19	2.59	6.25
Staveley		12.28	3.08	6.34
Windermere *arr.*	6.25	12.38	3.18	6.44

Up Trains	*am*	*pm*	*pm*
Windermere *dep.*	10.45	5.05	8.00
Staveley	10.52	5.12	8.07
Burneside	10.57	5.17	8.12
Kendal	11.05	5.25	8.20
Oxenholme *arr.*	11.11	5.32	8.26

* arrives 5.53. † arrive 5 minutes earlier. # arrives 4 minutes earlier. § 'Weekdays' in this period meant all days except Sunday. S denotes 'Saturdays only' and E denotes 'Except Saturdays'.

The 9.20 am and 8.30 pm on weekdays had through carriages to London. The 11.00 am had through carriages to London on Fridays only. In spite of this abundance of trains, the future would prove to have a strong element of uncertainty in it.

Down	*am*	*am*	*Sundays* *pm*	*pm*
Oxenholme *dep.*	5.54		2.50	6.30
Kendal	5.59	6.13	2.56	6.36
Burneside			3.00	6.40
Staveley			3.09	6.49
Windermere *arr.*		6.28	3.19	6.59

Up	*pm*	*pm*
Windermere *dep.*	4.30	8.00
Staveley	4.37	8.07
Burneside	4.42	8.12
Kendal	4.53	8.20
Oxenholme *arr.*	5.00	8.26

This war, rather like the last, did not, in most respects, impact significantly on the Oxenholme to Windermere line. Nevertheless, there was traffic associated with the war effort. The setting up of the 'Sunderland' flying boat project on Lake Windermere called on the services of the railway to bring in materials and personnel. German prisoners of war were also brought to the area on the railway and much has been made of the fact that one of those prisoners, detained in the area after being brought in on the line, included Franz von Werra, the man who became infamous as 'The One Who Got Away'.

The post-war period and nationalization

The war finished in 1945 and things slowly began to return to a level of normality. However, rather as had happened after World War I, the Government of the day had plans for changing Britain's railway system. This time the change would be even more radical than on the previous occasion because the policy was now 'ownership by the people'. In addition, with the war over, it would soon become apparent that far reaching changes would take place both in society and the ways in which the facilities for that society would be organized and operated. The running of the railways by four private companies would very soon end. Government control, seen as a strength for the unification of the nation, would lead to the nationalization of a number of sections of industry.

In 1948, only just over two years after the war had finished, the railways were taken under state control. From now on it would be 'British Railways' (later 'British Rail') (BR) which would take charge of the system. At first this did not seem to pose anything of a threat and certainly not to a short length of track between Oxenholme and Windermere. The post-war period would no doubt see services resume, the visitors would return and everything would be just as it had always been. This, however, soon proved to be a rather over optimistic view of things. Certainly the visitors would return to the Lake District but in significantly different ways.

The timetable for 1948 (*opposite*) shows a line operating a busy service together with some through trains between Windermere to Euston.

Kendal was an important railhead for bringing in agricultural machinery as demonstrated by this load of tractors. There is no date attached to the photograph but it was probably taken in the 1960s. Note the variety and quantity of vans and wagons in the background.

Margaret Duff Collection

Coal was a vital commodity carried on the railway. This is just one of the many private owner wagons to be seen in the goods yards pre-nationalization. *Margaret Duff Collection*

Changes, threats and closures

It soon became very apparent that the end of World War II meant the emerging science and technology, formerly applied to the war effort, could now be used for civilian objectives. A prime example of this was the continuing development of the internal combustion engine and this development was given a high priority. The outcome was that road transport was soon rapidly on the ascendancy. World War I, as mentioned previously, had to some extent stemmed the progress in this sphere of civilian development and the comparatively brief period, just 21 years, between the end of that war and the next, whilst seeing obvious progress, had not had enough rein to realize the full potential before the demands of another war effort diverted energies away from civilian endeavours to those of winning that war. In the mid-1940s, even with the war over, the railways remained, for the most part, and certainly in the North-West, reliant on steam traction as their motive power. As far as road transport was concerned, things were definitely changing and changing rapidly. This was demonstrated, in part, quite early on. Whitsuntide of 1948 turned out to be the hottest of the century so far, in the Lake District, with temperatures reaching 85ºF (30ºC) at times. The great British public, recovering from the restrictions of war, was to turn out in large numbers to take advantage of this weather. Excursion trains were busy; some 1,500 people went off to Morecambe from Kendal and district over the three-day period and around 500 in total came into Windermere on Sunday and Monday by rail. However, that was not all. On Saturday it was reported that 80 'motor' coaches each hour passed through Kendal en route for the Lakes with 110 in the same period the following day. Bus services, it was reported, had 'triplicated'. Some 10,000 visitors had come into the Lakes by coach. Here was a challenge, indeed a threat, to the railway! Yet there was one irony about all this. The result of ending the 'basic petrol' arrangement meant, for example, that although there were more than 200 coaches in the car park at Bowness on Saturday and 300 on Sunday, there were very few cars. Needless to say, this situation would soon change. The simple fact was that more and more visitors were coming to the Lakes by road than the number arriving by train. It was in this hot spell, when the fire services' resources were considerably stretched as they were called upon to tackle a number of fires, that there was a fire at Staveley signal box.

By the early 1950s there were growing concerns in the corridors of power; concerns which resulted in a view that the national railway system, including that in the North-West and the Lake District, needed to be carefully reviewed and appraised. Economic factors appeared to be uppermost and it was very apparent that the small branch lines were now losing money. Much of the freight, once taken by rail, was moving to the roads with the economy of the once-handling principle beginning to have a telling impact on costs. However, one ray of hope did appear in this period for many branch lines, including the line from Oxenholme to Windermere, and that was the decision by British Railways to introduce diesel-multiple-units (dmus). It was hoped these would be popular with the travelling public because the units were clean, comparatively comfortable and very airy, unlike some of the rather aged coaching stock in use, which had certainly seen better days. In addition to local services, by 1956, British Railways was advertising 'Scenic Excursion by Modern Diesel Train' to the Lakes, from

PLEASE RETAIN THIS BILL FOR REFERENCE F324/R (HD)

Sunday 4th August 1957

SPECIAL EXCURSION

TO

KENDAL & WINDERMERE TOWN

with

** BOOKINGS TO AMBLESIDE AND LAKESIDE

FROM	Departure Times	RETURN FARES SECOND CLASS			
		Kendal	Windermere Town	Ambleside	Lakeside
	a m	s d	s d	s d	s d
LIVERPOOL Exchange } A	10 10	10/3	11/6	13/-	13/6
ORMSKIRK } A	10 32	8/9	9/9	11/3	11/9
Going forward from PRESTON at	a m 11 30				
ARRIVAL TIMES		p m 12 43	p m 12 58	SEE NOTE**	
Return times same day		p m 7 20	p m 7 05		

LIGHT REFRESHMENTS WILL BE AVAILABLE AT POPULAR PRICES

NOTE— A Change at Preston in each direction

**Passengers for Ambleside and Lakeside travel by rail to and from Windermere Town making their own way to and from Bowness Pier, going forward to and returning from destination by any of the steamer services shown below.

		p m	p m	p m	p m	p m	p m	p m	p m	p m
Lakeside	Depart	—	—	—	—	—	3 10	3 45	—	5 00
Bowness	Arrive	—	—	—	—	—	3 45	4 20	—	5 35
Bowness	Depart	1 05	1 35	2 00	2 45	3 20	3 55	4 25	5 20	—
Ambleside	Arrive	1 35	2 05	2 30	3 15	3 50	4 25	4 55	5 50	—
		p m	p m	p m	p m	p m	p m	p m	p m	p m
Ambleside	Depart	1 45	2 00	2 15	2 45	3 35	4 05	4 45	5 25	6 00
Bowness	Arrive	2 10	2 25	2 40	3 10	4 00	4 30	5 10	5 50	6 25
Bowness	Depart	2 20	2 35	—	—	4 10	—	—	—	—
Lakeside	Arrive	3 00	3 20	—	—	4 50	—	—	—	—

SPECIAL NOTICE

Intending passengers may obtain tickets in connection with this Excursion available as from LIVERPOOL Exchange at any of the following stations:—

Aintree Sefton Arms
Allerton
Bank Hall
Bebington & New Ferry
Birkenhead Central
Birkenhead Park
Birkenhead Woodside
Bootle Oriel Road
Broad Green
Bromborough
Clubmoor
Cressington
Edge Hill
Fazakerley
Garston
Hoylake
Hunt's Cross
Huyton
Kirkby
Kirkdale
Knotty Ash
Leasowe
Liscard and Poulton
Maghull
Marsh Lane
Meols
Mersey Road
Moreton
Mossley Hill
New Brighton
Old Roan
Orrell Park
Preston Road
Rainhill
Roby
Rock Ferry
St. Michael's
Sandhills
Seacombe
Seaforth
Sefton Park
Town Green & Aughton
Wallasey Grove Road
Walton Junction
Warbreck
Waterloo
Wavertree
West Allerton
West Derby
West Kirby,

Such passengers will be required to make their own way to and from LIVERPOOL EXCHANGE at their own expense

CONDITIONS OF ISSUE

These tickets are issued subject to the British Transport Commission's published Regulaions and Conditions applicable to British Railways exhibited at their Stations or obtainable free of charge at Station Booking Offices.

Children under three years of age, free; three years and under fourteen, half-fares.

TICKETS CAN BE OBTAINED IN ADVANCE AT THE STATIONS AND OFFICIAL RAILWAY AGENTS.

Further information will be supplied on application to Stations, Official Railway Agents, or to T. C. BYROM, District Passenger Manager, Lime Street Station, Liverpool, (Tel. No. ROYal 8292, Ext. 40).

JULY 1957 BR 35000

BRITISH RAILWAYS

F 324/R (HD) A. GILMOUR, Garston

Special Excursion from Liverpool to Kendal and Windermere Town. British Railways, 1957.

places such as Carlisle and Liverpool. Yet in spite of attempts to win over the public by offering a more attractive way to travel by rail, there was a growing tide of tourists and local people who chose the alternatives. The motor car with its door-to-door destination facility and bus and coach travel with greater flexibility, were proving a big attraction. Increasing losses on the railway system, it was argued, were not acceptable now that the railways were in the public sector. The future of some lines became uncertain. One illustration of the way in which times had changed can be seen in the passing of the former glory of the Club Coach. Although there was what might be described as a token gesture for those who might use this type of service, it was only that; the first class coach set aside had, in reality, little to offer that could be considered outstanding. The fact was, the whole concept of such a service had really become anachronistic and even though it lingered on into the 1960s, it was hardly more than this provision of a coach for use by those who, for whatever reason, felt they needed this sort of facility. In any case its demise would have been assured when, towards the end of the 1960s, the through services to Manchester, the destination originally associated with this exclusive form of travel, were discontinued.

The axe began to fall in the North when Ernest Marples was Minister for Transport, although the really draconian measures to close lines came later under the direction of Dr Beeching with his 'Beeching Plan'.

More closures and concern

The Eden Valley Railway was closed in 1962 (by Ernest Marples) after a long and hard fought battle to keep it open. This, together with the Stainmore route, meant there was no obvious link for those living in the North-East around Darlington to access the Lake District by rail. The Coniston Railway also closed in 1962. Strategically it was poorly placed for tourism, branching as it did from the line north of Barrow, a considerable distance from the West Coast main line. There was a measure of concern growing about other links, including the line to Windermere and in August, Mr Wells, of Windermere, wrote to the *Westmorland Gazette* voicing a view which was no doubt shared by others. He pointed out that reports indicated the future of the line was uncertain because it carried less than 6,000 passengers each week. He argued a case for the minority and urged that decisions should not be made on the matter of cost alone but by bearing in mind resulting inconvenience for those who chose to use the train. He commented 'Man can now orbit the earth: soon he may not be able to travel from Oxenholme to Windermere with a trunk or a pram'. Although he was later accused of indulging in nostalgia there was no doubt that he was speaking for a substantial number as the developing situation gave rise to worried speculation. During this period, the line from Penrith to Cockermouth remained open for a time and it was assumed that if the line from Penrith to Keswick and beyond was secure, there was good reason to assume that the line from Oxenholme to Windermere would be so as well; Keswick and Windermere being seen as very much on a par when it came to tourism but (it could be argued) the branch from Oxenholme served a larger conurbation, namely Kendal, and this, possibly, gave it a greater advantage. It was during this year that the locomotive

ORGANISED RAMBLES

Led by Official Guides of the
Liverpool Ramblers' Association

SUNDAY 13th JULY 1958

SPECIAL EXCURSION

to

CARNFORTH KENDAL STAVELEY and WINDERMERE TOWN

**WITH BOOKINGS TO AMBLESIDE and LAKESIDE

FROM	Departure Times	RETURN FARES—SECOND CLASS Carn-forth	Kendal	Stave-ley	Winder-mere Town	Amble-side	Lake-side
	a m	s d	s d	s d	s d	s d	s d
LIVERPOOL LIME STREET	9 30	8 / 6	11 / –	12 / 3	12 / 3	13 / 9	14 / 3
HUYTON	9 46	8 / 6	11 / –	12 / 3	12 / 3	13 / 9	14 / 3
PRESCOT	9 52	8 / 6	11 / –	12 / 3	12 / 3	13 / 9	14 / 3
THATTO HEATH	9 58	8 / 6	10 / 6	11 / 9	11 / 9	13 / 3	13 / 9
ST. HELENS SHAW STREET	10 04	8 / 3	10 / 3	11 / 6	11 / 6	13 / –	13 / 6
WIGAN NORTH WESTERN	10 34	6 / 9	9 / –	10 / –	10 / –	11 / 6	12 / –
ARRIVAL TIMES		a m 11 45	p m 12 26	p m 12 37	p m 12 48	** See Note.	
RETURN TIMES SAME DAY		p m 7 42	p m 7 17	p m 7 08	p m 7 00		
		Due Liverpool Lime Street 9-46 p.m.					

LIGHT REFRESHMENTS WILL BE AVAILABLE AT POPULAR PRICES

**Passengers for Ambleside and Lakeside travel by rail to and from Windermere Town making their own way to and from Bowness Pier, going forward to and returning from destination by any of the steamer services shown below.

		p m	p m	p m	p m	p m	p m	p m	p m	p m	p m
Lakeside	depart	....	....	....	....	....	....	3 20	....	....	4 50
Bowness	arrive	....	....	....	....	....	....	3 55	....	....	5 25
Bowness	depart	1 05	1 35	2 05	2 35	3 05	3 35	4 05	4 35	5 05	5 35
Ambleside	arrive	1 35	2 05	2 35	3 05	3 35	4 05	4 35	5 05	5 35	6 05
		p m	p m	p m	p m	p m	p m	p m	p m	p m	p m
Ambleside	depart	1 45	2 15	2 45	3 15	3 45	4 15	4 45	5 15	5 45	6 15
Bowness	arrive	2 10	2 45	3 15	3 40	4 15	4 45	5 10	5 45	6 15	6 40
Bowness	depart	2 20	....	....	3 50	....	....	....	....	....	....
Lakeside	arrive	3 00	....	....	4 30	....	....	....	....	....	....

FOR FULL DETAILS OF RAMBLES—SEE OVERLEAF

CONDITIONS OF ISSUE.

These tickets are issued subject to the British Transport Commission's published Regulations and Conditions applicable to British Railways exhibited at their stations or obtainable free of charge at station booking offices.

Children under three years of age, free ; three years and under fourteen, half-fares.

TICKETS CAN BE OBTAINED IN ADVANCE AT THE STATIONS AND OFFICIAL RAILWAY AGENTS.

Further information will be supplied on application to the Stations, Official Railway Agents, or to T. C. BYROM, District Passenger Manager, Lime Street Station, Liverpool. (Tel. No. : ROYal 8292, Ext. 40).

PLEASE TURN OVER

LONDON MIDLAND

F.314/R (HD)

Organized Rambles to the Lake District with the Ramblers' Association. London Midland, 1958.

SUNDAY 13th JULY 1958

CONDUCTED RAMBLES TO

THE LAKE DISTRICT

Any Passengers travelling on this train are invited to take part in the Organised Rambles detailed below, but those not accustomed to long walks, should refrain from joining the STRENUOUS party. The rambles are led by Official Guides of the Ramblers' Association (Liverpool Area), who will wear green armlets and who are prepared to give every assistance to those desiring information regarding the district.

A. STRENUOUS. Book to Windermere but alight at Staveley to climb Ill Bell, 2,476 feet, though not the highest point, is the most pronounced peak in this range, and provides views amongst the most beautiful in the Lake District. The full length of Windermere can be seen to the south with its islands, sylvan shores and graceful hill-outlines, while in strong contrast to the north, west and east are the numerous Lakeland peaks and deep set valleys. The route is from Staveley for a most pleasant walk up the Kent Valley to Kentmere to climb up the Garbourn Pass and to Old Yoke, 2,163 feet, for the ascent of Ill Bell. The descent includes the summit of Froswick before joining the Roman Road track leading down Hagg Gill into the lovely Troutbeck Valley and through the village of Troutbeck, one of the most picturesque consisting of a main street nearly a mile and a half long with cluster after cluster of low roofed white and grey cottages contrasting beautifully with the emerald verdure of the valley, to proceed to Windermere via Orrest Head for the return.

B. MODERATE. Book to and alight at Windermere to climb Orrest Head, 784 feet, a small eminence behind the town of Windermere for the first extensive view of the Lakeland, including most of its peaks and the lake itself visible from end to end. The walk continues to the quaint straggling village of Troutbeck with its many picturesque dwellings, before proceeding to climb the easy accessible Wansfell Pike, 1,581 feet, for even more extensive views, The descent may be made to Jenkins Crag and down to Waterhead Pier, at the north end of the lake, for the lake steamer to Bowness for a short walk back to Windermere or the descent may be made to Ambleside to return to Windermere by bus.

C. EASY. Book to Ambleside and alight at Windermere to proceed through the town to Bowness Pier for the lake steamer to Waterhead. From Waterhead the walk, one of the finest in the Lake District, in fact in the whole country, proceeds to Clappersgate to ascend steeply up Todd Crag, 695 feet, and over Loughrigg Fell, although only 1,101 feet high provides fine views of Grasmere as well as Windermere Lake, and peaks such as Helvellyn, Coniston Old Man, The Langdales and many others. A steep but easy descent is made to Loughrigg Terrace, a really delightful walk which leads from Grasmere Lake to Rydal Water, an area visited and praised by many great poets. The River Rothay flowing between Rydal Water and Windermere Lake is then followed by a quiet road to Waterhead for return by the lake steamer.

If the numbers in parties are unduly large, additional guides will be provided to conduct these walks in a reverse direction, and routes will be altered at the discretion of the leaders to suit prevailing conditions.

Passengers intending to join one of the parties should carry food for two meals, and be equipped with strong footwear and a light waterproof.

Enquiries regarding rambles, etc., should be addressed to the Hon. Secretary, Ramblers' Trains Committee Mr. R. Gordon, 23 York Road, Maghull, Nr. Liverpool.

THE RAMBLERS' ASSOCIATION

LIVERPOOL DISTRICT AND NORTH WALES AREA

PLEASE MAKE A NOTE OF THE NEXT ORGANISED RAMBLE:—

BANK HOLIDAY MONDAY, 4th AUGUST, 1958 to CHINLEY, CHAPEL-EN-LE-FRITH, MILLERS DALE, and BUXTON for many delightful walks over the lovely Derbyshire Hills and along the picturesque dales such as Monsal Dale, Millers Dale, Chee Dale and many others all within easy reach of Buxton, a beautiful inland holiday resort and spa.

FULL DETAILS TO BE ANNOUNCED LATER

June, 1958 B.R. 35001

F. 314/R (H.D.) (Back) Hugh Evans and Sons., Ltd., Liverpool

Organized Rambles to the Lake District with the Ramblers' Association. London Midland, 1958.

A down express headed by Stanier class '5MT' 4-6-0 No. 45446 leaves Kendal *en route* for Windermere in the early 1960s. *Margaret Duff Collection*

Waiting to depart Windermere for Oxenholme in September 1961 is Stanier class '4MT' 2-6-4T No. 42571. *RCTS/HUO0398*

Fowler 2-6-4T No 42359 and Fairburn 2-6-4T No 42613 approach Oxenholme with a train from Windermere on 12th July, 1963. *Derek Cross*

Stanier 'Jubilee' class 4-6-0 No 45595 *Southern Rhodesia* nears Oxenholme on 27th July, 1963 with the up 'Lakes Express'. *Derek Cross*

Stanier 'Jubilee' class 4-6-0 No 45697 *Achilles* sets off from Oxenholme with a Liverpool to Windermere service on 27th July, 1963. Notice the locomotive is coupled to a Fowler tender.
Derek Cross

Ex-LMS '4F' 0-6-0 No 44440 waits at the signals on the Windermere branch with the daily pick-up goods on 27th July, 1963. On the main line Stanier 'Black Five' 4-6-0 No 44709 passes through the station with the Saturdays-only Newcastle to Blackpool service. *Derek Cross*

Stanier 'Black Five' class 4-6-0 No. 44982 heads the up 'Lakes Express' on the branch near Oxenholme on 31st August, 1963. *Derek Cross*

A double-headed train from Liverpool for Windermere near Oxenholme on 31st August, 1963. The bunker-first pilot engine is Stanier '4MT' class 2-6-4T No. 42613 and the train engine is Stanier 'Jubilee' class 4-6-0 No. 45717 *Dauntless*. *Derek Cross*

A busy scene at the junction at Oxenholme on 18th July, 1964. In the foreground two main line trains pass. English Electric type '4' (later class '40') 1Co-Co1 No. D336 is on a Crewe-Perth train and is being approached by Stanier 'Jubilee' class 4-6-0 No. 45726 *Vindictive* with a southbound freight. Between these two locomotives can be seen Stanier '8F' class 2-8-0 No. 48371 waiting to come off the Windermere branch with a freight train. *Derek Cross*

Branch passenger trains pass near the junction with the main line. Fairburn 2-6-4T No. 42147 is awaiting the signal to enter Oxenholme station as it is approached by Fowler 2-6-4T No. 42322 on 21st August, 1964. *Derek Cross*

shed at Oxenholme was closed. This was not really seen as particularly threatening as far as the branch was concerned but it was another sign of the general trend.

Another 'incident' at Windermere

During this period of uncertainty there was yet another incident at Windermere involving runaway coaches. On Monday 13th August, 1962, a train from Blackpool had arrived in the early afternoon and the passengers had alighted. Following this, the carriages were being moved to platform 2 in readiness for use later in the day. As the carriages were being gravity shunted into the platform, the brakes failed, two of the coaches became derailed and the train entered the station at 'considerable speed', smashing through the stop blocks and hitting a stone wall. The description of what happened next portrays a cataclysmic event. 'Stones, bricks and wood of the [station] canopy came crashing down as the thirty foot coach plunged into the forecourt. With one set of bogies torn off, the coach came to rest almost up against a fence, completely clear of the station'. Five pillars supporting the awning of the station forecourt were demolished and the brick and stone awning itself came crashing down. The entrance to the station master's house and a banana warehouse were both blocked. Perhaps the most remarkable aspect of this event was that nobody was killed or injured. The passengers had all left the station and because the day was dry there were no people, such as taxi drivers, sheltering under the awning. Colonel Hutchinson must have been turning in his grave but at least this was to be the last of this sort of mishap. There are no accounts of repairs but clearly they were done so that the station could function properly again.

1964 to 1968

In 1964 Staveley lost its goods traffic facility and also its signal box but on a brighter note there was still a good number of 'outings' possible by rail. There were trains from Windermere, Staveley, Burneside and Kendal to Blackpool, Bolton, Manchester, Southport and Liverpool three times each weekday in the mornings. Between 3rd and 30th March, on Tuesdays, Wednesdays and Thursdays, it was possible to visit the Ideal Homes Exhibition, although it meant a long day with departures from Windermere (at 8.30 am) and Kendal and returning from Euston at 11.15 pm. The 'day' returns to London on Friday nights until 20th March were a bit of a misnomer, leaving Kendal at 8.54 pm and returning the following day at 11.15 pm.

Meanwhile, any optimism about the future of the Cockermouth to Penrith line remaining open was short lived but when, in 1966, it was announced by Barbara Castle, the Transport Minister, that the section between Cockermouth and Keswick would be closed, there may have been some regrets but not much surprise. However, worse was yet to come.

It was at this time that in certain respects an era was coming to an end and a new era was beginning to open. Although there were two years left during which steam locomotives would still be at work on Britain's railways, including the

Fairburn '4MT' class 2-6-4T No. 42105 approaches Oxenholme with a passenger train bound for Lancaster on 20th July, 1965. *Derek Cross*

Fowler '4MT' class 2-6-4T No. 42309 on the down 'Lakes Express' on the Windermere branch near Oxenholme on 31st July, 1964. *Derek Cross*

A busy scene at Kendal station in May 1966. An Ivatt '4MT' class 2-6-0 is on the left of the picture. *John Alsop*

Fairburn class '4MT' 2-6-4T No. 42147 at Burneside in May 1966. *Margaret Duff Collection*

BR 'Britannia' Pacific No. 70021 on Monday, 30th May, 1966 heads a Liverpool to Windermere excursion, through Staveley. *John Dagley-Morris*

Brush type '4' (later class '47') No. D1843 departs Oxenholme with a Preston-Windermere passenger service in July 1967. *Derek Cross*

Oxenholme to Windermere branch, the withdrawal of steam traction was going on apace, although at this stage, steam on the branch continued to be used. The local was still steam hauled and, for examples, on 5th February, 1966 the 8.10 Windermere to Manchester service was hauled by 'Britannia' class No. 70027 *Rising Star* and on 25th March, the 17.22 Manchester to Windermere was worked by No. 45563. (The appearance of a member of the 'Clan' class seems to have been a fairly rare event but on 27th November in the previous year, 1965, 72007 *Clan Mackintosh* had pulled into Windermere with the 18.37 from Crewe. Shortly afterwards this locomotive became the only remaining member of its class.)

By this time the local services, for some years, had been in the hands of Fairburn class '4MT' 2-6-4 tanks. However, there was a significant change when from Monday 18th April, 1966, the local passenger services were handed over to dmus, usually of either two or four cars. In other respects, steam operation did continue and included two 'Britannia' turns, namely the 8.10 to Manchester and the 11.00 to Crewe and also two daily goods which were usually in the charge of class '5MTs'.

Even this arrangement changed as the year progressed and by July, the only steam workings were the two local goods and an early morning parcels. Through passenger workings were taken over by English Electric type '4' diesels.

On Wednesday 16th March, there came news that must have gladdened the hearts of those hoping the line to Windermere would not be closed. Barbara Castle announced in the Commons that included in her plans to give Britain a stable backbone of 11,000 miles of railways were 3,000 miles that would probably have gone, under the Marples - Beeching policy. Listed in this group was the line from Oxenholme to Windermere. (A cartoon at the time in *The Guardian* shows Messrs Beeching and Marples, dressed as surgeons and each carrying a saw, walking away with smug looks, from an operating table on which is strapped a BR employee. He is smiling as Barbara Castle approaches brandishing a large needle which is labelled 'social subsidy'.)

On a different front, innovation of sorts did appear in the same year, when the level-crossing at Staveley was converted to a half-barrier automatic system. The introduction of modern technology might have also been seen as an encouraging sign.

With the removal of the turntable at Windermere in late July 1968, it was reported that there had to be some workings which were tender first in one direction. During the first seven months of 1968 there were times when a Stanier class '5MT' and occasionally a class '8F' could be seen shunting and sorting out the local freight in Kendal goods yard and at Windermere. By August of that year, with the demise of steam on Britain's railways, it was no longer possible to see steam traction on the line. The freight workings were taken over by British Railways class '2' Bo-Bo locomotives (which later became class '25'). Few excursions were now visiting the line but in November two did come to Windermere. One came from the Midlands and was hauled by, what at the time was, No. D417. The second came from the North-East and had No. D256 at the head. This latter excursion included a number of Pullman cars. A reversal was necessary at Oxenholme. Later, in December, steam of sorts returned to the line when No. 75043 was used to provide steam heating on a Windermere to Euston service. The main motive power was No. D221 and both it and No. 75043 were taken off at Carnforth.

At 10 o'clock on a bleak January morning in 1968 a class '5MT' marshals the Kendal freight. This sort of scene would soon be a part of history although the long footbridge would survive as a section of a public footpath. *Author*

Towards the end of the steam era, diesel traction took over the through trains from Windermere to Euston. On 6th July, 1968 English Electric type '4' (later Class 40) No. D244 is about to pass under the metal footbridge as it approaches Kendal station. *Margaret Duff Collection*

On 16th July, 1968 as the steam era draws to a close, Stanier class '5MT' 4-6-0 No. 44871 approaches Kendal hauling a variety of goods wagons. *RCTS/HUO0798*

This scene from the final days of steam on the London Midland Region shows Stanier 'Black Five' 4-6-0 No. 44894 in the goods yard at Windermere prior to hauling a goods train to Carnforth in the summer of 1968. In the far distance English Electric type '4' No. D387 stands in the station platform with a London-bound train. *Derek Cross*

English Electric type '4' (later class '40') No. D387 waits to depart from Windermere with a train for London (Euston) (with incorrect headcode) in the summer of 1968. *Derek Cross*

During the year there was a track modification made at Oxenholme which considerably affected access to and from the branch. The junctions to and from the Windermere line with the main line at the north end of Oxenholme station were removed, leaving only the junction at the south end of the station. This resulted in trains which were leaving the up line of the branch no longer having to cross the down main line before passing through the station. The change was felt desirable, not least in view of the high speed trains which were now passing through. It also made it possible to extend the platform on the down main line at Oxenholme.

1969

In 1969 the goods facility for Windermere was withdrawn. It was, however, still possible to take a through coach from Windermere to Euston. The timetable for May 1969 to May 1970 was as follows:

Up trains					S						
Windermere	*dep.*	0805	0850	1100	1135	1233	1345	1615	1740	1800	2053
Staveley	*dep.*	0811	0856	1106	1142		1351			1807	2059
Burneside	*dep.*	0816	0901	1111	1147		1356			1812	2104
Kendal	*arr.*	0819	0904	1115	1151	1244	1359	1628	1753	1816	2107
	dep.	0820	0905	1116	1152	1245	1400	1629	1756	1817	2108
Oxenholme	*arr.*	0826	0911	1122	1158	1251	1407	1635	1800	1823	2114

The 0805 went through to Preston.
The 0850 and 1800 had through coaches to Morecambe on Mondays and Fridays between 9th June and 5th September.
The 1100 operated a through service to Euston from 16th June to 5th September. It did not run on Saturdays between 14th June and 5th September. There were dining and light buffet facilities on this train from Preston.
The 1135 was a 'Saturdays Only' train and between 14th June and 6th September had through coaches to Euston.
The 1233, 1345 and 2053 had through coaches to Carnforth
The 1615 had through coaches to Euston and had dining facilities
The 1740 was a similar service to the 1100 but unlike the 1100 had no dining or buffet facilities.
The 1100 and 1740 had through coaches for Blackpool North from 14th July to 22nd August.

Down trains					E		S			S		
Oxenholme	*dep.*		0818	0935		1205	1329	1335	1555	1620	1912	2047
Kendal	*arr.*	0522	0822	0938	1112	1208	1333	1339	1559	1624	1916	2051
	dep.	0527	0824	0939	1113	1209	1334	1340	1600	1625	1917	2052
Burneside	*dep.*		0829	0943		1213			1604	1630	1821	2057
Staveley	*dep.*		0835	0950		1220			1611	1637	1928	2103
Windermere	*arr.*	0541	0843	0958	1127	1228	1348	1353	1619	1645	1936	2111

The 1113 from Kendal ran from14th July to 22nd August and not on Saturdays.
The 1329 from Oxenholme was a 'Saturdays Only' train running between 14th June to 27th September.
The 1335 did not run on Saturdays between 14th June and 27th September.
The 1620 was a 'Saturdays Only' train and ran between 14th June and 30th August.

There were now no services on Sundays, a day when many would no doubt want to take a break and visit the Lakes.

The last main line diesels used on the line to operate the through trains were the English Electric class '50s'. No. D400 is seen here in April 1970. *Margaret Duff Collection*

Percy Duff was out with his camera to record the last through train between Windermere and London (Euston). It is seen here at Staveley on 2nd May, 1970 with an English Electric class '50' at the head. *Percy Duff*

A watershed

The timetable for the following period, May 1970 to May 1971 marked something of a watershed for services on the Oxenholme to Windermere line. It could well have been seen as another step in the process of downgrading the line because from now on it would no longer be possible to travel through from Windermere to London, Euston without changing trains. There would be through trains to Lancaster and Preston but at these stations a change would have to be made to travel onwards to the capital (or, for that matter, any other of the destinations south of these places). There was a train with through coaches from Windermere to Lancaster at 0815, stopping at all stations on the line, and the 1815 also had this facility to Preston but only on Mondays to Fridays between 13th July and 31st August. In a reciprocal service it was necessary to change when coming north and a connection at Lancaster reached Windermere at 0543 (but it did not call at Staveley or Burneside) and two others which did call at all the stations, one reaching Windermere 1044 and the other at 2254. From Preston there was a service which called at all stations and arrived at Windermere at 1932. A further service from Preston reached Windermere at 1207 but this train only ran between 13th July and 21st August, not on Saturdays and did not stop at Burneside or Staveley! There were other factors at this time which may have given rise to some concern. There remained no Sunday service to Windermere but a Sunday service was reintroduced on the line from Penrith to Keswick. This may have been seen as an indication of which of these lines was seen to be the more important when it came to visiting the Lakes.

During 1971 with downgrading reaching even further, the track layout at Windermere was modified to be made more appropriate for current needs.

Another period of uncertainty was experienced when the line from Keswick to Penrith was closed in March 1972. This was seen as a very significant and alarming move. Where would the axe fall next? The obvious answer might have been 'On the Oxenholme to Windermere line'. However, on Monday 18th June, 1973, Richard Marsh, the British Railways Board Chairman, published his 'Railway Policy Review'. In it he urged the Government to retain 'somewhere near the present track network'. With a general election only two years away his words did not go unheeded. The outcome was that the closure of the Keswick and Penrith did not turn out to be some sort of an omen. The Oxenholme to Windermere line would remain open. The importance and significance of Kendal had helped to swing the balance in reaching this decision. That would have given Cornelius Nicholson a great deal of satisfaction. The threat now seemed to be over. The aftermath was that the line from Oxenholme to Windermere would be the only surviving line to serve a destination in the Lake District.

In spite of all this good news, 1972 did see the last freight working on the line when, on 28th April, class '2' Bo-Bo No. D7620 was at the head when it left Cropper's Paper Mill for the final time.

Another 'last' for the branch as BR type '2' (later class '25') Bo-Bo No. D7620 is photographed heading the final goods at Kendal on 28th April, 1972 *RCTS/HUO6144C*

This petrol-engined locomotive belonged to Cropper's paper mill and is seen at Burneside in May 1972. *Margaret Duff Collection*

More rationalization

Nevertheless, it was gradually becoming more and more apparent that 'remaining open', could and would not mean 'remaining the same'. Over these years of uncertainty, it soon became clear that further rationalization (as seen from one point of view) or 'downgrading' (from another point of view) would be inevitable. Consequently, a series of measures was taken which would greatly reduce the former facilities which the line from Oxenholme to Windermere had to offer.

By this time, there were growing concerns about the poor state of some of the infrastructure. On Tuesday 1st May, 1972 during a meeting of Kendal town council (ironically, at which rental to be paid by Ribble buses for use of the new bus station was discussed) comments were made about the state of Windermere station. It was described as 'a shabby eyesore' with paint peeling from the walls. Rain would lash through the bare girders of the roof because the glass panels had been removed in case they fell in. The canopy supports were shrouded in rust and it was alleged that the station had not been repainted since the 1950s. In addition there were no refreshment or toilet facilities. With only two staff members remaining from (it was said) the 60 in the past, the whole place presented a sorry sight and hardly a welcoming one for visitors, many of whom had made complaints. In spite of all this, there was no immediate prospect of improvement. A spokesman for British Rail had said that it was already realized the structure was too large for current requirements but there was no money available for demolition or replacement. Economy was paramount (it was reported) because the station was at the terminus of a grant-aided service between Preston and Windermere, with a grant of £131,000 for 1972. It was suggested that if new building work was to be undertaken, there might be a loss of £151,000 incurred and this would fly in the face of Ministry regulations!

It was during this period that considerable sections of the buildings at Windermere were let to Lakeland Plastics (now Lakeland Ltd). These included the goods shed, the old waiting rooms and the station master's house, along with the car park. This company also rented a number of the buildings at Kendal station. Although negotiations were opened, British Rail was not ready to sell off any of the area at Windermere at this stage. The discussions became very protracted with a number of proposals being put forward, some of which involved the local council. Ideas included a conference and exhibition centre and also an overnight caravan park, the latter to be sited on what is now the present Lakeland site. A lack of decision making on the part of British Rail resulted in what was felt to be a state of limbo. In April 1979 an event occurred which was reminiscent of the one at Windermere in May 1853. A guard on duty at the station noticed that a fire had broken out in one of the buildings in the station yard and so he called the fire brigade. In 1853 this had meant horse-drawn appliances coming over from Kendal but things had moved on a long way since then! Six fire engines and over 30 firemen were soon on the scene. The building contained stock belonging to Lakeland Plastics (as it still was) resulting in the fire blazing fiercely and destroying £200,000 worth of items. However, the prompt action by the brigade contained the fire and although rail services were held up whilst the track was checked for possible damage, all was well. Shortly afterwards, in May, British Rail had a change in policy and consequently it agreed to lease three acres of the former goods yard

History repeated itself when in April 1979 fire broke out at Windermere station destroying stock owned by Lakeland Ltd (then Lakeland Plastics). Unlike the previous outbreak in May 1853, the fire service was able to respond swiftly. *Sam Rayner, Lakeland Ltd*

A dmu leaves Burneside in 1986. *Stewart Hookins/Author's Collection*

for 100 years to Lakeland Ltd. Having acquired the area to the north of the station it has been able to build its flagship premises. Eventually, following this, Booths, the supermarket chain, was able to acquire and develop the old station area.

The sense of uneasiness about what the future intention for the line might be was demonstrated to some extent in March 1980 when it was claimed that British Rail was deliberately running empty trains on the Windermere line. This assertion was made by a councillor at a Public Works Committee in South Lakeland. It appeared that passengers were being excluded from the last train which left Windermere on Friday nights. This service, made up of a two-coach dmu, left Oxenholme at 10.49 pm, went down the line to Windermere, waited a few moments and then at 11.19 pm returned empty towards Oxenholme. Nobody was allowed to board it for the return trip. The rationale for this, according to British Rail, was that it did not consider the few fares that might be taken were worth collecting. It was felt by some on the committee that any income would be welcome. 'Running half a service was ridiculous' was a view shared by the group. British Rail then came up with the argument that it was pointless allowing passengers to travel because the stations on the line were closed at that time of night. It was then argued by British Rail that the train was a 'special', being run for those people who were coming to Windermere for the weekend. The train, British Rail insisted, was considered to be 'empty stock' when returning from Windermere to Carnforth and was therefore not available for the travelling public. To those who wondered what British Rail might be up to, these were seen as unconvincing arguments and not at all reassuring.

Seeing the changes after travelling the line in 1970 and then in 2010

An observant traveller, with a good memory, returning and making the journey which included the section from Oxenholme to Windermere, after an absence from, say, the late summer of 1970 until 2010, would notice many differences from the earlier ride. If such a traveller had arrived at Manchester airport, intending to make the journey to Windermere, there may well be delight to discover, if it was not already known, that there is now a rail service linking the airport directly with Windermere. Steam had gone by the time of the first trip in 1970, with diesel locomotives replacing it on the main line services. However, the use of diesel power had evolved over this period. Not only that, the result of the privatization of the railway system in 1994, and the awarding of franchises, had resulted in numerous liveries appearing on Britain's railway system. The service from the airport, introduced in 1994, would now be operated by a well appointed diesel unit of the '185' series, in its mainly blue and pink livery. Run by 'First TransPennine Express' (the company which took over the franchise from First North Western in 2005) it provides both first and standard class facilities. (The traveller might find the reference to 'Trans Pennine' rather bemusing but trains of this company operate over a wide area.) It would be necessary for the passenger to board the appropriate section of the train at the airport, because the carriages would be in two sections. These sections would be divided at Preston; one section going to Windermere, the other to Barrow-in-Furness.

A Birmingham RC&W class '104' arrives at Windermere in the summer of 1986. Diesel-multiple-unit services were introduced on the branch on 18th April, 1966.

Stewart Hookins/Author's Collection

BREL-Leyland class '142' 'Pacer' units also saw service on the branch. No. 142052 approaches Kendal. Note the accumulation of unsightly rubbish at the side of the track.

Margaret Duff Collection

On arriving at Oxenholme (where no change of train would be necessary) first impressions might be that the station had not been altered to any great extent. Some refurbishment would be visible, although perhaps not that carried out to the great wall which is on the Kendal side of the station. There would be less paraphernalia about, especially on the platforms, and fewer staff would be in evidence. Arrival at Oxenholme, and therefore departure for Windermere, would be at platform 3, as, indeed was the case in 1970. Following the modification of the track layout in 1968, platform 2 was no longer an alternative. The extended platform on the down main line might be noted and also the addition of a waiting room as a separate building. Passengers for Burneside and Staveley may well be told (both at the station and on board the train) that it is necessary to inform the train conductor if they wish to alight at either of these stations. They will also be informed to use, or at least move to, the centre carriage as this is the only one where the doors will be opened at these stops. This is a consequence of the short lengths of the platforms.

On leaving Oxenholme, the traveller would possibly become aware that the branch consists of a single track. When the announcement was made in April 1972 that the branch would be reduced to single line working, there was a lot of local opposition, especially from trades people at the Windermere end. The local press, clearly not enamoured by the prospect, referred, rather emotively, to the track being 'torn up'. In spite of this, 1973 saw the proposal put into effect. There are no passing loops, not even at the Windermere end, and so some have been moved to describe the present line as 'just a long siding'. There were timetable changes resulting from this decision; the 2205 Lancaster to Windermere train was withdrawn and replaced by a 2110 Lancaster to Oxenholme, linking with the 1705 Euston to Barrow. There was another at 2220 from Oxenholme to Windermere, linking with the 1805 Euston to Carlisle. It was also announced that the 1200 Windermere to Oxenholme would stop at Staveley and Burneside. With the main line through trains being discontinued, this element of rationalization was intended to reduce costs of maintenance. The singling of the track meant the signal boxes were no longer needed but, in any case, some had already been taken out of service. The one at Staveley had closed in 1964 and the one at Kendal suffered the same fate in 1973. In the same year the ground frame at Burneside station was also shut down. These moves were part of the drive associated with effecting further economy. In addition, the decision to have a single track also had the effect of putting an end to excursion trains, although the number of these had, in any case, reduced considerably after the 1960s.

The arrival at the station in Kendal might well be the cause of some surprise and possibly dismay. The scene would be very different from that on the occasion of the previous visit. There would be no bustling staff; no porters and nobody on the station to announce the arrival of the train (although a message might be heard over the tannoy system which is linked to Oxenholme). In fact the traveller would find that the station is devoid of all railway staff; in 1973 it had become an unstaffed halt. There is now only one platform, which is on the former down side. The station building, too, or the apparent lack of it, might cause something of a shock, though not perhaps as much of a shock if the traveller had made the journey some years earlier. In 1974 the section of the station, as seen from the train, on the up line was demolished, having seen the effects of a period of considerable neglect; the rest was boarded up to await further consideration. In 1980, during the discussion of a draft

Metro-Cammell class '156' 'Super Sprinter' units were used on the branch in the 1990s. This one is seen crossing the bridge over the River Kent. *Margaret Duff Collection*

Relaying the track at at Burneside in summer 2002. *Percy Duff*

document 'Public Transport Plan 1980-81' which was produced by Cumbria County Council, British Rail had stated that it hoped to improve Kendal station, possibly including the demolition of part of what remained, but, as it turned out, it was some time before there was any real progress on that front. A solution was eventually at hand, however, because in 1991, the 'Lakes Line Action Group' (a body formed some seven years earlier and which had already proved it had clout when it was successful in taking up a challenge to ensure Windermere had a suitable station) brought pressure to bear on those putting forward new (and what were considered inadequate) proposals for passenger accommodation at Kendal. The recommendations of the group were heeded and the result was the provision of a scheme deemed more appropriate for such an important stop on the line. The station buildings at the top of the former approach road are now used as a medical practice and a pharmacy although this would not be obvious from the train. On the platform side of the old building, a fence has been erected. Sadly, the old station frontage has lost much of its former visual impact. On leaving Kendal, the traveller would notice that the goods yards have gone. On the previous visit in 1970, although there would not have been a great deal of activity in the yard there might well have been the sight of a lone diesel locomotive in charge of an incoming freight, probably destined for Cropper's Mill. Eventually, following the closure and clearance of the site, an industrial estate was built where the yards had once been. The traveller might just catch a glimpse of the long metal footbridge which spanned the yards and remains as part of a public footpath.

Burneside, where the three level crossings in this section of the line are still extant (but none are automatic), is the next place which still sports a station of sorts but it would be apparent that it is just a shadow of what it had been. One platform, which is on the old up side, replaces the two offset platforms which the station had before the line was reduced to a single track. Nowadays provision for passengers is little more than what looks like a bus shelter. There is, however, telephone communication and a help line.

The traveller would find the same to be true of Staveley. Like the other stations along the line, this has become an unstaffed halt with the minimum of facilities. Also like Burneside, the platform is on the old up side and the remnants of the platform on the former down side can still be seen under the vegetation which has grown over much of it. The train may well stop at Staveley but the conductor will almost certainly have been checking tickets regularly on the journey and the procedure, adopted before the 1960s, of checking all tickets at Staveley, because Windermere was an open station with no barrier, has ceased.

As the journey progressed, the one thing which would not have changed significantly would be the scenery. This is pleasant, it would probably be recalled, but not dissimilar to many other rural areas in the country. The really impressive vistas in this part of the district are to be found much further on, beyond the end of the line. It may give cause to reflect that it was surely not the possible spoiling of *this* scenery which lead to the real opposition when the line was first proposed; there were other factors and ulterior motives about what might happen next, which were the reasons for all the fuss! As the train moves along, the really discerning traveller might note the smoothness of the ride. By the end of 2002 the whole of the track had been re-laid with continuously

A class '185' unit for Oxenholme stands at Kendal station. The verdant surroundings belie the fact that the station stands in a busy part of Kendal. *Author*

A class '185' unit bound for Oxenholme passes over Staveley crossing. This is the only automatic crossing on the line. *Author*

welded rail. Yet what might be the greatest surprise for the traveller would be the one experienced when alighting at Windermere.

Almost certainly, it would have already been realized, on the approach, that the goods yard at Windermere had gone. (It had been closed to traffic just a year before the previous visit.) On the south side, where sidings and the turntable had been, there is now a substantial car park. As the train approaches the station, it is possible to see an impressive building on the north side of the line and this is owned by Lakeland Ltd. On this latter journey, the train would not pull into the once glorious canopied station platform (although by 1970 it was in a rather sorry state) with all the usual accoutrements of a busy station; it would pull in to a single platform, most of which is open to the elements. In fact, there may well be a feeling, when stepping onto the station platform, that arrival is at a supermarket rather than a station. The sign 'Booths' is very conspicuous. In the years running up to 1980, it had been decided that the station at Windermere was, by this time, far too large for contemporary requirements and therefore impractical. Eventually the station building was sold to the Booths supermarket chain. In developing the site for a new store, some consideration was given to retaining certain of the old features of the station, which the LNWR had included in the plans drawn up at the beginning of the 20th century. These features, in part, still remain but have lost much of their former impressive character. And, when it came to making new provision for those arriving at Windermere or those coming to catch the trains, it was felt the proposals being made fell well short of what could be deemed appropriate. As mentioned earlier, in 1984, the Lakes Action Group stepped in and convinced the planners that something more than what was seen as 'adequate' was actually inadequate. Something more suitable was needed for the station at the head of the line and the gateway to the Lakes. The group backed its conviction with money raised towards the cost of a 'new' station and this was opened on 17th April, 1986 with souvenir tickets costing £10 being issued, allowing travel 'Any Station to Windermere and back'.

The result, the traveller might well feel, on closer examination, is an impressive facility, given the needs which it is now required to meet. The area inside the little building feels light and spacious. There is a ticket office, a waiting area and toilet facilities (but no porters!). The overall effect creates a pleasant ambiance and for those days when the weather is dry and warm there are seats placed along what is a lengthy platform The decision to create a station of this form was clearly vindicated by the fact that in 2008 Windermere station won the 'Best Small Station in Europe' award.

The 'Lakes' Line

In April 2008, Tom Harris, the Rail Minister, announced that the Lakes Line between Oxenholme and Windermere would be designated a 'Community Rail Line'. This step was greatly applauded by those determined to promote a successful future for the branch. It put the line in a category in which, at the time, there were only 20 others in the country. There had already been a Rail Community Partnership which involved operators First TransPennine and the Lakes Line User Group but this latest move was hailed as 'a really exciting development'. The designation gave official recognition to the policy that local communities could have a say in how services might be run, forging stronger links between those who operated the line and those who used it and, it was hoped, as a result, not only encourage more people to use the facility but also attract external investment. So, in just over 160 years, the line, which in that period has passed through so many transitions, had entered on yet another, very different, phase of its development.

Motive power during the post-war periods

In the post-World War I period, especially after the formation of the LMS, a very wide variety of motive power could be seen on the Oxenholme to Windermere stretch at various times, although most of this variety came from visitors to the line. There was originally a strong flavour of former LNWR types which passed into the LMS stables. Oxenholme shed saw Bowen-Cooke's 'Precursor' tanks into LMS days but these were eventually phased out and in 1951, for example, by which time the railways had been nationalized, Oxenholme shed is listed as having five locomotives, four of which were Fowler class '4MT' 2-6-4T engines, with the fifth being a Stanier class '4MT' 2-6-4T; all of LMS origin.

Later, in the sixties, after the closure of Oxenholme shed, and before the withdrawal of steam-hauled local passenger traffic, in April 1966, Fairburn class '4MT' 2-6-4Ts, which were based at Carnforth, were used for local passenger work. In the 1930s ex-LNWR '19 in. Goods' engines (actually designated as 'mixed traffic' by the LNWR but later designated '4F' by the LMS) were included in the motive power which handled freight on the branch. Latterly, jumping to the post-nationalization era, freight was usually handled by a Fowler class '4F' 0-6-0 or more usually, later, by a Stanier class '5MT' 4-6-0 engine; there are reported sightings of Stanier class '8F' 2-8-0 locomotives being used.

In the inter-war period, in the 1930s, the LMS introduced the 'Royal Scot' class, designed by Fowler, together with his 'Patriots' and later Stanier's 'Jubilees' and, subsequently various developments of these, and it became a common occurrence for the excursions which came to Windermere to be hauled by these classes, as well as the through services to and from Windermere. Later, locomotives of the 'Britannia' and 'Clan' classes introduced by BR also made appearances (although the latter was quite a rarity) towards the last days of steam. It was the Stanier class '5MT' (possibly No. 44709, a Carnforth engine) which appears to be the last steam class to use the line when it left the branch on 3rd August, 1968.

There was an overlap of the steam and diesel eras. English Electric type '4' 1-Co-Co-1 (class '40') and class '50s', were brought in, the latter, for a time, also being used in tandem on the West Coast main line before being transferred to the Western Region. As mentioned earlier, freight traffic was taken over by British Railways class '2' Bo-Bo locomotives which were later given the classification '25'.

The classes of diesel-multiple-units used on the line have included Birmingham RC&W class '104', Derby class '108', the BREL-Leyland class '142' 'Pacer' units and the Metro-Cammell class '156' 'Super Sprinter' units. At present (2012) it is Siemens Desiro UK class '185' units, operated by First TransPennine Express, which can be seen on the line.

Chapter Nine

The Line

After the line opened there were numerous modifications carried out over the years and some of these are dealt with earlier. It was during the period when the LNWR owned it that the various facilities reached a zenith although this continued for some years beyond the Grouping of 1923. The line leaves the main London to Glasgow line at Oxenholme.

Oxenholme

The station at Oxenholme was owned, initially, by the Lancaster & Carlisle Railway and later by the LNWR. When first constructed it was situated to the north of what has become the B6254, linking Kendal to Kirkby Lonsdale. The railway crossed over this road and so the route of the latter remained unchanged when the line was built. The main station building was approached from the east and this had a substantial platform. There was a smaller building and platform on the west side. An engine shed was situated to the south and on the down side of the main line. Access to and from the Kendal & Windermere line was (and remained) to and from the south only. At no time were there any plans for a north facing junction. Even if such a development had been felt desirable, the terrain would have presented the builders with a very difficult challenge. Eventually the station would be enlarged with the B6254 diverted to make this possible and enabling the facilities to be extended.

Following the modifications, the Kendal & Windermere Railway left Oxenholme in the down direction by junctions to the north and south of the down platform of Oxenholme station. The branch had double tracks and so the junction from the up line of the branch to the up main line had to cross over the down main line to join it. The track layout, as mentioned earlier, was eventually rationalized.

From Oxenholme, the branch descends on a steep gradient of approximately 1 in 80. There were occasions in the early days when this proved to be the undoing of some drivers who were not used to the railway and, also, in the up direction, the need to provide banking assistance for some trains. The line follows a gradual curve down, crosses the A6 by way of Longpool Bridge and enters the first station on the branch, which is Kendal.

Kendal

Kendal station served (and still does) by far the largest centre of population on the line and one of the important objectives in building the line was to serve this town. The station was initially of modest dimensions with the main station building and platform on the south side; the 'down side'. Initially there were

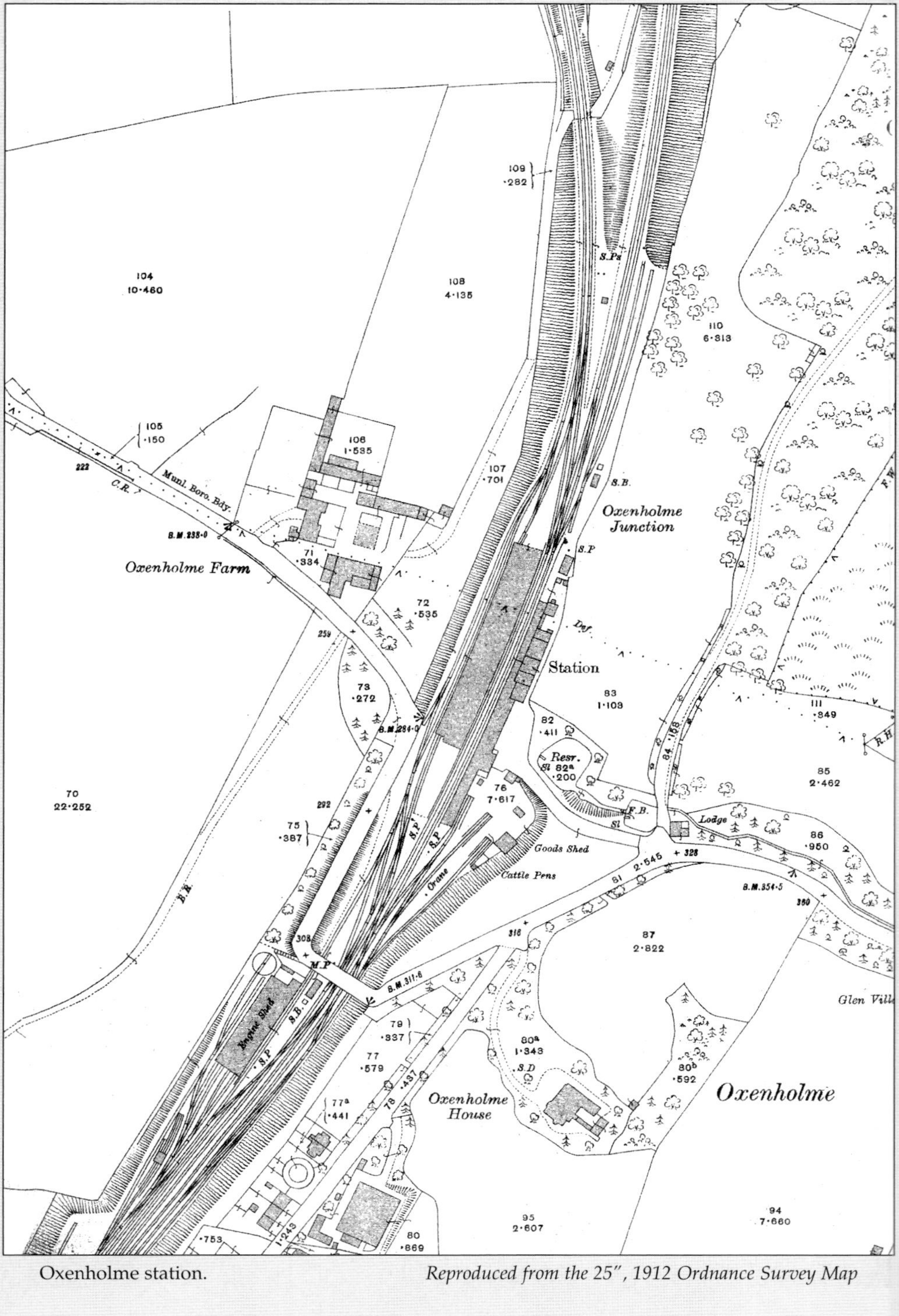

Oxenholme station. *Reproduced from the 25", 1912 Ordnance Survey Map*

Oxenholme looking south in May 1966. *John Alsop*

Oxenholme looking north in May 1966. *John Alsop*

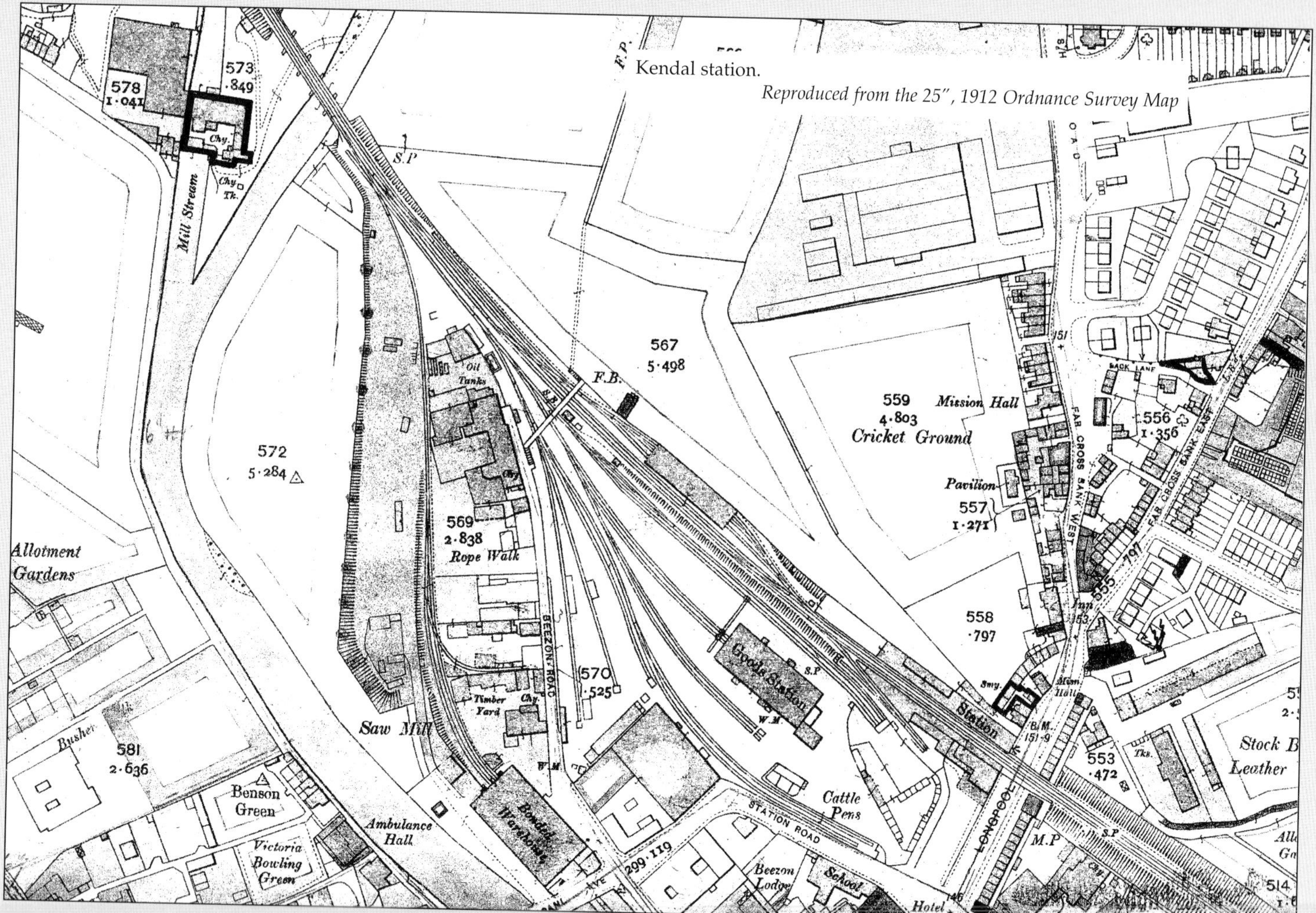

Kendal station.

Reproduced from the 25", 1912 Ordnance Survey Map

Kendal station frontage in May 1966. *John Alsop*

After closure, the original Kendal station building was considerably enlarged as can be seen in this 2012 photograph. The section to the extreme right with the gable and the similar but lower section on the left now almost hidden, in this view, behind the new building in front of it, together with the ground floor between the two are, in effect, the original building. The extended centre section houses a pharmacy and a medical practice. No part of this building now forms part of the station. *Author*

View from a train travelling towards Windermere of the down platform at Kendal station in July 1970. Note what appears to be a disused carriage possibly being used for storage.
Author's Collection

Kendal station, looking west, August 1960. *RCTS/HUO0969*

A view of the goods yard at Kendal. Horses are in use although in the left background another form of transport is apparent. *Margaret Duff Collection*

This box at Kendal with its 'modernistic' design was built to replace the LNWR box and was opened in the summer of 1955. For a time the two boxes existed side by side during the changeover. This box closed in 1973. *RCTS/HUO0970*

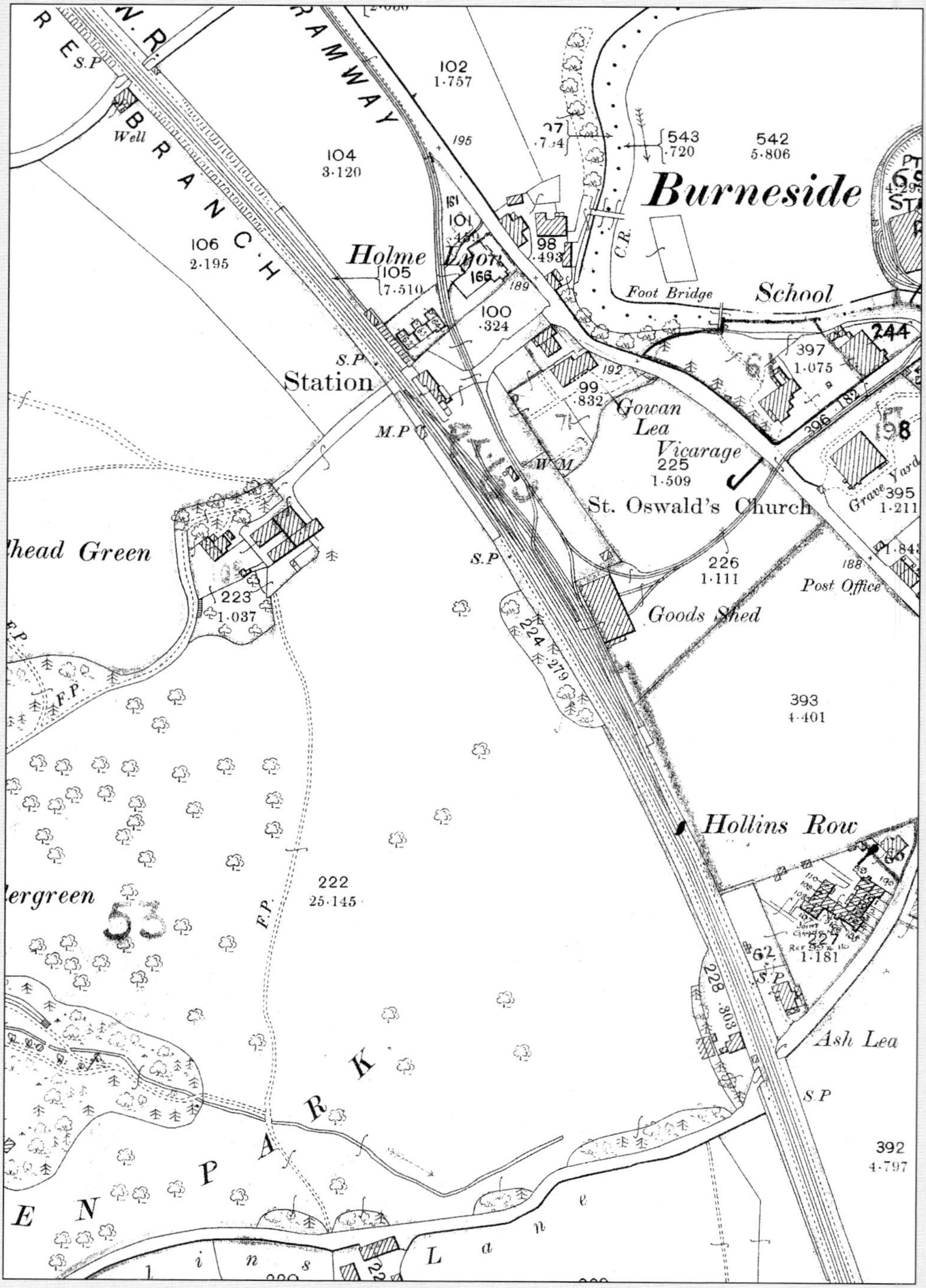

Burneside station and Hollins crossing. *Reproduced from the 25", 1912 Ordnance Survey Map*

two 'goods stations' and a cattle enclosure. Eventually a major goods terminal was developed adjacent to the station and this included goods sheds, coal yards, cattle pens and facilities for storing a variety of commodities as it was a distribution centre for both incoming and outgoing items. The site at Kendal would be considerably developed over the years with station platforms on both up and down lines.The signal box at Kendal station was situated at the side of the down line and towards the west end. At one stage this box had 30 levers with some of these being spares.

After leaving Kendal the line takes an uphill gradient in a generally north-westerly direction, crossing the River Kent and then the road between Kendal and Burneside. It eventually passes over the first of a group of three level crossings, Burneside Higher, on the approach to the station, and then reaches Burneside.

Burneside

Burneside station at the outset, was a comparatively simple structure. It would later be rebuilt and additions made over the years. When there were two platforms, these were staggered and the second of this group of crossings was an access crossing which passed between these two platforms. The station at Burneside, although serving a relatively small community, became an important centre as the nearby Cropper's paper mill grew in size with the resulting need to bring raw materials in and carry finished products out. At this stage sidings were laid down on the up side of the line and rail links were made to the mill which had its own railway system, initially narrow gauge. Later, for reasons of compatibility, this was replaced by standard gauge, in the 1920s. A ground frame was installed at the south end of the station and eventually this was housed in a covered annex attached to the station building. The station at Burneside is in a slight dip and in the early days this would be seen to have a nuisance value for trains stopping at Burneside station and when they struggled to set off again.

From Burneside the line continues to climb and passes over the third crossing of the group, Burneside Lower.

Before the building of the Staveley by-pass the main road from Kendal to Windermere passed through the village and on the approach to Staveley another level crossing was made. This is also still extant but is now controlled by an automatic barrier. The line now reaches Staveley.

Staveley

At Staveley the station was much the same as that at Burneside. It eventually had a signal box with 22 levers although not all were in use. During the early period, after the line was opened, the village of Staveley had three bobbin mills; Rawes mill, Newgate mill and Chadwick's mill. The railway provided a much easier way of moving the bobbins from these mills to places further than just local markets, for which carts were used. The line gave the producers an

Burneside station in LNWR days. Notice the station ground frame on the extreme right.
John Alsop Collection

Burneside station on 10th May, 1966. By now the ground frame has been enclosed in a wooden cabin.
John Alsop

advantage over those mills which were, for example , at Ambleside. (One of the arguments for promoting a rail link to Ambleside was because the producers in this part of the Lakes felt keenly that without a rail link, they were disadvantaged when compared to the producers in Staveley.) Some 60 years later, by the beginning of World War I, there was just one bobbin mill left and that was Chadwick's. It had its own small internal railway system. Rawes mill, by this time, was making garden furniture. At Staveley there was a goods shed on a siding on the down side of the line.

From Staveley the line continues the climb in a westerly direction, passing through open countryside which is quite bleak in places; Black Moss being one of them. The line now levels for a short distance and then, about a mile from the terminus, begins a steep descent similar to that on the approach to Kendal. This down hill run would prove to be a particular challenge, especially, again, in the early days, when those drivers unfamiliar with the line misjudged the severity of it and in the comparatively short distance of it before reaching Windermere.

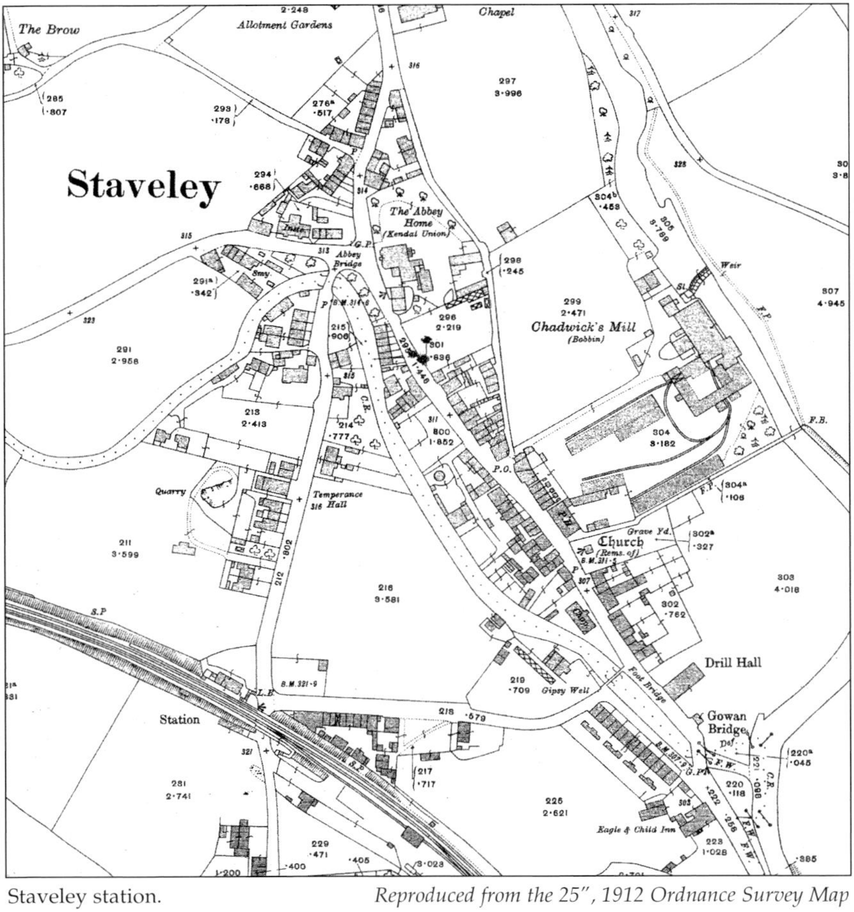

Staveley station. *Reproduced from the 25", 1912 Ordnance Survey Map*

Staveley station, looking towards Windermere, in May 1966. *John Alsop*

The branch looking from Windermere towards Oxenholme; Windermere signal box, right.
Margaret Duff Collection

Windermere

The original station at Birthwaite (Windermere) was designed by Miles Thompson and built by Abraham Pattinson. Early illustrations depict it as having a sense of grandeur. It was clearly seen as something of a showpiece, given that it was considered by many to be the most important station building belonging to the Kendal & Windermere Railway, not least because it was at the head of the line. It cost £1,109 1*s.* 10*d.* to build. Sidings and sheds were provided. Originally, each of the three main running lines had on it a small integral turntable. In connection with the work done by Abraham Pattinson, the following items and costs are listed in the accounts book for period including April 1847:

	£	*s.*	*d.*
Public road bridge near Orrest Head	25	0	0
Six sets of points and crossings	150	0	0
The west siding to the turntable	54	12	6
Siding to engine and carriage house	44	3	6
Siding through station	55	2	0
Road across turntable	12	16	6
Ballast	101	2	6
12 girders for coal depot	47	10	0
32 boats for coal depot	1	0	0
Cutting rails for turntables in main line	2	0	0
Timber in foundations of three turntables	11	14	0

Windermere signal box. This photograph was taken in August 1960, the box was closed in 1973. *RCTS/HUO0981*

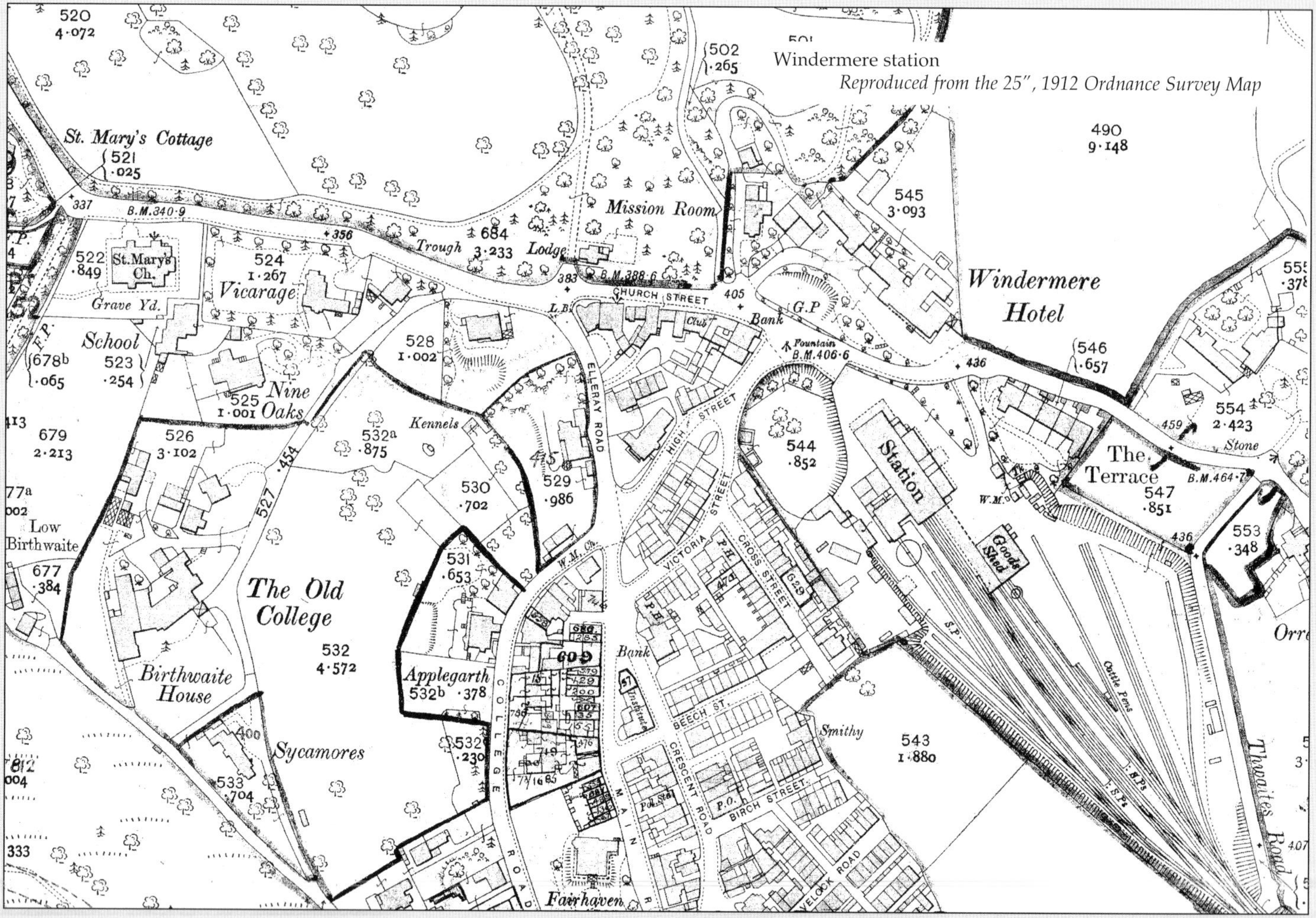

Windermere station

Reproduced from the 25", 1912 Ordnance Survey Map

A Stanier class '5MT' 4-6-0 shunts in the yard at Windermere during the early part of the 1960s. The picture gives an idea of the extensive siding facilities. *Author's Collection*

This view taken at Windermere station in August 1951, shows a variety of coaching stock that was in use at that time. *John Alsop Collection*

This view taken in August 1960 shows the turntable and engine shed at Windermere. The shed by this time has been boarded up. *RCTS/HUO0983*

Change is on the way, as depicted here. It is January 1984 and the station at Windermere is being converted into a supermarket. The engine shed is just visible beyond the fence on the left. *RCTS/HUO3285*

Abraham Pattinson would go on to be involved in much of the building work which would take place in Birthwaite, following the arrival of the railway

Like the other stations, Birthwaite/Windermere was eventually extended and developed to meet the growing demands placed upon the railway both from the point of view of goods and of passenger traffic. The access and regulation of Windermere station and yards was eventually controlled by a signal box to the south of the down line. This held some 40 levers and it was reported in 1911 that there were 33 levers in use. There was also (as will be seen on the maps) a sizable goods yard including, to the south of the station area, a turntable. Windermere was the terminus; it was at the head of the line and so as the level of traffic grew, it had to be able to accommodate a considerable amount of that traffic and to hold some of it. Under the LNWR, plans were drawn up in 1906 for a much enlarged building with enhanced facilities. At the peak of its use there were four platforms with platform 2 and platform 3 being the lengthier ones. There was also a siding between these two which ran the same length.

This view was taken recently (July 2012) from a similar position to the one depicted in the LNWR postcard (*see page 172*). *Author*

Epilogue

A Gateway from the Lakes to the World

And so the saga of a railway for Kendal and the Lake District reaches a point where, for the moment, the future of the line would seem to be assured. The early days, when the railway was being planned and built and, later, when it became operational, had often proved to be difficult ones. However, the tenacity of those early pioneers with their faith in what they were doing, carried the project through. The railway for which they were responsible altered and enhanced the economic pattern of the region, not least by bringing in large numbers of tourists and with them a level of commercialization which, in their day, would not have otherwise been possible. In the 21st century, the Lake District relies more and more on this factor of tourism to provide a realistically sustainable local economy. The railway from Oxenholme to Windermere, which thankfully has survived when others have been less fortunate, continues to play a significant and increasing role in this state of affairs.

Sitting in the Lakeland restaurant at Windermere and watching a train arrive, especially in the high season, can witness to this fact. When the carriage doors open, considerable numbers of passengers alight and most of these are no doubt visitors to the area. The railway acts as a shuttle between Oxenholme and Windermere, bringing in tourists who arrive at Oxenholme on the main line train services from many parts of the country. In this way it helps to boost the local economy. Further, with its direct link from Manchester Airport, it provides another important gateway for visitors coming from abroad. But it does more.

Cornelius Nicholson would certainly be delighted because the line now has what can be thought of as an extended role. All those years ago, the railway enabled businessmen to come and live in the area, whilst being in easy reach of the centres of industry, such as Manchester, where they had made vast fortunes. They brought with them their wealth which would help to bolster the local economy. In the present era the service from Windermere (and stations along the line) to Manchester International Airport can be used by local businessmen and businesswomen, who wish to travel not only throughout the United Kingdom but, more significantly, further afield, into mainland Europe and, indeed, to destinations worldwide. In doing this, with the aim of promoting local commodities, there is a beneficial impact on the local economy; the railway has a significant role in all this.

These two elements of tourism and business, with the all important link to the airport, mean that the railway is not only 'a gateway to the Lakes' it has also become 'a gateway from the Lakes to the world'.

Postscript

In a report prepared by the Association of Train Operating Companies and issued in August 2011, the Kendal and Windermere line was named as being in the top 10 of the branch lines in the country that had enjoyed significant growth during the previous four years. Figures released indicated there were 409,860 passengers who used the line between April 2007 and March 2008 but in the same months for 2010 and 2011 there had been 491,078 users, an enormous leap of 81,218; in other words in the region of 20 per cent. However, there were those who argued that in reality the increase had been even greater than this because other factors had not been taken into account.

Whatever the pros and cons of this happen to be, the message is very clear. The line with its terminus at Windermere remains highly successful and those who, in the past, have fought for its continued existence and those who now maintain it as a vital link can feel well pleased with their efforts.

Passengers board the train, a Siemens Desiro UK class '185' at Windermere. The cases are possibly an indication that many will be travelling to Manchester International airport. This link can be used to travel throughout the world. *Author*

A synopsis of the various schemes for the line north of Lancaster towards Carlisle

1835 Locke carries out an assessment (not a formal survey) at the request of the Grand Junction Railway. He favours a route which takes a line from just south of Lancaster towards Claughton, passing near Tunstall, Kirkby Lonsdale, Sedbergh, Tebay, on to Shap Fell and thence to Penrith. This is in spite of the fact that he has said Kendal is a town which would merit inclusion in a scheme. He has also considered a route via Longsleddale.

1836 Stephenson is asked to look over and comment on a route which could be included in a coastal scheme and to compare it with an inland route. He favours a coastal route.

1837 Job Bintley is asked to consider surveying a route through Longsleddale.

1838 Locke puts forward two other proposals. The first he refers to as the Appleby Route. This still takes a wide sweep by Kirkby Lonsdale and Sedbergh. The second, the Kendal Line, approaches by Stainton, passes east of Natland then to Oxenholme and Larch Hill, leaves Kendal about a mile to the west and then takes the high ground to Meal Bank, crosses the River Mint, takes a western detour by Garnet Fold to Otter Bank, over the River Sprint at Cat Barrow, thence along to Longsleddale and Back Barrow, where there will be a tunnel. The line then passes on the west side of Hawes Water and on to Thornthwaite and Bampton and by way of the valley of the Lowther, eventually to Penrith.

Locke still appears to favour his first proposal namely what is referred to as the Shap route.

Job Bintley agrees to survey the route through Longsleddale.

Hague surveys the southern section of the coastal route.

1839 Larmer puts forward his own proposals for a route which would leave Lancaster and after passing near Kirkby Lonsdale would go through the Lune Valley, passing near Orton and on to Shap. This, in effect, is just a modification of Locke's route.

1840 Larmer is asked by the Kendal Committee to investigate other possible routes and puts forward the Grayrigg Junction route. This route, which would bring the railway close to but not through Kendal, is put forward too late to be considered by the commissioners when they carry out their first review.

In May the commissioners recommend that the Lune Valley route should be adopted but almost immediately, Lord Lowther successfully petitions for a review which would include the Grayrigg Junction proposal.

In November, the commissioners revise their recommendation and favour the Grayrigg route.

When put in charge of the project, Locke decides to reject the recommendation of the commissioners and to revert to his preferred route which would pass to the east and so by-pass Kendal.

The Kendal Party raises objections and is successful in making representation. Following this, the Grayrigg route is eventually adopted.

... and then

1884 Attempts are made to press ahead with building an extension to Ambleside.

1887 A Bill for the Ambleside Extension line goes before a Select Committee and is thrown out.

Sources

Minutes of meetings, plans, letters and other documents held in the National Archives at Kew.
The Kendal Mercury
The Westmorland Gazette
The Railway Record
The Illustrated London News
Wyld's *London and Birmingham Railroad Guide* (Published 1838)
Measom's *Official Guide to the London and North Western Railway.*
Ahrons, E.L., *The British Steam Railway Locomotive from 1825 to 1925*
A Well-Spent Life by Cornelia Nicholson (A biography of her father Cornelius)
Timetables; Various
'Contemporary knowledge'

Places

The National Archives
The National Railway Museum Archive
Kendal Archive
Kendal Library
Lancaster Library

My thanks – to those who, in the various places where I sought material, were so helpful in their support and guidance. Thanks to Mrs Diana Matthews for the details about Abraham Pattinson and to Mr Sam Rayner for the information concerning the involvement by Lakeland Limited at Windermere and Kendal. Thanks, also, to others who provided me with information and gave leads, which were possible to follow up, about the more recent 'history' of the line. (At what point is the term 'history' inappropriate?) A special word of thanks to the ladies of the Local Studies section at Kendal Library, not least in acquainting me with the latest technology (the reader-printer or, as I tended to call it, 'search and scan'!) and for coming to my aid when it and I seemed to be at variance. (The reader-printer is an absolute boon to the researcher.) Also to the staff at Kendal Archive. I remember with gratitude my good friend, the late Percy Duff, who, during the 40 years that I knew him, was a fount of knowledge of all things 'Kendal' and provided me with a wealth of information on the Kendal & Windermere Railway. Finally, thanks to John Hitchens for his help and guidance in unravelling some of the problems which arose during the preparation of this book.

Index